FALSE PAPERS

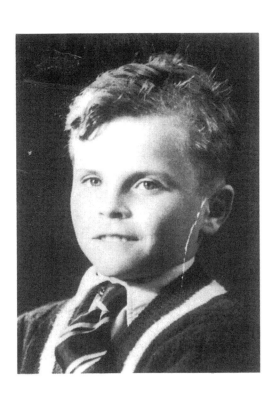

ROBERT MELSON

False Papers

DECEPTION AND SURVIVAL

IN THE HOLOCAUST

Foreword by

Michael Berenbaum

UNIVERSITY OF ILLINOIS PRESS

URBANA, CHICAGO, AND SPRINGFIELD

♾ This book is printed on acid-free paper.

The Library of Congress cataloged the cloth
edition as follows:
Melson, Robert, 1937–
False papers : deception and survival in the Holocaust /
Robert Melson ; foreword by Michael Berenbaum.
p.   cm.
ISBN 0-252-02594-6 (cloth)
1. Melson, Nina Ponczek, 1912–1985. 2. Melson, William.
3. Melson, Robert, 1937– 4. Jews—Poland—Biography.
5. Holocaust, Jewish (1939–1945)—Poland—Personal
narratives. 6. Poland—Biography. I. Title.
DS135.P63M4486   2000
940.53'18'092—dc21   00-008309

PAPERBACK ISBN 978-0-252-07250-5

To Gail, as always, and for Irenka

In memory of ז״ל

*Sara (Sylvia) Blumenfeld Mendelsohn
(d. Davos, 1916)*

*Joel (Julius) Mendelsohn
(d. Stanisławów, 1941)*

*Stefania Bathsheba Gromb Ponczek
(d. Treblinka, 1942)*

*Leib (Leon) Judah Ponczek
(d. Warsaw ghetto, 1942)*

Nina (Natalia) Ponczek Melson (1912–85)

*William John Melson (b. Wolf Mendelsohn)
(1907–80)*

Wanda Lili Goldblum Ponczek (1920–89)

Tadeusz (Tadzo) David Ponczek (1916–91)

*Maria Moszkowksi Goldblum (Pani Marylka)
(1897–1959)*

Compassion and brutality can coexist in the same individual and in the same moment, despite all logic; and for all that, compassion itself eludes logic.

—Primo Levi, *The Drowned and the Saved*

Contents

Foreword

MICHAEL BERENBAUM

False Papers is a work that stands on its own. Its author, Robert Melson, is not only a child survivor of the Holocaust, one who spent his early years living with a false identity, but also a distinguished scholar of the Holocaust and genocide. Hence, he speaks with the authority of his life experience *and* his learning. Both add weight to the book.

Children's memories are suspect; so too are their memoirs, especially since the controversy surrounding Binjamin Wilkomirski's *Fragments*. Again and again, Melson fights for the integrity of his memories against adults who would challenge them. "How could *you* know?" they might ask. "How could *you* remember?" As adults we often speak in the presence of children—especially young children—confident that they do not understand, they will not remember. Melson attempts to distinguish between the stories that he heard and the moments he recalls. Children may not remember events because events have context, they have a past, and children may not be familiar with either. They will recall, often quite vividly, emotions such as fear and terror, excitement or anticipation. They may even recall colors and smells, which later knowledge permits them to interpret into a more complete narrative. The reader should be mindful of two things. Despite how young he was at the time, Melson insists on the integrity of his memory, and he keeps the reader informed of the difference between what he has remembered and what he has pieced together as an adult.

Some mistakes are inevitable in children's memories, not because adults mislead with regard to what they remember but precisely because children experience the world as children. A personal example may illustrate. Ten years ago I was invited back to the synagogue in which I was raised as part of its fiftieth anniversary celebrations. I had last seen this synagogue some two decades earlier and was shocked by its size. What I remembered as large was in reality quite small. I had remembered the synagogue as imposing and impressive, which it most properly was to a six-year-old or ten-year-old boy, but since then I had grown, seen other synagogues, and this synagogue seemed so small. I who had been trained to read blueprints and understand square footage would have been off by a factor of three or four if I had been asked the dimensions of the synagogue before I went back.

When we interview children survivors at the Survivor of the Shoah Visual History Foundation we try to ask questions that reflect the way in which children experience the world. For example, if adults are asked to describe their parents, they will usually give you an adult narrative of what they have learned of their parents, but if adults are asked to describe their bedrooms and to answer some specific questions, such as what was on their beds, what books were on their shelves, or what was in the desk drawers, the only way they can answer is to return to their childhood rooms and see them again in their imaginations. Some part of the recollection may be distorted, but much that they can share will be rich in memories that describe their childhood homes and families.

The return to fresh recollections may also be instructive in another way. In a CD-ROM created by the Shoah Visual History Foundation, Paula, an adult in her sixties, is asked to recall deportations from her ghetto when she was seven. She vividly describes the colors of the snow—pink and red—which she then correctly surmises was the result of red blood mixing with white snow. She remembered the colors. As an adult she could correctly interpret their significance.

Melson insists that he remembers what he remembers but he fortifies his personal memories by allowing the reader to understand how the fragments of his memories have been pieced together into a coherent narrative. Bobi's voice is the voice of a child, but he brings his adult insight to bear on understanding his parents. His methodology is straightforward and also appropriate. He interviewed his parents over an extended period of time and then presents their stories in their own voices. Nina, Willy, and Bobi each emerge with integrity, and each has an opportunity to tell a story. It is remarkable how much Nina and Willy were prepared to share with their son. At many points while reading the memoir I wondered if my parents could ever talk so frankly about their past or if I could talk so openly about my past to my children and thus cast off, in part, the parental role. I was surprised by their candor. In the home where I grew up, sex was not discussed so openly, nor would a mother have been willing to reveal quite so candidly how she used her beauty to save the family. At times, I envied that candor, but only slightly. A steep price was paid for such knowledge. The reader will not require me to summarize the clarion narrative that emerges, but some brief amplification may be helpful.

Melson's choice of title, *False Papers,* is appropriate. When most people think of life in hiding during the Holocaust, they think of attics and basements, barns, and life in an actual hiding place. For Jews in this type of hiding, the danger was discovery or betrayal, someone finding your hiding place, an informer turning you in to the police, a landlord growing tired of the pressure of providing for additional mouths to feed or getting ever more reluctant to endanger his family. The requirement for such a life in hiding was a rescuer willing to court danger with or without the possibility of remuneration in order to save some Jews. Often ties of friendship bound the rescuers with those they saved; less often the motivation was ideological opposition to the Nazis and the "Final Solution." Some saved others to earn money, others merely because it was right. We often label these people righteous, but if we listen closely to what they say, it was not righteousness but ordinary human decency that was their basic motivation.

Willy, Nina, and Bobi, however, did not live in hiding. They lived in the open but concealed the most important—and most dangerous—aspect of their identity. Because they were educated and assimilated Jews, they spoke Polish fluently and without accents. When Willy and Nina first met before the Holocaust, even after they were intimate, they could not tell that the other was Jewish. They were so fully Polanized and so fully assimilated that they did not reveal, even in passing, the lingering remnants of their Jewish identity. It is remarkable to note that what they most loved in each other was their "non-Jewish" characteristics, even though each felt more comfortable marrying one of their own; i.e., a highly assimilated Polish Jew. Because they were young—Nina was beautiful and Willy was clever and daring—they were able to pull off the ruse. Others who spoke with an accent, whose appearance, mannerism, or language was too Jewish, could never have attempted such a deception. Still, this life involved a deep renunciation of the past that would haunt them after the war.

For Jews who lived with a false identity, there were different sorts of dangers. Anyone, at any time, who knew you from your past could recognize you and might immediately reveal you as an impostor. Thus, the more widely you circulated, the more dangerous the problem of recognition. Willy and Nina fled a far distance from their homes and found relative safety. Willy and Bobi could also reveal their identity or have their identity forcibly revealed merely by dropping their pants. The Covenant of Abraham, a circumcised penis, was a death sentence. It was the indelible mark of the Jew. But as Melson describes the life he lived, we understand that self-betrayal was also a danger. A remark that was too candid, an expression of sympathy for the Jews or for the plight of a Jew in a mixed marriage, or even an expression of interest in the Jews' fate could also give away one's hidden identity. Many Holocaust survivors believe that Jews could "sense" fellow Jews. Perhaps the scent of fear is unmistakable, especially to those who are also afraid.

The skills that enabled Willy to succeed in the heart of Europe during World War II did not easily translate themselves into ingredients for success in less turbulent times. After the war, he maintained his drive and determination along with his cleverness and the ability to adjust and shift paths quite quickly. But perhaps because of the absence of danger, he came close, but could not quite pull off his postwar schemes. Ordinary times meant that there could be checks and balances, inspections and investigations, and not the free-for-all and wild atmosphere of wartime. And Willy's work could not survive such scrutiny.

In his book *Against All Odds,* William Helmreich, a City University of New York sociologist, explored why survivors succeeded. He might also have wondered why some of those who could pull off the impossible during the war years could not quite adjust to less turbulent times. Willy Melson was not alone. Tuvia Belski, who created a family camp in the forests of Eastern Europe and provided food, shelter, ammunition, and life itself not only for fighters and partisans but also for women, children, and the elderly during the Holocaust, comes to mind as a prime example of a man whose skills were suited to battle but not to peace. Many of those he saved prospered in America. He did not. I am not prepared to draw large conclusions, but the paradox should be noted.

I know that Robert Melson the scholar is faithful to the truth that he discovers, the documents he studies, the witnesses he interviews, the experiences he encounters, and the reality he describes. Writing of himself and his family, he is no less faithful. Readers will be drawn into this tale and charmed by his insights. In *False Papers,* Robert Melson is restrained. He neither romanticizes his parents nor settles scores with them. He does not denounce his father, nor does he take sides with either of his parents. Despite his strong feelings during many of the events he described, now he is more grateful than angry, more understanding than judgmental. Melson even treats himself as but another part of the story, neither seeking the final word nor vindication, except with regard to the integrity of his memory. Bobi has come out of hiding and will be cherished for his courage to come forth.

Acknowledgments

This book was a difficult personal and literary project that took years to complete, and it would not have seen the light of day except for the generous help of family and friends. It gives me great pleasure to be able to acknowledge their attentive reading of earlier drafts of the manuscript, their editorial suggestions, their steadfast encouragement, and their many acts of kindness: Renata Arnold Alperin, Christopher Browning, Robert Channon, Barry Chazan, Naomi Chazan, Thomas J. Cottle, Aria Edry, Alan Gold, Joseph Haberer, John Indyk, Mary Indyk, Michael Kaufman, Ted Korman, Jacques Kornberg, Mona Kornberg, Angela McBride, William McBride, Joshua Melson, Irene Morgensztern, Vitor Morgensztern, Samuel P. Oliner, Nancy Patchen, Ivone Ponczek, Roberto Ponczek, Samuel B. Ross, Herbert Selesnick, Rona Sheramy, Roger W. Smith, Kathleen Spivack, Hinda Sterling, Colin Tatz, and Shimshon Zelniker. All errors found in the book are, of course, my responsibility.

I wish to single out Neil Myers and Lilian Price, talented writers and old friends, who spent weeks of their valuable time in helping to edit the manuscript. Thomas C. Andrews and Peter Balakian, poets and brilliant memoirists, gave me the courage to be a narrator as well as a chronicler. Michael Berenbaum, a scholar and nurturer of survivors' memoirs, added practical to moral support when it was most needed and urged me to add an epilogue, which rounded out the story.

Yisrael Gutman and the staff at Yad Vashem assisted with research on Stanisławów. Peter Black, Wesley A. Fisher, Michael Gelb, and Severin Hochberg of the United States Holocaust Memorial Museum helped to verify crucial details of the story. The Department of Political Science and the Jewish Studies Program at Purdue University and the Center for International Studies at MIT provided welcome support. The staff at

Purdue included librarians, secretaries, and teaching assistants who helped in ways large and small, notably Jean-Pierre Herubel, Michelle Conwell, Marty Dahlstrom, Betty Hartman, Tanja Dresp, and Elizabeth Frombgen.

Anne Edelstein, who took this project on as an agent, was a constant good-humored advocate who believed in the book from the start and fought for it when my own resolve weakened. Willis G. Regier, director at the University of Illinois Press, was open-handed in his encouragement and lent his great expertise to the honing of the final product.

Gail Freedman Melson and Sara Melson, my wife and daughter, were there every step of the way, helping to read and to edit numerous drafts. Their love sustained me when I wavered, and their sensibility guided me when I went off course.

FALSE PAPERS

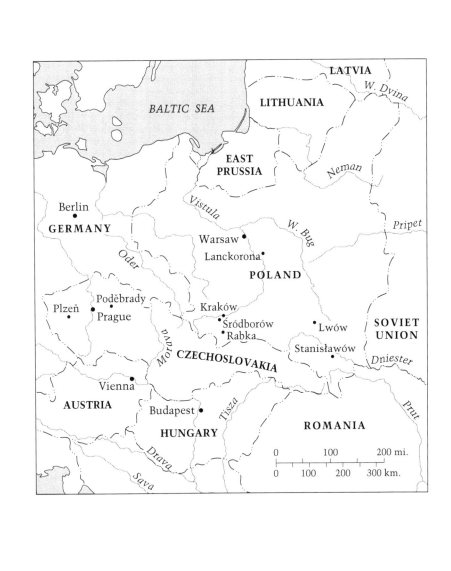

LATVIA

LITHUANIA

W. Dvina

BALTIC SEA

EAST
PRUSSIA

Neman

Vistula

Berlin

GERMANY

Oder

W. Bug

Pripet

Warsaw

Lanckorona

POLAND

Poděbrady

Plzeň

Prague

Kraków

Śródborów

Rabka

Lwów

SOVIET
UNION

Morava

CZECHOSLOVAKIA

Stanisławów

Dniester

Vienna

AUSTRIA

Budapest

Tisza

Prut

HUNGARY

ROMANIA

Drava

Sava

0	100	200 mi.
0	100	200	300 km.

Prologue:
Our Faults Make Us Real

On October 12, 1941, the Jews of the little Polish town of Stanisławów were murdered by special units of the SS and the German police under the command of Hans Krueger. My mother had a premonition the night before, and the morning of the massacre she and my father carried me—I was four years old at the time—to the outskirts of town, where we hid in a cellar of a house owned by friends. We had mistrusted the Germans' motives and had refused to go to the center of town, where the Jews had been told to assemble before the killings, but now we had to go into hiding and find some way to escape. Our only hope was to acquire false identity papers that would allow us to impersonate "Aryan" Polish Catholics. This is the story of how my mother, by sheer chutzpah and bravado, was able to acquire the identity papers of the Zamojskis, a Polish family of noble lineage, how my father was able to wheel and deal to get us money, and how my parents and I were then able to elude the Nazis for the duration of the war.

Thus my father, Wolf ("Willy") Mendelsohn, started to pose as Count Jan Ferdinand Zamojski; my mother, Natalia ("Nacia") Ponczek, took on the role of Countess Janina ("Nina") Victoria Zamojska; and I, born Sylvio Mendelsohn, became little Count Bogusław ("Bobi") Marian Zamojski for the remainder of the war. My parents invented new lives and new pasts for us; they were the authors, actors, and impresarios of a grand charade. I got towed along, but without realizing my true identity, as I had no memory of being Jewish, of being called Sylvio Mendelsohn, or, for that matter, of being anything but Bobi Zamojski. Even after the war my parents continued to call me "Bobi" or "Bogusiu," the affectionate diminutives for Bogusław.

Neither did I realize that I provided a critical ingredient to the impersonation. I was blond and blue-eyed. My pug nose looks like a potato that has been screwed into the middle of my face. And with my golden curls, I resembled a saccharine angel in a Christmas pageant. Given the Nazi stereotype of what a Jew looked like and how this differed from how an "Aryan" appeared, my face could have been designed by central casting to put the Nazi bloodhounds off the scent. I had what Polish Jews during the war called a "dobry wygląd," which is literally translated as "good looks"—looks that allowed a person to pass as a non-Jew.

My mother, who was in her twenties at the time, also had such "good looks." She too was blond and blue-eyed. Her nose was small and straight. She was very pretty, but more importantly, like me, she looked Slavic and easily passed as "Aryan" during the war. Moreover, she had the attractive woman's easy flirtatiousness around men. That too was essential when she had to face down (or charm) Gestapo officers who had our fate in their hands. She had a wide and ready smile and the vivaciousness, sexiness, and confidence of a born entertainer. Before the war she had been a singer in one of Warsaw's most popular nightclubs, the Adria. As an actress she intuitively understood the world of make-believe, of playing a part. She couldn't know before the war that her greatest role would be that of a Polish countess, a part she would have to play day and night for nearly four years.

My mother's native tongue was Polish, and she spoke it without a Yiddish accent. This too was crucial during the course of our impersonation as Polish Catholics. She was born into a middle-class "assimilated" Jewish family—only one in ten Jews in Poland before the war came from such families. Although my grandfather Leon ("Leib") Ponczek was an observant Jew, my grandmother Stefania Bathsheva, known as "Sheva," was not. Both of Nina's parents were great admirers of Polish culture, despite the prewar antisemitism.

My father was not as well equipped as my mother for survival under the Nazis. He was a handsome man, but he had straight black hair, liquid brown eyes, and a strong nose. In a Polish population that was largely blond, blue-eyed, and pug-nosed, some of these traits could have incriminated him as a Jew. Ironically, it was not he but my mother who was once suspected of being Jewish because, as one of her German acquaintances said, "She had the sad eyes of a Jewess." (No doubt there were many reasons for having sad eyes while she was laughing and impersonating someone else, at the same time fearing what was happening to her parents in the Warsaw ghetto.)

My father too had been born into an "assimilated" upper-class German-speaking home in Austrian Galicia and hence grew up speaking German without the Yiddish accent of most Jews; this was essential to our impersonation. He was also quite beguiling: glib, charming, a *macher*—a smooth operator.

During World War I, while his father, Julius, was serving as an officer in the Austrian army, his mother, Sylvia, fled with the little boy to Vienna and then to Davos, Switzerland. There in 1916 she died of tuberculosis. Willy was nine years old when, the night before her death, Sylvia called him into her room. "What is your name?" she asked.

"My name is Wolf Mendelsohn," Willy had replied.

"Yes, your name is Wolf, and you'll have to fend for yourself like a little lone wolf when I'm gone." And he did.

After his mother's death, Willy was called into the head surgeon's office, where he was given an urn of her cremated remains. He was then left on his own. A teacher who taught at the clinic where Sylvia had died took him in for the duration of the war. All that time he dreamed about his father coming to Switzerland to take him home. By 1919, a full year after the war's end, Julius remarried and only then sent for his son. Willy kept the urn of his mother's ashes until the Nazi occupation. Then he disposed of them, and he never forgave his father for abandoning him.

As a young man Willy lived in Vienna, Berlin, and Paris, where for a time he worked as an assistant to a movie producer. By the time he met my mother in 1936 in Warsaw, he had his own wholesale business, but the Polish government passed a law that made it illegal for Jews to sell to government agencies. To get around that ruinous provision he changed the name of his firm and started to call himself "William Melson," a non-Jewish-sounding version of "Wolf Mendelsohn."

"So you were passing as a non-Jew even before the war!" I remarked to my father during an interview. "Even your mother, when she first met me, figured that I was Swedish or something!" he replied, laughing. In fact, when they first met, neither suspected that the other was Jewish. Even after they were living with each other, they weren't sure. He thought she was Polish, and she thought he was Swedish, and that was before the war, when one's life didn't yet depend on such deceptions. Antisemitism was so pervasive in the Poland of their day that they were afraid to raise the subject of their Jewish identity to each other even in private as lovers. Finally one day, out of exasperation, my mother demanded to know if he was Jewish. Then, as she put it, "We embraced because now everything was just right."

We survived the war in part because my parents were extraordinarily well cast for the roles they created for themselves, but most other Jews were less lucky. My mother's parents were interned in the Warsaw ghetto and were later murdered in the Treblinka death camp. My grandfather Julius Mendelsohn committed suicide before the Stanisławów massacre of October 12, 1941. I have since heard about other relatives who were killed, but either I didn't know them or I don't remember them.

During the course of the war, first under Soviet occupation and then under the Nazis, Tadzo, my mother's younger brother, came to live with us. Then in Kraków in 1942, by sheer chance, we met three Jewish women whose fate became intertwined with ours. Wanda, Irenka, and their mother, Pani Marylka, were also in flight, posing as "Aryans," and like us were living on false papers. Wanda married Tadzo during the war, and thus the seven of us, impostors all, survived together.

Most of this story is based on seventeen hours of taped interviews that I conducted in separate sessions with my mother and father in July 1978 and on my own recollections and recreations of the past. Over the years I have also spoken to Wanda, Tadzo, and Irenka about our survival, and some of their reminiscences are used to supplement my parents' recollections. Pani Marylka, unfortunately, died before I started this project.

My parents and I agreed that it would be better to conduct separate interviews, so as to get each person's individual perspective on past events. Their stories—as well as Wanda's, Tadzo's, Irenka's, and my own—corroborate each other, but they also contradict each other in places. I listened to each person tell his or her version of our story without trying to square each telling and have it "come out right." The interviews with my mother were conducted in Polish, her mother tongue, which I later translated into English. Those with my father were conducted in English, although he would have felt more comfortable speaking German, the language of his birth. While writing this book, I tried to preserve the freshness of their voices, but I didn't hesitate to rewrite passages that I thought were flat or obscure.

Even after the war and when she recalled her past, including her childhood, my mother mostly referred to herself as "Nina," the name she assumed during the war, and not "Natalia" or "Nacia," her given name and its nickname. It was to honor her own sense of self, therefore, that I have labeled her sections "Nina." Even my father, who did resume his given name after the war, introduced "John" as a middle name. "John" is the English equivalent of the Polish "Jan," as in Jan Zamojski, which was his assumed name during the war. As will be seen at the conclusion of our story, neither Willy nor Nina could easily switch back from their Zamojski to their Mendelsohn selves. The effects of the war and the impersonation persisted for years and never quite dissipated.

Much of the story I knew already from having lived with my parents through some of the experiences they described and from having heard them tell their stories many times before, but some of the details were a surprise. I was two when the war started and eight when it ended. I have my own childhood snatches of memory of that time, which start out rather dimly but become clearer near the end of the war as I was getting older.

I conducted the interviews with my parents in their apartment in Cambridge, Massachusetts, off Central Square, in a decaying part of town. They had been living with my younger brother, Richard—he was born after the war—for a number of years, ever since my father's business had failed. That same year, my father underwent open heart surgery and discovered that he had cancer. Earlier my mother had suffered a severe depression, which left her speechless and nearly immobilized until she received electroshock therapy. Neither was in good health, and both were in strained economic circumstances.

Given their situation at the time of the interviews and our awful memories of the war, one would think that our sessions would have been permeated with gloom, but that was far from the case. At some moments we recalled the past with sorrow, but at others we dissolved in laughter at the recollection of some ridiculous event. The interviews transported Willy and Nina to a terrible era, but also to a time when they were young, attractive, strong, and resourceful. Although at points in the interviews we were overcome by grief, the truth is that we also felt a measure of pride in our survival. After all, we had not gone up in smoke as Hitler had wished, and we had eluded and outwitted his Nazi killers.

Since I am a survivor and the son of survivors, in writing about our experiences I felt a special responsibility to be true to my parents' and my own memory of the events. I felt like I was a witness at a supremely important trial. My testimony had to be pure and true, out of respect for the memory of those who could no longer speak for themselves and for the deliberations of future generations. Yet I also wanted to tell a compelling story that would bring our experiences to life. The result was that I felt uneasy being a son—privy to his family's secrets—and a chronicler of his family's history, both a witness and a storyteller.

I tried to be truthful by neither denying nor embellishing my parents' exploits nor suppressing incriminating or embarrassing moments. My parents showed extraordinary courage, resourcefulness, and kindness during the war. Indeed, they managed to save not only our immediate family but also my uncle and three Jewish women—chance acquaintances, one of whom became my aunt. It was risky business to include such strangers in our charade, since at any moment we might have been betrayed for being Jews trying to pass as "Aryans." However, neither Nina nor Willy nor I was a candidate for sainthood.

At one point in the interview, when she recalled being a young woman in prewar Poland, Nina said that she had rejected a suitor because "he looked so Jewish." "I despised that look," she added for good measure. I should add that she fell head-over-heels in love with my father, who was quite handsome and distinctly "Jewish looking," in a blond and blue-eyed Polish context. At another juncture, Willy discussed his wartime affair with a Czech woman as if it were inconsequential. In each of these instances, as their son and memoirist, I was tempted to suppress the incriminating evidence. I was startled that my mother, whom I adored, had a streak of Jewish self-hatred, and I worried that my father's wartime exploits, during which he saved all our lives many times over, would somehow dim because of his propensity to promiscuity. But I left these things in on purpose.

I wished to pit our very bodies, our quirky, sexy, funny, wicked, frail, ordinary selves against the totalizing, flattening, unrelenting, undifferentiating, grotesque, murderous fantasy concerning race and the Jewish World Conspiracy that had Germany and so much of Christian Europe in its grip during the war. Let our faults stick out, I thought, they only make us real.

I was determined to commemorate my parents not as martyrs and heroes but as the authentic people I knew. It was, after all, not caricatures but living human beings, with their light and their dark sides, their strengths and their weaknesses, their goodness and their badness, who perished. And it was real people like my parents and I who survived. As Isaac Bashevis Singer, writing of the Polish Jewish generation preceding the war, put it in *Shosha*, "The generations that will come after us . . . will consider all of us holy martyrs. They will recite kaddish after us and 'God Full of Mercy.' Actually everyone of us will die with the same passions he lived with" (New York: Fawcett Crest Books, 1978, 264). My family, I know, lived and died with many passions.

The original interviews with my parents took the conventional question-and-answer format, with me posing the question and them responding; this book is a continuous story based on the interviews but not on their protocols. I wished to be as truthful as I could; however, unlike testimony at a trial, the structure of a narrative creates its own demands for continuity, pacing, color—all the elements that make for a "good story." I supplied historical information that my parents didn't know, details that they had left out. In places I had one say things that were said by the other. I also changed the names of two minor protagonists in order to spare their families any embarrassment. In sum, I shaped these interviews into a narrative somewhat in the manner of a novelist. And that's why I felt additional unease about being both a credible witness and a good storyteller.

The story of our survival is told in chronological order from before to after the war. Each chapter is narrated by Nina or Willy with a brief section at the end labeled "Bobi," in which I add some of my recollections. These "Bobi" sections get longer and more detailed as the story progresses because I could remember more from later in my childhood and had more to say.

During the interviews I felt tension between me and my parents. This stemmed not only from the usual aggravations and misunderstandings that exist between parents and children. It also derived from my parents' unwillingness to admit that I remembered anything significant from the war. "But, Bobi, you were only a child during the war! How can you remember anything?" When either one of them would say that I felt a stab of anger that would take my breath away. By questioning my memory, they were denying me my past and a share in our story.

In 1976, two years before the interviews, my uncle Tadzo and my aunt Wanda visited my parents in Cambridge. They had come in from Brazil, where they had settled after the war, and I flew in with my pretty little daughter, Sara, to proudly introduce her to my beloved relatives. We had not seen each other for nearly thirty years, so the reunion was overwhelmingly emotional. The last time we had said good-bye I had been a child; now I was a man holding them in my arms. I felt so grateful for the love, protection, and the sense of humor with which they had surrounded me during the worst moments of the war. They wept as the three of us embraced.

Tadzo and Wanda had done well in Brazil. They were still vigorous and attractive. Wanda was a bit more plump than I remembered, but she was as vivacious as ever, and her black eyes flashed with affection and humor. Tadzo was more stooped, but he was still tall and thin, with a rueful grin on his face. He broke us all up with his wry sense of humor and wore the characteristic expression of a man for whom life in the deepest sense was an absurd comedy.

That night when Sara was asleep in the bedroom, the five of us sat around the kitchen table reminiscing and telling stories. At one point the subject of reparations from Germany came up. Out of sheer pride my parents had at first refused to apply for reparation payments when these first became available in the 1950s. However, by the 1960s and 1970s they were in serious financial straits, and they had hired a German lawyer in Munich to pursue their case. As my father was explaining the kind of claims he and my mother were making, Wanda interrupted and asked, "What about Bobi?"

"Bobi?" My father looked bewildered.

"Sure, Bobi. Aren't you putting in a claim for him? Bobi, how about it? You must put in a claim for yourself," she said, turning to me.

Before I could answer, both my parents turned on Wanda with the only annoyance they expressed that night. My father said, "Bobi? Bobi knows nothing!"

And my mother added, "Bobi was a child during the war. Leave him out of it."

It was Wanda's turn to be annoyed. "What are you talking about? A child remembers nothing? He was there right from the start. The Germans owe him plenty."

I wasn't going to claim reparations from the Germans, but I knew what I remembered. I knew about our past. Neither of my parents had ever wanted to admit that my childhood had coincided with the years of the war, the years of terror and flight. They had created an illusion for themselves that I remembered nothing of the war and that my real life had started when we arrived in New York in 1947. Mine may have been a difficult childhood, but it was the only childhood I had, and now my aunt had finally confirmed it for me. I leaned back in my chair and felt a wave of love and gratitude sweeping over me for Wanda that left me quite speechless.

Bobi knows something, I thought to myself, and that is one of the reasons that when I transcribed the interviews with my parents I supplemented their versions of our story with my own.

———————

As I think about the conversations with my parents, I realize that the silences—what was not said—may have been even more important than what was said. For example, when my father tried to describe what he saw in the first few months of the German occupation of Stanisławów, he lapsed into silence. I asked him, "What did you see?" When he still didn't answer, I volunteered, "You saw them humiliating Jews in the street. Pulling out the beards of religious old men. Hitting them. Killing people at random. Things like that." To this he replied, "Yes," and looked away. Many years after the war when I visited my uncle Tadzo in Brazil, he was able to recall some of what he experienced, but he refused to talk about what happened to him when he and my father failed to save my grandparents from the Warsaw ghetto. The memories were just too excruciating.

Throughout my life, including at these interviews, my parents had not told me the worst of what they had seen or experienced, possibly to shield me, possibly to shield themselves from terrible memories. That may explain why they insisted that I remembered nothing of significance from my childhood. The most terrible memory must have been that of having abandoned my grandparents in the Warsaw ghetto in order to save me and themselves.

I *Before the War*

Nina

My father had a beautiful pure tenor voice, and he loved to sing. Every Sunday afternoon during the opera season, he would take my mother, my brother, Tadzo, and me to the Warsaw Opera, where we had a loge to ourselves. My mother loved music too, but she was tone-deaf. Stefania Bathsheva Gromb was her name. In Yiddish she was called "Sheva," but people called her "Stefcia."

She was a beautiful woman, much younger than my father, a restless person, a *coquette*, who dressed like a movie star. My father was very much in love with her, so he doted on her. Before the depression, when he was still well-to-do, he'd throw banknotes wrapped in tissue paper on her bed. "Stefciu, here is some money; buy yourself a nice dress," he'd whisper, while she slept. He adored her, despite the fact that she had many admirers. I knew many men were very much in love with my mother. From time to time flowers from strangers were delivered to our home. I remember azaleas.

I was a very perceptive child. I thought, What will my father say? Azaleas like this. My father said, "That's wonderful! I have two daughters. I am happy when my two daughters are happy."

All her life my mother had an affair with Abram Juwiler. She was crazy about him. She told me they had met in a garden when she was seventeen years old and they were both on vacation. They had shared a swing. He was her first and only true love. My father knew all about it, but said nothing.

Her parents forbade her to marry Juwiler; he was too assimilated for the Grombs. They wanted somebody respectable and religious, like my father. In their eyes Abram was a vagabond. They thought he was too handsome, looked like a movie star. He had been a diamond polisher in Brussels, spoke French beautifully, very well dressed—white slacks, blue blazer with gold buttons—that kind of guy. When he arrived in Warsaw he started a jewelry business, but he was a gambler. He'd play the horses every day. He'd win, he'd lose, win, lose. Every evening he was at our house, except on Friday because he would not be allowed to smoke cigarettes. My father was observant, while Juwiler was a freethinker and a chain smoker. On Sunday we'd go to the opera, but without Abram.

When I was a child I didn't know that there was anything wrong with the arrangement. I liked Abram very much. And my father liked him too! As a matter of fact, when Juwiler lost his business, my father hired him as an agent. Didn't I have wonderful parents? My father was an angel. He looked just like Tadzo—a more handsome version of Tadzo, although he had a slightly pockmarked face. He was taller than Tadzo, but he had absolutely the same personality: gentle, funny, and ironic.

And I'm like my mother. If I weren't happy in my marriage, I too would become a very big flirt. Because in a way life is so empty. I have my music, but just to be a housewife, I can't. If I were not in love with Willy I would have three boyfriends. It's not the sex, it's the boredom.

———————

My parents had one of the most attractive apartments in the Jewish section of Warsaw, such that young people planning to marry would stop by to see how it had been furnished. In the bedroom—they had made it to order in golden oak—there were parquet floors. The curtains were lilac, and the lampshade by their bed was in the shape of a half moon, lilac and gold colored. The walls were gold. The dining room furniture was black, and from France my parents had brought Gobelin tapestry of the Three Musketeers. My mother had gone to Czechoslovakia especially to buy water and wine glasses.

My parents invited fifty people for my sixteenth birthday, including the directors from the Bank of Vienna and the Agriculture Bank. Before the party my mother had a pale blue crinoline dress with white embroidery especially made for me. They hired an orchestra. The tables were beautifully laid out with silver and porcelain. Two maids circulated with trays of hors d'oeuvres, while the guests danced and drank until morning.

My father imported tea—a family tradition. He told me that when he was fourteen years old, his father sent him to Yalta in Russia to learn how to mix tea. And then he was sent to India to learn how to mix orange pekoe with other teas. He owned four cars: a Chevrolet, a Ford, a Talbot, and a special truck for the tea. The truck had the company name on it, Japończyk, and in the back was the trademark: a Japanese water carrier. My father had twenty agents working for him, and some had also been invited to my birthday. These were my surroundings before the depression and the war, when I was young.

He was a very religious man, and when I think about him, I don't understand him. Why did he choose my mother, who was such a beauty, so much younger than he, and such a freethinker? He had a difficult life because he loved her but didn't show how he felt. Of course before they were married, he didn't know that she was in love with Abram. There were other things that didn't make sense: My father, who was so religious, still exposed me to nonreligious teachers. Why did he sent me to the conservatory of music and urge me to become an opera singer, when at first he didn't want me to go on the stage?

My grandfather on my mother's side was Tewel Gromb. He was in the textile business, but his hobby was to study literature. I remember him only vaguely because I was a small child when he died. He was a handsome man who didn't look Jewish at all. He was blond and blue-eyed and had a very gentile-looking face. My mother looked like him, and so did I, and so did Sylvio. He was also very assimilated. In his youth he had gone to the yeshiva, a Jewish seminary, but also to the university. When I visited him as a child he took me for a stroll around his study to examine his manuscripts. He spoke perfect Polish, French, and German. It was a very cultured house.

His wife, grandmother Helena, was a very gifted woman, especially in languages, and she had a superb memory. She spoke French and German fluently. Her Polish was impeccable, like mine. I never heard her speaking Yiddish. Maybe it was because of antisemitism in Poland, our people avoided speaking Yiddish even at home. We would speak Yiddish only when an uncle came from the country who didn't know Polish. I don't know how to speak Yiddish, although I understand most of it.

Grandmother Helena was quite the lady, but she was a bit weird. She loved jewelry to the extreme. When she came to our house for *Pesach*, Passover, she would wear twenty brooches—I'm not kidding!—everything she owned, and a lilac mantilla with laced borders. Usually her hair was uncovered, but on the sabbath and on high holidays she'd wear a wig like a traditional religious Jewish woman.

When Grandfather Tewel died of cancer, Grandmother Helena would spend a week at Andzia's, one of my mother's sisters, and a week at our house. Friday evening, following the "benching," the-grace-after-meals, she would pick up her pince-nez and start to read articles about Hitler. Already, by 1934–35, they were trying to get us ready for war, but no one believed it.

The paper was called *Nasz przeglad,* "Our Review." We sat drinking wine, while grandmother would read the paper. She'd start with the date when the paper was printed and then proceed with an article. "Children, listen to what Hitler says. There will be war. Nacia, we have to flee from here!" she'd warn over her pince-nez.

"Why, Grandma?" I'd ask.

"I'll read what the paper says: 'November 21–27. Senior Reporter, Jakub Apenszlak, Junior Reporter, Jakub Frankel. Quoting from *Mein Kampf . . .*'" She would go on this way. Then she'd lay down the paper and quote from memory parts of the article. An extraordinary memory . . . People would sit and listen, but nobody took her seriously when she said, "Let's run away."

Sometime I'd say to my father, "Dad, we've got the money, why don't we go to London, maybe to America?"

My father would respond, "Nacia, there won't be any war. I'm no longer so young. I'll now start looking for a new position in London? We have a beautiful home. There won't be war. I know about such things—more bark than bite." So we stayed in Warsaw.

For the most part, I had a happy childhood, but at times I felt neglected and very lonely. My brother, Tadzo, was younger than me, and at the time we had nothing in common. Even as a child I was grown up in a way. I knew many things. I observed many things. When I was in my room, I'd hear people playing cards: "Pass! Bianco! Pique!" I had nobody to talk to. I was close to my mother when she had time for me, but mostly she was busy with her own life, with cards, with Abram.

The only thing is that my father was crazy about me and thought that I was the best child in the world, and I was very pretty and beautifully dressed. When I was older, twice a week he'd take me to a movie. In the evening after work I'd pick him up in the factory, we'd have a bite, then at nine we'd take the car and go to a movie together.

I was very close to my father. I was eighteen years old, and still I would sometimes sit on his lap! I loved him beyond everything. Today when I open up a package of tea and smell the orange pekoe, I'm reminded of him. The fragrance of orange pekoe clung to his suit. Whenever I get even a whiff of it, I want to weep.

Later, when I finished the conservatory, because I felt so lonely, I started having one date after another. Every evening I went dancing with a different young man. I slept with none of them, but I flirted a lot. I'd get all dressed up, I'd go out. I'd feel important when the young men would shower me with compliments. For me it was all a big joke, just not to have to stay home. It was too boring. What was I to do? I could read a book for two hours, but you can't read all evening long! And I didn't want to hang around watching my parents and their friends play cards. It bored me to death.

I won three beauty contests in Warsaw. I was very happy to be pretty and gentile-looking, because if you looked Jewish you were lost in Poland. Wherever you went, you felt the weight of your Jewishness. One day when I was singing some songs of Leoncavallo at the conservatory, I noticed that my fellow students were whispering among themselves. They had seen my father drop me off at school and had figured out from his looks that we were Jews. All my Polish girlfriends dropped me from that moment on.

Warsaw was a very elegant city—a smaller, more intimate version of Paris. Jewish women, especially in my circle, were very well dressed. They'd go to Italy and to Paris to buy clothes. We had beautiful nightclubs and coffee shops. And the most beautiful nightclub I saw in my life after Paris was called Adria, where I performed. It was built from white stone and had red carpeting and chandeliers made out of crystal, real crystal. Beautiful tables, delicious food, people in tuxedos in the evening, and women in long gowns—very elegant. During the day women like my mother would meet for lunch and gossip at various restaurants and coffee shops. Galicki, on Nowy Świat, near where I lived when I was married, had especially wonderful cakes and cookies.

When I was little we lived on Nowolipki Street, in the heart of the Jewish area. During the depression, when things got harder, we had to move a few blocks south to Prosta, but our apartment on Nowolipki 23 was in a brand new building with an elevator. Next to our building was a *shul*, and you could hear the men *davening*, praying, day and night.

Much of life was in the street, especially for the Jewish poor. When you left your apartment, you'd see groups of Hasidim talking with their hands: politics, Hitler, *dus yens*, business. Not everybody was religious, of course. There were Jewish workers who belonged to the Socialist party. There were even communists who didn't believe in God. Everybody was mixed up together.

In the little Jewish stores you could get everything. The best food, the best dresses, the best cakes . . . store after store, building after building, everything in my neighborhood was Jewish. We were separated from the Polish side. It was not a real ghetto, but in a way it was a ghetto.

In 1940 the Germans surrounded my neighborhood with a stone wall and imprisoned everyone, including my parents. Nowolipki was six blocks south of Mila Street. Mila 18 became the headquarters of the Jewish underground that led the Warsaw ghetto rebellion. Nowolipki was also five blocks north of Krochmalna Street, where the writer Isaac Bashevis Singer lived when he was a boy. That was also my neighborhood, and I remember it clearly to this day.

My father was a Hasid too and a follower of the Rabbi of Ger of Gora Kalwaria, but he refused to wear a *kaftan*. Only on Yom Kippur when he went to *shul,* he'd wear a *kaftan*. Otherwise he was very well dressed. Once a year there was a congregation of the followers of the Rabbi of Ger, and my father would go.

But he separated his religious life from his home. He never had any of his Hasidic friends over. Some religious Jews would come to our door every Friday evening before prayers, and my father would give to charity. They would come—poor rabbis, students—and my father would give them money for *Shabbes,* but it was really for the week.

———————

All of a sudden the world depression hit Poland very hard. Everybody lost their business, including my father. I was eighteen at the time. I remember going to our office. He looked so pale and unhappy! When business was good, my daddy would mix the tea, while 113 girls packed it in boxes of different colors. Weak tea in a yellow box. Stronger tea in a red box. Our best tea was packed in a white box with gold letters. The package looked like Lipton's.

I saw that my father was very upset. Dressed in a white laboratory coat, he was sitting on crates, popping aspirins.

"Daddy, what's wrong?" I asked.

"Nacia," he said, "you see these crates, they're not full of tea, they're full of unpaid bills!"

He had to close the factory. He had saved a little money and tried to get started, but a year later his business failed again. Terrible depression. It came to this, that we had to leave our apartment, and we moved to Prosta 19, about eight blocks south from Nowolipki. At this point, we didn't have much money, but somehow we managed. My poor father couldn't continue in his business. He put an ad in the paper that he was looking for a job as a mixer of teas, and through family connections he managed to get a job in Radom. He worked there all week and came home only on *Shabbes*. Such was his life.

On Prosta Street the apartment was very modest, but my mother was very brave. People still came to the house to play cards. She kept up appearances—went to the hairdresser at least twice a week. In the evening Juwiler would come over with friends to play cards, and there were still good things to eat. We still had a maid, but things had changed.

I thought to myself, What to do? I'm so bored. My boyfriends were just an annoyance. They just wanted one thing, but I cannot go to bed without emotion. So I returned to the Chopin Conservatory of Music, and I resumed my singing lessons. For me it was an escape. Maybe most young girls feel like I did, but I was very, very lonely.

———

One day as I was on my way to the conservatory, I said to myself, Nacia, why not try to get a job and bring some money home to Mom? Maybe they'll take you at the Adria. You're a pretty girl. You sing well. That evening I got all dressed up and made-up and went to the Adria.

The director of the Adria was a very big, fat, red-headed Jewish fellow named Moskowitz. When the door opened and I walked into his office, I tried to make a grand entrance, like a movie star. Meanwhile Moskowitz, his huge belly sticking out like a mountain, was lying on a couch. He was drinking champagne out of a bottle.

"Pan Director, my name is Natalia Ponczek. I'm a singer. I'm nineteen years old. Do you think there might be a place for me here at the Adria, the best club in Warsaw?"

He moved over on the couch and pointed to a tiny spot next to him. "Lie yourself down here," he growled.

"But Pan Director, there is no room!" He grabbed my hand and dragged me on top of him, while I held on to my hat with the other hand and struggled to get off his huge belly and maintain my dignity. "Pan Director, this is a most uncomfortable position . . . Perhaps later, but first, please listen to what I have to say!"

"Okay," he said and pushed me off. "Go sit over there. Do you want a glass of champagne?"

"Yes," I replied.

He got a glass and poured me some. Then he asked, "So what do you do, and what do you sing?"

"Cole Porter, Gershwin, Kern. Or classical music."

"Listen, tomorrow there's going to be a meeting here of all the nightclub managers in Warsaw who work for me. If they like your stuff, then we'll talk."

After that I went home. Mom helped to adjust one of her long gowns, a white dress, and I went to get my hair fixed.

Before the war, Warsaw had some wonderful shows—political satire, musical and dance revues—with wonderfully talented actors, singers, dancers. There was a famous *rewja*, revue, directed by a Hungarian Jew named Jarosy. He was a marvelous master of ceremonies. Such a charming, witty, elegant man, dressed in a tuxedo! After him would come Zosia Terné, a girl singer with a great voice. She was pretty but tiny. Made herself out to be French, but she was a Polish Jew. After her came a trio of comics, Dymsza, Olsza, and Krukowski. Their act was political satire. They criticized everything—the government, all governments in the world. The audience was elegant and knowledgeable, the food was good, there was plenty to drink. Jarosy's revue in Warsaw was so wonderful that since then I haven't experienced an evening's entertainment that was as much fun. Every month they changed the program, and all of us had to see what was new.

We had radio, of course, but we had no television, so we went often to the movies and to the theater. I went to the theater at least once every two weeks. The theater was not just Polish, but French and American productions would come through. The Warsaw theater was at a very high level.

The performers of the Jarosy review, the comedians, singers, and dancers—Jarosy himself!—were going to be my judges at my audition for the Adria! I was thrilled and nervous just thinking about it.

I didn't want my father to be bitter and unhappy about my singing in public, so I spoke to him about it. People in our circle would be very much against it. Warsaw, when it came to that, was a small town. Everyone knew everybody else's business. It was a *harpe*, a shame, for me to sing in a nightclub. For a girl to sing in a club meant that she was a whore. Plain and simple. That was the opinion of the Jews of Warsaw.

"Nacia," said my father at first, "I'm very much against it. Becoming an opera or operetta singer is one thing, but to become a nightclub performer is something else again. Why don't you learn how to type? You can become a secretary. If you perform at the Adria, you'll hurt your chances of getting married."

Of course he was right about that. I didn't want to worry him. I was an obedient daughter, so at first I dropped my plans. My mother, by the way, had nothing against my singing at the Adria. She was all for it.

In the meantime, without telling him, I had my audition. The Adria had loges above the dance floor. Below, in the mezzanine, was a stage, an orchestra, and a place for people to dance. I was on the stage singing with the orchestra, while my judges were sitting in their boxes above me. I brought my own notes and sang a popular Polish tune, a tango, "Nie dziś, to jutro, dziewczyno, będziesz moją," "If not Today Then Tomorrow, Girl, You'll be Mine."

When the moment came, I wasn't at all nervous! I said to myself, What will be, will be. I don't give a damn. I'm not about to perish from hunger. Jarosy, wearing a camel's hair coat and a foulard, came down and smiled at me. They all liked me. After all, I was just a kid, and they were taken with me. I stood and sang, and they applauded.

Afterward Moskowitz with the fat stomach sidled up to me and in a loud voice ordered, "Come to my room!"

Oy vey! I said to myself, *nicht git,*this is not good, but I went. It was so ridiculous, but extremely funny!

When I got to his office, he looked at me and said, "What do you think, that you'll sing here for free? Every vooman"—he mispronounced *woman* in Polish—"every vooman must spend some time in bed with me."

I said, "Fine, but I'm not yet a woman, I'm still a teenager, and I've never done anything like that. If you'll insist, I won't sing."

So he said, "At least kiss me." So I kissed him on the cheek. He was plainly embarrassed and said, "Okay, come tomorrow morning, we'll sign a contract."

After this experience I went to see my father, but I was very unsure of his reaction. He was resting in bed after his *Shabbes* nap. What a wonderful treasure of a man! I sat next to him and took his hand.

"*Tatusiu,* Daddy"—I was so nervous that I had rehearsed my speech— "I can earn a lot of money at the Adria if I sing daily from nine in the evening until two in the morning and even more if I sing on Sundays from five to seven in the evening. After all, it's money that we can use, and if you're worried about me, then Pan Juwiler can accompany me or Mommy can come, even you can come. You can sit at a table and keep an eye on me."

My father thought about it, and then he said, "You know, Nacia, had I not been religious, I would certainly have tried to sing for the opera. But my own father didn't want me to take singing lessons. I'm sorry that I didn't follow my dream. Go and sing!"

He had changed his mind! As a result, this lovely religious man would accompany me to the Adria and sit at a table by the stage until I was done with my act. He allowed me to sing, but he kept an eye on me.

The Adria had two floors. On the second floor was a cafe, and on the first was a dance floor with an orchestra. Half the evening I sang upstairs in the cafe, and the second half I sang downstairs. You could see my pictures in each window of the cafe with my name, Natalia Ponczek, boldly printed across each one. Van Dyke was the name of the photography studio that did my photos. They were first class. The head shots were very artistic.

I was dressed in a long ball gown, and earlier that day my mother had taken me with her to have my hair done at Elizabeth Arden—the company had a large salon in Warsaw. I looked good, but I walked out trembling with fear. This was the first time I had sung in public, and I expected a sophisticated and critical audience.

At first my eyes were downcast because I was too scared to look out at the audience, but when I looked up I saw before me all of Kalecka, my high school! The kids had passed by the Adria and had seen my picture, and the word got around that I was singing, so they all came down that first evening!

I have no idea if I sang well, but I was young and pretty, and the audience was packed with my friends, so I was received with great enthusiasm and prolonged applause. After my number was up, my girlfriends climbed up on the stage and began to kiss me. Moskowitz was very pleased, of course. It was great publicity for him and the club. The papers picked it up, *Nasz przegląd* had an article about it. The following evening even more people came, out of curiosity perhaps.

In the evening I sang downstairs from about eight o'clock to two in the morning. At first just my father but later my mother or Pan Juwiler would come, sit at a table, and take me home after my performance.

But after three months I was exhausted. Not only was I tired but I was tired of the whole thing: The raffish atmosphere of the club—I was smoking a lot—the constant flirting and innuendoes. When my parents were not around, men would sit at my table before I went up on stage, and they would stroke my face, proposition me. You know how men are around a pretty young girl. It got very tiresome—after all, I was still a kid. I told my parents I'd had enough.

———————

Meanwhile, I resumed studying music and voice. I sang for my friends. Once in a while my mother and I would meet in town for lunch or coffee in the afternoon. We especially liked to meet at Cafe Gajewski on Nowy Świat—on the same street where later Willy and I had an apartment, where Sylvio was born. Many assimilated Jews from Warsaw made it their hangout. Wonderful cakes and cookies. Never in my life, never since, have I tasted such wonderful pastries! Especially freshly baked jelly donuts, *ponczki,* and *rurki,* blintz-like tubes filled with cream—out of this world! For my birthdays, mother would buy a dozen or more of such *rurki.*

At Gajewski's I met a young man, Tadek Reichman, a physician who fell head-over-heels in love with me. He came from a very wealthy family. The father was a prominent Warsaw philanthropist. Tadek was not bad looking. He dressed beautifully, was rich, and had a great car. He began to court me. We'd go out to the theater, to restaurants, to the movies. Finally he asked my father for my hand in marriage.

At this moment when things were bad for us financially, such a match would have been a great coup. But I did not love him, and I refused him. I could not. I couldn't have even kissed him. He did not appeal to me, he looked so Jewish. I despised that look. After he was refused he left for Cairo, Egypt, where his brother, Moshe, had a gynecological clinic. In Poland there were quotas on Jewish doctors, so the two brothers left the country.

One spring day, out of the blue, I got a phone call from a young man, somewhat older than I, whom I had admired a great deal. He invited me for dinner and dancing. "Nacia," he said, "let's go out to dinner at Phillips. It'll be fun."

Phillips was a well-known restaurant and dance club where, when the weather was nice, you could dance outdoors. I answered, "With pleasure." I was bored.

"In that case I'll pick you up at eight. I'll have a car, and I'll ring downstairs." I fixed myself up. I had nice things from the days at the Adria. He rang, and we were off.

Cafe Phillips was quite unique—perhaps in Paris you'd see such things. By the shore of the Vistula River they had constructed a huge dance floor in the shape of a wheel, which would turn like a lazy Susan or a slow-moving carousel. All the rooms were decorated with flowers and balloons, and they were lit up by rose-colored lamps. The waitresses, dressed like little Dutch girls, wore wooden clogs, short skirts, and those cute white bonnets. It was all a lot of fun and very original.

When we were shown to our table, my escort introduced me to two other attractive, elegant young men. He explained that they were friends who had come to Warsaw recently. The four of us had dinner. We had a few glasses of wine. We chatted. We laughed. We danced.

After I returned from dancing with one of the young men at my table, I sat down and saw sitting at an adjoining table an exceptionally handsome man. I had never seen anyone like him before. He looked like Gregory Peck. He was gorgeous! The eyes so sad, so melancholy, long black hair, a mustache, dressed in the latest style, so elegant . . . It was Willy! I lowered my eyes, but I realized that he was looking in my direction. I raised my eyes. We exchanged glances!

I completely forgot the other people at the table. Meanwhile, he was sitting with his girlfriend, a blond, but he was not looking at her, but at me! He raised his glass to me and mouthed, "*A votre santé!* to your health," with his girlfriend looking at him. I lifted my glass and responded, "*A votre santé,*" with my escort and his friends looking at me! When I resumed dancing with one of the young men at my table, Willy got up with his girlfriend. They danced very close to me and my partner, with Willy staring unashamedly in my direction. At one point he and his girl danced so close that he practically thrust his face up to mine. What a ridiculous moment! It looked as if he had forgotten about the woman in his arms and only had eyes for me!

After Phillips closed, my escort, behaving like a gentleman, took me home. At two o'clock in the morning, my mother was still up—she had been playing cards. I called her over and said, "Mom, tonight I really fell in love. The man I saw was so attractive, but I will probably never see him again. I don't know who he is. I don't even know his name. It seems to me that he's not from Warsaw. I know everyone, but I've never seen him before."

When I had won a beauty contest I had met hundreds of people. I knew most of the young people of my circle, but I had never seen him before. My mother answered, "If it is fated that you are to meet him again, then you will meet him again. Don't worry about it. It will be okay."

Later I lay in bed wondering how to meet up with him again. I didn't know his name, his address, his phone number, nothing. And he didn't know a thing about me.

This was on Wednesday. By Saturday afternoon—my mother was a very lively lady—she said, "Dad is asleep. How about you and me going out dancing?" In Warsaw it was customary for people to go out on Saturday afternoon to such "dancings." There was an adorable little club, a *boite,* situated toward the end of Nowy Świat. It was called Le Mirage, and nearby was Le Paradis; both were linked together. I went with my mom to Le Paradis. In Warsaw it was the custom at these "dancings" for men and women to sit separately and for a young man to approach a young woman to ask her to dance.

Of course these were middle-class and upper-class women and girls—

students mostly—people like me. The "others" had their own places. My mother and I had coffee and cake. Many young men asked me to dance. Some asked my mother to dance—she was, after all, a beautiful woman. When it became seven o'clock, my mother said, "Nacia, hurry up, let's leave. People are coming over for bridge tonight, and I'm already late." So we put on our coats and left Le Paradis.

My mother and I are strolling arm in arm down the street when I see Willy coming from the opposite side! I'm walking one way, and Willy is coming the other. He is dressed in a gray flannel suit, a light blue shirt, a crimson knitted tie. He wears a black Borsalino hat at a jaunty angle and carries black kidskin gloves and an umbrella. What a dandy! What a strutting peacock! It makes me laugh when I think of it. He stands in the middle of the street blocking our way. Staring at me he says, "We have met before, haven't we?"

"No, sir, I have never seen you before."

"What are you talking about? The other night we couldn't take our eyes off each other. We drank a silent toast. Come to dinner with me right now!"

Meanwhile my insane mother whispers, "Nacia, he's gorgeous! You'll never meet anyone better looking. Go out with him."

And he overhears this! But I say to him, "I'm very sorry. I'm busy. I have a rendezvous this evening."

"You have no rendezvous," he replies, rolling his eyes. "You don't know it yet, but you are in love with me, and I'm in love with you. And we are meant for each other. Let's go out to dinner."

That's Willy! Right there in the middle of the street. The first time he met me—I swear it was like in a movie, and so comical! He takes my mother under one arm and me under the other, and we're off to dinner! For a minute he ducks into a telephone booth and calls a friend to join us. He didn't realize that the woman accompanying me was my mother. He took her for a girlfriend, and he called one of his friends so that we could all go out together!

My mother says, "Sir, I must tell you that I am very busy this evening. I have people waiting to play bridge."

"That's all right. We'll get a *droshki* and take you where you want to go."

After we had taken my mother home, he turned to me and asked, "Are you acquainted with the Proarte cafe?"

The Proarte cafe looked like a fabulous furniture store—gorgeous couches, cocktail tables, rugs, end tables, lamps with red, black, and yellow fixtures, dining tables made of glass. However, Proarte was also a cafe, filled with people. You could have a meal. You could also buy the furniture if you wanted. A very unique place.

We ordered a corner table, and we got into a conversation that lasted for hours. We spoke seriously about our lives; we had so much to tell each other. We didn't ask about social or religious origins—you didn't do such things in Poland—but we talked about everything else. I told him about my parents, my brother, the conservatory, piano lessons, and my love of music. He told me about his past, the death of his mother, his father's neglect, and the factory in Stanisławów. We spent a lovely evening together.

When the time came to leave, Willy turned to me and said, "Nacia, I want you to come home with me, right now."

And without hesitation I replied, "I will." We spent a delightful night together. We fell head-over-heels in love with each other.

Willy's apartment was decorated with great originality. There were seven rooms plus a kitchen. Some of the rooms I recall had orange walls and black doors. There were striking pictures on the walls and decorator lamps. In addition there were gorgeous kilim rugs that his father manufactured hanging on the walls. He had two maids. Things were going very well for him at this time. Sometimes when I stayed over, they'd bring us breakfast in bed, sometimes it was dinner. We saw a lot of each other and went out every evening. We were very much in love.

Meanwhile, I told my mother everything. Willy was my first true love. She was very understanding, a modern woman. However, she asked me, "Is he Jewish? For me it's not a problem, but for your father it's a major issue. If you married a non-Jew your father would die."

"I'll ask Willy," I replied, not quite sure what the answer might be.

There was a club called Plutos, named after a brand of chocolates that were popular in Poland at the time. Plutos were almost as good as Wedel chocolates. One evening Willy and I went there for a cup of coffee. It was a tiny place—red walls, black furniture, poorly lit, but with lots of atmosphere, packed with students. I was determined to find out if he was Jewish or not.

The day before I had spoken about Willy to my mother and my aunt Eva Korman, who later immigrated to Australia. My aunt, my mother's sister, had come to stay with us for a few days. She too was a contemporary and enlightened woman, and she too had had a lover before getting married.

"William Melson?" she asked. "That's his name? He's probably a Swede or a Norwegian, maybe an American. You'd better ask him. If it's serious, you'd better know and not waste your time in case he's not Jewish. You would not hurt your father and do something outrageous like marrying a non-Jew. Your father adores you, and you adore him. You just couldn't do that to him."

So Willy and I are at Plutos. We're having cups of coffee. We're chatting and smoking, flirting with each other. We were a very attractive couple. When we walked together down the street heads would turn. People thought we had recently arrived from Hollywood.

I turn to Willy and ask, "Willusiu, your father has a kilim factory in Stanisławów?"

Willy says, "Yeees?"

I continue, "When I was on vacation, I met a very nice man, a Jew, whose name was Horowitz. Do you know him?"

And Willy says, "Nooo," and he has this dumb look on his face.

Then I ask, "My mother once knew a lawyer from Stanisławów, his name is Halpern, do you know him?" Horowitz and Halpern were Jewish names.

Willy says, "Nooo."

It was getting to be ridiculous. Then I ask, "Are there many Jews in Stanisławów?"

Willy says, "I have no idea. I didn't count them."

By this time I'm so mad that I jump up from my seat and away from the table. I glare at him and demand in a loud voice, "Willy, are you or are you not a Jew?"

Willy jumps up, glares back at me, and replies, "Yes! I am a Jew! What of it?"

We laughed and laughed. I still laugh when I think of the scene.

I swear to God that's how it was: "Are you a Jew or aren't you?" It was important for me because it was important for my father. And when Willy replied, "I am a Jew," we embraced because now everything was just right. Later I started to cry. I was so in love with him, but I had been afraid that he wasn't Jewish and I would not be able to marry him.

That evening I came home. My father was lying in bed. What he would say had weighed like a heavy stone on my heart. When he had lost the tea business, Japończyk, he had had a heart attack. I had to be careful not to upset him. I took his hand in mine and kissed it. "Daddy," I said, "I've found a man whom I really truly love, someone I'd like to marry."

My father replied, "Nacia, you deserve to find a fine man. As for him, he has discovered a rare and precious jewel." When he said that, I burst into tears. Then my mom came into the room, and she started to cry too.

The week after, my parents invited Willy to a traditional Friday night,

Shabbes, dinner. The wine glasses were from Prague. The tablecloth, the place settings, everything was just so for Willy's arrival. Of course as bad as things were financially, we still had a maid. The dinner was scrumptious—gefilte fish *mit allen guten Sachen*, with all the trimmings.

Tadzo, Pan Juwiler, my mom, my father—we were all there by the table. When Willy came he asked for a yarmulke out of respect for my father. My father was very touched, and so was I, because so many of the young men no longer covered their heads at meals. Pan Juwiler, for one, sat at the table with his head uncovered. Even Tadzo did not wear a yarmulke. He fought with our father all of his life. It was only when my father was in the ghetto that Tadzo began to show him respect.

We lit the candles and said the blessings. It was a delicious meal. People began to relax. Pan Juwiler started to tell stories and jokes. We chattered and laughed. When dessert came along we discovered that there was no ice cream. Pan Juwiler asked, "Who wants ice cream? Raise your hand." He then ran out and came back with ice cream.

"Nacia, come over here," said my father, and I stood by him while we sang arias together, from *Carmen, Madame Butterfly,* and *Aida . . .* I'm not sure that I'm saying this right, because whenever I speak about him a gauze curtain falls over my eyes, and I want to weep.

Willy actually never proposed to me. One day he said, "Nacia, you love to play the piano, don't you?"

"Of course," I replied.

"I have an offer: Tomorrow I'm going over to your parents' home, and I'm going to bring your piano here to my apartment."

"How is that? My parents will let you take my piano out of their home to bring it to your apartment? It's a very expensive object—costs thousands of zloty." I made myself stupid. I often do that to appear dumber than I am.

"It doesn't matter," he said. "Your piano teacher can come along."

"What are you saying? That you want to marry me?"

"Yeah!" he said, looking down at his feet.

And that's what happened. We moved my piano over to his apartment, and six weeks later we got married.

The ceremony was at a rabbi's house not far from our home. At the wedding were Pan Juwiler, my parents, Willy and I, and that's all. Willy understood what our financial situation was. He didn't want to embarrass my parents by having them pay for a huge wedding, so we kept it small. After the wedding we came back home, and there I met my father-in-law, Julius Mendelsohn, for the first time.

He was a character, a weirdo. Right in the middle of the wedding meal, he starts complaining. The meal was just scrumptious—I love good food and so did my mother—but when they served the carps in gelatin— just delicious—he looked them over and said, "The fish portion is too small!"—said it in German. Then he proceeded to stuff himself.

He could be extremely charming, but there was something missing. I don't know how to put it . . . He wasn't all there. He had a lovely smile and beautiful eyes. He loved to crack jokes. He couldn't finish a sentence without adding a little joke. Earthy guy with a big belly, big laugh, big handsome man, but there was a coldness about him.

In a word that was our wedding. I was very happy. My parents were relieved. Tadzo was just delighted. My dad had been worried that I was alone and didn't have a profession. He wanted me to get married to someone who could take care of me. And for all of us, Willy was that someone.

I quickly became pregnant. Sylvio was our love child, and Willy and I were delighted. However, when I was pregnant, Willy was scared that I'd miscarry. He had lost his mother as a child, and because of that, for some reason, he feared that something might happen to me. So he coddled me. He sent me to Śródborów, a place in the country an hour's drive from Warsaw. There was a marvelous Jewish pension, Rosenblum's—excellent modern facilities, good food, orchestra playing for lunch and dinner. The place was first class, but very expensive. He got me two rooms and commuted to Warsaw by car, all to make sure that I and the baby were safe.

Although the pregnancy had been easy, the delivery was very hard. I was very narrow, and the child's head was too big. The birth took nearly twenty-four hours. Even though I was given injections to speed things up, the kid refused to leave! Finally Sylvio appeared. When I woke up, they placed him in my arms at my breast. I looked down at him and laughed, "Oh my God! This kid is my exact copy!" He was so tiny, blond, with blue eyes staring up at me. It's a strange feeling to have a child—or at least for me it was. After all, I was just a girl myself, and I had created a new person. It seemed such a miracle to me.

When I came home, Willy hired Maria, a governess. It was like that in Warsaw—all young mothers had governesses. Maria was a *goyishe kind*, a gentile girl. I nursed the baby, and she took care of him. But I had so much milk that some of it had to be drained. Slowly he began to develop—a sweet and gorgeous child. Maria and I taught him how to walk back and forth along the halls of the apartment, and Willy played with him after work.

Right about this time people started talking about the possibility of war with Hitler. My father, of blessed memory, didn't believe that anything would come of it. Willy also didn't believe in it. The German people would not allow it, he said. They were too ethical for that. My father had an offer to go to London, but he didn't want to.

One day the three of us went to my parents' apartment for dinner. Because it got very late we decided to stay the night on the couch. My mother, dressed in her bathrobe, came and sat on the couch near me. She took my hand and Willy's hand and said to us, "Children, go to Stanisławów."

Willy said, "Not for all the money in the world! I don't get along with my father. Stanisławów is a hole in the wall. Never!"

My mother said, "Children, I know. I have a premonition that there will be war. Leon and I are too old to flee, we have nowhere to go, and we don't have the money. But, Willy, you have a well-to-do father in Stanisławów. I would take Sylvio and go there."

That night I said to Willy, "Your business is bad. Our rent at Nowy Świat 36 is enormous. We have nothing to lose. Let's go to Stanisławów for a year. We'll go with Sylvio and see—perhaps things will get better at your father's. Beyond that, perhaps your father will finance our trip to America." Willy had dreamed about going to America ever since he was a young man.

We listened to my mother and went to Stanisławów. That my mother urged us to leave and that we left is surprising, because in Warsaw people simply did not believe that there would be a war. Neither the Jews nor the Poles believed in it.

We took the train. Sylvio was dressed in a little white rabbit's fur coat with a matching fur cap. A gorgeous child—with his golden locks, he looked like Shirley Temple. At the train station my mother and Pan Juwiler saw us off. My father was at his job in Radom. I never saw any of them again.

Bobi

It's a warm, sunny, spring day. The windows of our apartment are open, and the curtains are blowing in a gentle breeze. I follow my mother and a maid around the house, holding a little dustpan and a toy broom. I'm helping them to sweep up dust and bread crumbs into a pile. "Why do we have to sweep up bread crumbs?" I ask my mother.

"It's for the holidays. We can't have any crumbs around the house," she explains, smiling down at me.

This is my first memory of my mother. I assume it was spring 1939 and the holiday was Passover.

2   *The Russians*

Willy

Look, I'm a *macher*, an operator, that's what I am. I get things done that other people think are impossible. It's not only in business, it's also in small things. You want to get into a show where all the tickets are sold out? Call me, I'll get you in. You need a table in a restaurant, where there is none to get? I'll get it. How? You have to have the right approach. You can't just go up to the head waiter and say, "Here is ten dollars. Get me a table." That's insulting. You've got to take him aside, make him feel that you and he have this problem—how to get you a table—and because he's so powerful and good looking only he can solve it. You give him the ten dollars out of gratitude, not because you're such a wise guy. Bullying mostly fails, but then again sometimes it's the only way.

When she was dying of tuberculosis at a hospital in Davos, my mother called me to her side and said, "What is your name?"

I said, "My name is Wolf Mendelsohn."

"Yes, your name is Wolf, and you'll have to fend for yourself like a little lone wolf when I'm gone. Do you understand?"

"You'll be all right, Mom!" I sniffled and tried to hold her hand, but she wouldn't let me touch her. After she died, the doctors gave me her ashes to keep in an urn. I was ten years old in 1916, and I kept her ashes until we had to flee from the Gestapo more than twenty-five years later. Meanwhile, my father was in the Austrian army on the Russian front, and it wasn't until 1919, a year after the war was over, that he sent for me. By then he had already remarried, and he had no time for me, but I didn't care. I've always remembered what my mother said—that I'm on my own, and I have to survive.

I love it when someone tells me, "Willy, it can't be done." It can't be done? Are you kidding? Watch me! I was twenty-four when I graduated the Handelshochschule, a famous business school in Berlin. I didn't want to go home to Stanisławów, so my father cut me off with out a *grosz*. I was on my own. My first job was with the Kartro corporation, an outfit that sold business equipment and stationery. Soon I became one of the crack salesmen. One day I was on the train from Berlin to Vienna when it stopped for fifteen minutes at a small railroad crossing. To test myself, I decided that in the ten-minute interval before the train started, I would persuade the railroad agent to purchase Kartro's line of office stuff. When I got to my customer at the station, I realized that I had forgotten my sample book on the train. This was a challenge! In the little time I had, I persuaded him to buy my stuff sight unseen. I laugh when I think of it now—twenty-four-year-old Jewish boy with chutzpah coming out of his ears!

I had heard about Paris. Paris, people told me, is the center of the world: The most elegant city, the most beautiful women. I had to go. At the time I was intrigued with the movie business—not the acting. I'm no actor, but producing or directing a movie, that might be exciting. But how do you break into the business? I met this Hungarian Jewish producer—I was always in his way trying to be helpful. One day he tells me, "Willy, I'm making a movie about Napoleon. I need hundreds of people for a crowd scene." What to do? I ran down to the river and rounded up all the *clochards*, hobos, who were sleeping under the bridges. The next day I came leading an army of a few hundred ragged-looking men to the studio. From then on in I became the producer's assistant.

I was making money. I had Madeleine, a gorgeous black-haired, blue-eyed French girlfriend from a good family, who wanted to get married, and I was happy. Then my father writes me, "Willy come home. You're my only son. I need you in the factory. Blah, blah, blah." So I left Paris and Madeleine and went home, but it didn't work out. My father and I simply didn't get along. We had a huge fight, and I left for Warsaw.

Before the war in Poland you couldn't change your name legally, and, because of the antisemitism, Jews had trouble in business. So I listed my name in the telephone book as "William Melson," and that's what I called myself while I was in Warsaw, "William Melson." It sounded American.

All my dreams were to go to America. I read all the American books—Dreiser, Sinclair Lewis. I admired Ford. I loved American movies, went to see every one of them when they came to Warsaw—Humphrey Bogart, Clark Gable, Edward G. Robinson, George Raft. Nacia's and my favorite movie was *It Happened One Night* with Clark Gable and Claudette Colbert. I knew so many things about America, and Melson—this was my way of taking an American name. Look, fascination with Poland was difficult for a Jew. With Stanisławów, even more difficult. In Berlin, antisemitism. Vienna, a provincial, sleepy town. But America! I'll go there, and the people will say, "Bill! Bill! People like you we need!"

There was rampant antisemitism in Poland. The most popular party was the Endecja, the National Democratic Party. They wanted to kick the Jews out of Poland. Jews were prevented from doing business and prohibited from selling to the government. Jewish students were beaten up at the university, if they were even allowed to attend. The government wanted to expel the Jews. But I wouldn't say the Jews were completely innocent. They didn't behave like guests, they behaved like a separate nation, with another language, another dress, another culture—completely different. And, really, they looked down on the Poles. If they admired anybody, it was the Germans. And the Poles understood this.

Look, I never felt like a Pole. I never felt like anything. I never felt like a Swiss. I never felt like an Austrian. I never felt like a German. I felt nothing. I felt like "William Melson." It's an abbreviation of Mendelsohn. I didn't want another name. It's very logical: Mendelsohn, Melson. There was violence against Jews at this time in Poland, but it had nothing to do with me. When people heard the name, they thought I was Swedish. "We came to Poland three hundred years ago... blah, blah, blah." That's the story I cooked up. I was passing as a goy even before the war!

When Bobi was born we called him Sylvio after my mother, Sylvia. Her real name had been Sara, but she went by Sylvia. Nina's Jewish name is Necha, but she was called Natalia or Nacia for short. All the Jewish families Christianized and modernized their names. In America you can call yourself Sara, but in Poland it was no advantage to be called Sara or Necha.

A week after meeting her, I called Nacia from a famous swimming pool and asked her to join me. She said no, blah, blah, but tomorrow at three o'clock. The next day I was there at three. She arrived at four. Kept me waiting for an hour. Nicely dressed. At this time her father was not so prosperous. He had lost his business during the depression, but she was very well dressed—flamboyant, but in good taste. And we went to Proarte, a coffee shop where they also sold antique furniture.

We had so much to talk about, and we immediately became very intimate. We were like two lost souls that had found each other. I looked into her eyes, and I saw my mother's reflection. She told me about her life, and I told her about mine. She was very beautiful, had a lot of admirers, but she too was lonely.

We met every day. We were practically living together—that's when I realized that she was tremendously spoiled. There were two Jewish beauty queens of Warsaw; one of them was Nacia. She was sought after everywhere we went. She'd go on vacation an hour from Warsaw and her admirers would send her flowers, face powder, perfume, lipsticks, stockings—such idiotic things. I knew it, but I didn't like it.

Once we went dancing at the Adria. Adria was a very famous club where Nacia used to sing. Later when I was already dating her I recalled a young girl who had sung at the Adria, and unbeknownst to me at the time, it was Nacia! It was customary to cut in at a "dancing," but I told her I didn't like it. "Don't do it," I warned her. A guy comes, cuts in. Off she goes with him. "Darling, darling." They're dancing cheek to cheek. When she returned I told her, "Let's go." I pulled her behind an entrance door of a house. I gave her two slaps across the face. Clap! Clap! "Never cross me again!"

Look, it's my philosophy. It worked out fine. It worked out. I've always understood that with women you have to break them in. Either you are riding the horse or the horse is riding you.

"I'll leave you if you do that again!" she cried.

"My dear, I don't give a damn," I replied.

Another little incident: One day she tells me that she's going to the theater with someone. I say to her, "That's okay, but I don't want to know you anymore." It's ten o'clock. I get a telephone call from Tadzo, her younger brother: "She didn't go, blah, blah, blah." Always, always such things. She was testing me.

The third little incident: It's the high holidays. Nacia comes to me, and without saying hello she says, "Cigarettes, where are the cigarettes?"

I took her and threw her out of the apartment: "Get out!" A few minutes later she came back. She was very young. A very young, a very spoiled girl, but I loved her. She was my lover and my mother. In my own way I worshipped her.

One day I said to her, "Why don't you move your piano here?"

"What do you mean?" she asked.

So that's how I proposed.

———————————

It was the summer of 1939. War was brewing. My business was bad, so I returned to Stanisławów to work in my father's factory. I had to swallow my pride. I had a wife. I had a child. My father met us at the station and brought us to the factory grounds, where he gave us the use of a small villa that came with a maid. I was supposed to work with him in the factory, take care of the business side, while he and my uncle Moritz looked after production. For the first few weeks things went off without a hitch.

Nacia redecorated the villa and hired Hela, a young Ukrainian girl, to look after Sylvio. I worked in the factory, and in the evenings we'd try to find something to do. There were one or two restaurants and a movie house, but after Warsaw, Stanisławów was deadly dull, especially for her. Then she had this bright idea. Instead of trying to find entertainment, she would do the entertaining! I spoke to my father, and he agreed that twice a week there would be a concert on the factory grounds, "An Evening of Music and Songs with Nacia Mendelsohn." She had a guitar, we got her a piano, and she'd sing folk songs and pop tunes. She was a big hit. The workers loved her, and that proved damn useful when the Soviets came.

A few weeks after I had been working at the factory, I found out that by buying wool from local suppliers, instead of from Holland as we usually did, I could save the business a lot of money. Since my father and uncle were out of town I decided to act on my own. After all, I wasn't a child anymore—I was in my thirties and had run a successful business in Warsaw, so I made my own decision. When my father returned and found out what I had done, he became so enraged that he lost control of himself and began to shout and humiliate me in front of the office staff and the workers. I was about to tell him to stuff it, that I was going back to Warsaw, but then my uncle rushed in and shouted at my father to shut up: "The Germans attacked Poland this morning! The war is on!"

Just before I left Warsaw I visited the American embassy to ask about a visa. When they found out that my father had a factory, immediately they gave me a visitor's visa. There was an exhibition in 1939 in New York. I had this friend Glowinsky who worked for me, and he took care and prepared everything. He reserved the tickets. Everything was ready for the trip. When I got to Stanisławów I said to my father, "I have the tickets to go to America," but my father said no. The whole trip came to about 1,000 zloty, about $250, but my father said no.

"Willy, there will be no war," he said, but I knew different. Maybe yes, maybe no. I felt that war was coming. I didn't know all the details. I heard rumors. A few years before, when I was at a swimming pool in Berlin, the Brown Shirts came and beat up Jews. It was the beginning. It wasn't the heavy stuff like Kristallnacht in 1938, when the Nazis staged a pogrom in Germany. I didn't look Jewish. I lived my life separately. I didn't live in a Jewish community. I had nothing to do with this. But I knew. I saw. I understood there would be war. My father swore to me, "I give you my word that there won't be war." Suddenly there was war.

I'm supposed to go to the army. I get out my uniform and stuff a backpack, but before I can report, there is no army. The Polish army had been defeated before I could even join my unit. Polish cavalry against German Panzers. Forget about it!

The Germans attacked Poland from the west and the Russians grabbed it from the east. Stanisławów was in the east, so we were invaded by the Russians. They were heavily motorized. Even their horses were transported on trucks. The trucks were mounted with machine guns—not one, but four. Four machine guns mounted on the trucks. They came, you couldn't stop them. There was no resistance. What resistance?

At first things were not so bad. Most places remained open. The Russian soldiers behaved well, not like the Germans. They strolled in the streets and tried to flirt with the girls. The regular soldier was a Russian at heart: open, warm, a good soul who loves potatoes! But the NKVD, the Russian secret police, was something else entirely. They started to arrest, shoot, and deport people to Siberia. We tried our best to stay out of their way.

Now here is the situation: I am still living in the villa on the factory grounds, while my father is in his apartment in town. He's got all the money, and he asks the Russians what to do. They tell him, please put it in the bank immediately and sign the papers. Then they tell him to resign. He asks them to allow him to work in the factory for nothing, for a small salary. But they won't let him. Nothing. Not only can he not work, he can't even stay in Stanisławów—a man who had given his life to his damn factory!

The ID card they gave you was called *Soc. Pohozenie,* social background—a little booklet with your picture in it and your class background. We were all "capitalists"—very dangerous for us. Immediately he gets an identity card stamped "Capitalist." And his wife: "Wife of a Capitalist." And me: "Son of a Capitalist." And Nacia: "Wife of a Son of a Capitalist"! And a certain number, and this meant that you could not get any job. Impossible. You were banned. It was like the Germans who later stamped *Jude,* Jew, on people's ID cards. It determined your fate. My father fled Stanisławów for Kolomyja, a town nearby, where the NKVD arrested him.

Nacia and I were ordered to move out of our villa, so we packed all of our belongings, including all the furniture, which was put into a couple of trucks. At the entrance of the factory were huge iron gates. That's where the two trucks full of our stuff were stopped by Russian guards. "Halt!" they said, and they would not let us through. But for us, our furniture was our fortune. Without the furniture to barter we'd starve, since I had no money, and as a capitalist I wasn't allowed to work.

Nacia got out of the truck and went back into the factory to speak to the workers. She climbed up on a table, stopped their production, and made a speech like Lenin!

"Listen, brothers and sisters. You know me from before the war. You know that I'm no capitalist or aristocrat. I'm just like you. Give us a hand with getting our furniture out because without it we won't be able to barter for food and we'll starve."

So they consulted with each other, and then the factory representatives walked over to the Russian guards and told them in Russian: "You must let them go. If you don't, there will be trouble." So the Russians asked why.

Then a woman worker stepped forward and said, "Pani Mendelsohn was very good to us before you came. She sang for us. She organized evening entertainment for us. She was like a sister to us. She never acted as if she was the boss." So the Russians let us through. We took our stuff to Hela's cottage in a very poor neighborhood.

Hela was a Ukrainian girl, short, dark, red-headed, and plump, who loved Nacia and adored Sylvio. She loved him like a mother. She used to kiss him and fondle him for hours. When the Russians came Nacia told her, "Hela, I can't employ you anymore. We have no more money."

To which she replied, "I don't want any money from you. I just want to be with you. You can live in my house. Just give me a bowl of soup and we'll stay together." She was an orphan who had been left a small dacha on the outskirts of town. The three of us—and later Tadzo too—moved into the top floor while Hela lived in the kitchen downstairs.

By the winter we were freezing. In the factory we had these round cast-iron stoves that were heated with wood logs. I installed one of these in our house, but at first it didn't work, the smoke came into the room. Later when I got it working, we ran out of wood. Then we started to run out of food. It's winter. It's very cold. How do I live? The peasants are coming to the market, and you can barter with them. We bartered our furniture for food, potatoes, and this is how we ate. However, I don't have wood. It's cold as hell. Sylvio is playing with the maid, and Nacia and I are sitting on the bed. Freezing. Suddenly I hear whistling from outside. It's a friend of my father's, a friend of ours. "Willy, what are you doing?" So I explain to him. He says, "Why don't you throw in some furniture?" We were trying to avoid burning our furniture, but there was no help for it. I threw in the kitchen chairs, otherwise we would freeze. Such crazy things!

One day while we were out, a fire broke out, and the house was engulfed in flames. Of course we lost almost everything, even though I helped the fire brigade to douse the flames. To add to our problems, the next day we got a visit from the NKVD. They accused me of sabotage. They took me aside and began to question me. This was not the first or the last time that Nacia showed that she could be very daring, very brave. Later she told me that she gets a feeling of I-don't-give-a-damn— *vas banque*, as they say in roulette—and like a gambler playing for high stakes she risks it all.

While they had me pinned to their truck and were interrogating me, Nacia walked up and with her hands on her hips and a bright smile on her face she interrupted them right then and there.

"Listen," she said in broken Russian. "Why should we have burned down our own house? It's not logical. We lost everything. We don't have a penny, so just for that reason we'd burn down our house just to get your attention? Why?"

So the NKVD investigator says, "Mendelsohn is a son of a capitalist. This is sabotage."

Nacia got mad and interrupted him again, "Some capitalist!" she laughed. "He's got nothing to eat and is dressed in rags. My son and I are starving. We don't have a *grosz*."

I don't know if it was because of her bullshit or her good looks, but somehow we crawled out of that mess. That was the first visit from the NKVD, but there would be more.

The Halpern brothers were pint-sized little guys, friends of mine, who made their living making candles before the war. They had candle-making machines that the Russians confiscated and labeled them all "capitalists"! So now what? Three brothers with their families, perhaps fifteen people or so, and they're coming to me and asking, "Willy you're such a *macher*, what are we going to do?"

"We can starve to death," I tell them. However, there was one possibility.

Under the Russians there were three powers: the army, the NKVD, and the Party commissars. We had nothing to do with the army, and the NKVD would arrest and deport you on the spot. The only people you could talk to were the commissars because they needed goods, all kinds of goods, to send back to Russia. They needed craftsmen to make brushes, little mirrors, ink, all sorts of consumer junk. For this they allowed people to organize craft cooperatives that they called *artils*. If you worked in such a cooperative, they didn't ask you where you got the raw materials, and you had the privilege to buy bread.

Once I started working there was such a rule: "For each hand one bread." I'd get home, and I'd have two loaves of bread—perfect bread, very good bread. So you didn't have to starve. But what kind of craftsman am I? I know nothing. So the Halpern brothers told me, "The Russians have a wagon. A whole wagon of wax to make candles, but we have no machine to make candles, since they've confiscated it."

So I said, "You know what? I'll go and tell them that I'm an expert. I'll make a chemical *artil*, and we'll make candles."

"What kind of expert are you?" the brothers asked me.

"An expert for making candles!" I replied.

I went to the Russian commissar. "I'm a chemist. I want to make an *artil*. I have ten, fifteen people who can go in with me. We can make all sorts of products. We'll start with candles and call it Artil Krushcheva."

I didn't know then that Nikita Krushchev was head of the whole Ukrainian region. *Weiss Ich?* What did I know? But I knew he was important. The commissar was very pleased.

"And could you use a wagon of wax?" he asks.

"Oh, da," I say. "Please, yes."

On Kazimierzowska Street I rented a store, and the Halpern brothers and I started the Artil Krushcheva. We rolled candles by hand because the Russians stupidly had confiscated their candle-making machine. We used up the whole wagon of wax and stacked up thousands of candles. Delivered, we got the money from the commissar. Fine. We were in business!

Usually at eight o'clock I went to the *artil*, and then I went to the Russian commissars for a *schmooze*. They liked me. When they heard that I was listening to the forbidden BBC, the British radio, they asked me, "What's new? What's going on?" And I told them. Around ten o'clock I went to the bakery to make sure that the bread was ready for us, but then I looked around for maybe meat, maybe wood—I was the *farzorger*, scrounger, head of the outfit. After a week or so the Russians said, "We have another *artil*, forty people, they're making brushes. They are going to be attached to your *artil*. Take care of them."

I gave myself a title, Technical Director of Artil Krushcheva. The people wanted to elect me as their president, but that was impossible. I persuaded the *balagula*, the porter who used to drive the *shmates* and other rags to my father's factory, to become the president. To show me his appreciation, he would sit with me over a cup of coffee. This was a big favor because to sit with the "capitalist Mendelsohn" was dangerous for him. And yet the difference in salary between us was very little. I think I got 350 rubles and he got 400. That's all.

Every few weeks another group would be added to the *artil.* One week it was fifteen people who had an oil press. Then another group of sixty people who made little mirrors. In this Artil Krushcheva they had consolidated all the little *scheiss,* shitty, crafts. Finally we had over a hundred people. Without me there would have been no *artil,* and they all would have starved. I knew how to talk to the commissar and how to scrounge around for resources and food. I was the whole business.

Ordinarily there was nothing to do in the evening, so one day when I heard that an opera troupe was in town and they were going to do *Aida,* I told Nacia, and she was thrilled. I like operettas—Franz Lehar, *The Merry Widow*—but opera bores me to death. I went only because Nacia insisted. Most people, including us, just went dressed in their ordinary everyday clothes, but these Russian women—trying to make an impression, I guess—arrived dressed in the sheer nightgowns that they had confiscated from the "capitalists" like us. These were expensive transparent nightgowns that they must have taken for ball gowns. For the most part they were short and stout middle-aged wives of commissars and NKVD officers. "Look at them!" Nacia whispered, poking me in the ribs. "It's all the potatoes they eat. Such fat *babas.* Such huge *tzitzkis!*"

I shushed her like a child: "Be quiet. Do you want to get us arrested?"

After a few months under the Russians Nacia started getting letters from her parents in Warsaw. Her parents and all her aunts and uncles had moved in together. About fifteen people in one apartment. They had no work, no money, no food. Soon they became destitute, and little by little they began to die of typhus.

One day she got news that her father was dying. Then, after a few weeks, she received a letter: "My beloved child, I'm still alive. God wants me to live. I was close to the end and was worried about your mother, what she would do without me. But the Lord wants me to live. There was no medicine, and food is scarce, but somehow the typhus is gone. Now I believe that I'll survive this war. Such is our fate." And her mother added a note: "My dear, if there is some way for you to get us a bit of food, we'd be most grateful."

Nacia made up packages of flour, oil, whatever we could get our hands on that would not spoil, and at first her parents got them. Her mother wrote: "My dear child, you don't realize it, but you are saving our lives." But then increasingly the letters became more desperate. One day her mother wrote: "I hid your package from the rest of the family because I can't afford to divide up our food anymore." The next day we went into town and bartered our winter coats to get food for them. We made up a big package and sent it to Warsaw, but they never received it.

———————————

One day Tadzo, Nacia's brother, arrived at Hela's. He had been living with his parents in Warsaw, but he had escaped and somehow was able to find us. I remembered him as tall, thin, well dressed, and jaunty when I knew him before the war, but now he looked like a starving homeless beggar, so that I hardly recognized him. He was ill, and for the first few days he could hardly speak. Nacia nursed him back to health.

At first he didn't want to talk about the ghetto. We had to drag it out of him little by little. It came out in fragments.

People were starving, there were bodies lying in the street. There were thousands of refugees from all over Poland, some from abroad. Most couldn't find housing because even before they came, there were seven to ten people living in a room. So the refugees were homeless and some froze to death. It was the intelligentsia that had it the worst. Professors from the university, composers, actors, directors, writers—all had been reduced to beggary. They stood on street corners, dressed in rags, their hands out, begging for a few groszy. *The Germans seized men and women for forced labor and treated them brutally. People were whipped and beaten for the slightest infraction or for no reason at all. Many were killed right at the job. Polish hooligans would steal into the ghetto sometimes at night, where they would go on rampages of rape and destruction. There were attempts at self-help and self-defense. Each apartment block had a housing committee that would try to take care of its own, and a small underground counterfeited identity papers and helped people to escape to the "Aryan" side, but any physical resistance was crushed with great brutality.*

His parents had pleaded with him to escape so that at least he could survive, but he had refused, feeling that his duty was to stay with them. It was only after his father insisted that he save himself that he escaped

*and managed, after weeks of wandering, to cross the border into the
Soviet zone.*

*On his way to Stanisławów he had stayed a week in Lwów, where
he had run into some of his friends who belonged to the Zionist youth
movement, Hashomer Hatzair, the Young Guard. They told him that in
a small village in the German zone, the Germans had rounded up all
the Jews in a synagogue. They had set fire to the building and had shot
anyone who tried to escape.*

The next day he found us. He felt as if he had betrayed his family
and his people, and he finished his story by holding his head in his hands
and staring at his shoes. Nacia was crying softly.

I realized that Tadzo was upset, but I didn't believe what he said.
I thought that he was exaggerating and slightly hysterical. The story
about the Jews in the burning synagogue is what did it. It sounded like
World War I propaganda to me. I knew that the Germans could be brutal,
but this, no. It was impossible. Moreover, life for us was not exactly a
socialist paradise. Not only was there a problem with getting enough to
eat but there was also the ever-present fear of arrest, and soon rumors
reached us that thousands of people were being deported to the east. It
all seemed fantastic and slightly insane.

The NKVD deported thousands of Poles, Ukrainians, Belorussians,
and Jews. Among them were political enemies like Trotskyites and An-
archists; what they considered to be class enemies, including aristocrats,
landowners, well-to-do merchants, bankers, industrialists, and hotel and
restaurant owners; also priests, rabbis, ministers, refugees, people who
had traveled abroad, Esperantists, and stamp collectors.

My father was too old to be deported, so they imprisoned him. Nacia
went to the NKVD to plead for his release. She tried to explain that he
loved his factory and his workers. She told them that he was just like
another worker, but a worker who really loved his job. "Listen, be a de-
cent person. You're dealing with an older man. How long do you think
he has to live? Let him go," she said. But they wouldn't do it, told her to
mind her own business or she would be arrested next.

The prison where they kept him was an old converted barn surrounded by little wooden huts guarded by Soviet troops. Later when he
got sick they let him out, but they had beaten him so badly that he had
lost sight in one eye. I saw him briefly before he and his wife—she had
been his maid before the war—moved to the country. There he committed suicide when the Germans came.

My father was arrested plainly because he was an industrialist. I am not sure why the NKVD hunted Tadzo when he escaped the German zone and came to live with us—maybe because he was suspected of being a German or a Zionist spy or an illegal Jewish refugee from the Warsaw ghetto or possibly because he enjoyed collecting stamps.

———————————

After he had been with us for a few months, Tadzo read in all the papers and saw placards posted in public places that persons with higher education—professionals, scientists, doctors, teachers, and so on—were to report to the railroad station. They would be taken by train to work in the Soviet Union, where they would contribute to the glorious building of socialism.

Before the war he had started his pre-med studies in biology at the university, and he was tired of working for me at the artil, *so he was tempted by the possibility of working in his profession, even if it was far away in the Soviet Union. Without telling me, his sister, or anyone, he packed his small leather doctor's bag and a satchel of books on the assigned day and walked down to the station.*

A few blocks from his destination he saw a large crowd making its way, and he recognized a few of the better-educated people from the artil. *Before he reached the train, however, the* balagula, *the coachman who had worked for my father in our factory and now headed up the* artil, *somehow recognized him and sidled up to him.*

"Listen to me good," said the coachman in Yiddish. He was dressed in a leather coat and was wearing a cloth cap that almost hid his broad face. "I'm in the party, and I know, if you want to go on breathing, don't go near that train."

Tadzo hesitated. He had crazy hopes of a new life in the Soviet Union, where he might be able to complete his medical training and where, after the war, he might be able to bring his parents. But then, wisely, he decided to listen to the coachman. He turned around and went back to the artil.

Once the train was full, it stayed in the station for three days and no one was allowed to get on or off. All over town you could hear the cries for water and food coming from the railroad station. Finally it left for a three-week trip to Siberia, where most of its passengers disappeared into the taiga, *the frozen forests. Many people perished; still, the Jews had a better chance of surviving Siberia then the ghetto. Meanwhile, Tadzo went back to live with us, and that's where the NKVD came to look for him.*

We were having dinner—mostly pea soup and potatoes—when we heard a whistle and a strange commotion in the street. Hela looked out of the window and whispered, "NKVD!" My first thought was that they were coming back to arrest me for the fire. Then I realized they had probably come for Tadzo.

"Hela, it's Tadzo," I said. She understood immediately and led him up to the attic, where she covered him under a pile of laundry.

A few minutes later three guys dressed in civilian clothes barged in and surrounded us, while we stayed seated at the dinner table.

"Do you know Ponczek?"

"He is my brother-in-law."

"Where is he?"

"I have no idea. He was here, but now he's gone back to Warsaw."

At a signal from their commander they started to search the house. Then Sylvio got up without permission and ran up the stairs to the attic. Nacia went after the child. One of the NKVD guys followed both of them upstairs. I didn't know what was going on, but a few minutes later the NKVD guy comes down eating a pickle and Nacia follows him, holding Sylvio in her arms. They looked for about a half hour, and then, after giving me all sorts of warnings, they left. Later Tadzo came downstairs, shaky but okay. What had happened in the attic?

Nacia explained that Sylvio was about to show the NKVD where his uncle was hiding, but somehow she managed to distract the guy by giving him a pickle. On such things depended our lives!

One night in June 1941, I hear on the BBC that millions of Germans attacked the Russians and had started the invasion of the Soviet Union. That meant us! The next day I go to the commissar, he tells me not to worry, the Russians would quickly drive the Germans back. But then a few days later I hear that the Germans are advancing everywhere and the Russians are fleeing. I go to the commissar—this time he is very grim and tells me that it's true. The Germans will be here any day. There is a proclamation: Those who want to flee with the Russians can do so. He tells me that trucks will be available the next day and that I should take my family and flee to the Soviet Union. "Why?" I ask.

"Because people like you don't have a chance."

That night Nacia and I discussed it. I didn't know what to do. "How are you going to survive in Siberia?" I asked. I decided that we'd risk living under the Germans. After all, German is my mother tongue; I have a German university degree; My father served in the Austrian army, and I have his papers. I was sure that things would improve with the Germans, especially for a person like me. Of course, I could not have been further from the truth.

Bobi

I remember chasing Hela around the kitchen table in her house. It was winter. There was wood crackling in the huge hot iron stove, and we were getting sweaty from the exertion. Hela was wearing a long peasant skirt, but I was determined to lift it to see what she had under it.

"You're such a naughty, naughty boy!" She cried as she picked me up, out of breath from laughing, and hugged me while I pulled the bobby pins out of her long red hair. Just then *mamusia*, my mother, came in looking mock-stern, but I knew she was kidding, and came to Hela's aid by taking me into her arms.

I was playing in the dirt road in front of our house when I saw *tatusiu*, my father, riding his bike around the bend. He was wearing a worker's cap with the brim raised up, and he was waving to my mother and me. Before he could dismount, I ran up to him, and he hoisted me up on the handlebars. These dug painfully into my butt, but I shrieked with delight as we careened together the few yards back home. Then *tatusiu* swung me up to the sky, set me down safely, and leaned the bike against the wall. I ran after him to where *mamusia* and Hela were waiting.

My uncle Tadzo was a tall, blond, blue-eyed, skinny guy with a sweet but crooked smile and an off-the-wall sense of humor. When he first came to stay with us, he and I hit it right off. At first, before he became employed in my Dad's *artil*, he had a lot of time to play with me. He showed me a trick where a spoon could be made to disappear up your sleeve. We'd build forts out of the living room furniture, and we'd play hide-and-seek in the attic among the laundry.

Before the three NKVD men came through the door and started looking for him, Uncle Tadzo disappeared. I figured that he was playing hide-and-seek, the way we usually did, so I went looking for him too. And I was better at it than the policemen, because I found him hiding in his usual place in the attic—under a pile of sheets behind the barrels of pickles. The policemen were still looking downstairs when I cried out my delight at being the first to find my uncle. Meanwhile, he tried to shoo me away and gestured that I should be quiet. My mother, who had followed me, caught on to the dangerous game and shushed me just as one of the three NKVD types appeared on the stairs.

Still holding on to me, she stuck her right arm through the left arm of the Soviet policeman.

"Tell them you looked here, Comrade," she laughed, "and all you found was pickles."

"Wait," said the policeman as he disentangled himself from my mother and went to the barrel. There he fished for a pickle and followed us downstairs.

3   *False Papers*

Nina

The morning of October 12, 1941, I woke up toward dawn. I'd had a disturbing dream and was drenched in sweat.

"Let's get out right now," I said to Willy. "We don't even have time to wash up." I was getting dressed as Willy examined me with the dumb look of someone just awakened from a deep sleep. "I am certain the Gestapo will come this morning to arrest us. We'll be killed. We've got to leave immediately."

"You're insane," Willy said.

I usually go along with him, but I knew we were in grave danger, and I had to get us out of the house. "Let's take Sylvio and let's get out now!" I pulled the child out of bed and started to dress him. Sylvio was confused and kept falling back asleep in my arms. He smelled sweet, like newly mowed hay.

Ever so grudgingly, Willy got out of bed. "What makes you think we're in danger?" He slipped a black ski parka over his head.

"Last night I had a dream: My father stood in the middle of a town square. He was surrounded by a bright light and was holding up a placard with the number twelve printed on it over his head. He then waved me over. When I approached him, he said, 'Take care, you're in grave danger! You're in grave danger!' I tried to touch him, but he turned away and faced a blank wall. That's when I woke up. Today is October 12—something terrible is going to happen."

Without further questions, the three of us fled to friends who lived out of town. The Offenbergers, Jews who had converted to Catholicism, knew the Mendelsohn family from before the war. We walked for three hours. Sylvio was cranky, so Willy and I took turns carrying him part of the way.

When we arrived, we simply said that we feared for our lives. Could they help? During the war no long explanations were necessary. I didn't tell them about my dream—I was too embarrassed and they'd think I was hysterical. They didn't question us further.

"Of course," they said. "First let's have lunch, and then we'll show you where you can stay."

They were a middle-aged couple, possibly in their forties. He wore glasses and had thinning blond hair, while she was short and plump and looked very Jewish to me. In every room of their two-story house hung a crucifix, which made me feel uneasy because I still thought of them as Jews. Willy told me that they had become Catholics way before the war, not because of any advantage it might bring them, but because they were genuine believers. That made no difference to me. All I cared was that they were kind and brave. Everyone knew that they could be killed for hiding Jews.

After a midday dinner of hot vegetable barley soup and baked pigeons with potatoes—luxuries during the war—they took us downstairs to a cellar filled with straw and told us to make ourselves at home.

I heard some scurrying and scratching under all that straw. I'm terrified of mice and rats, but I was so relieved to be out of Hela's house and in a safe place that I stretched out with great pleasure. Willy lay down next to me, and Sylvio, having jumped up and down on the pile of straw, crawled in between us and fell asleep. Willy and I said very little. What was there to discuss? We listened to the sounds of the Offenbergers moving above us, but somehow I found that comforting, and I fell into a deep sleep.

———————

While we slept the Jews of Stanisławów were being killed. Preparations had started in July 1941 when the German army had marched into the city. Willy's hometown had a population of about sixty thousand people, half of whom were Jews. First the Germans established a *Judenrat*, a Jewish council, that was supposed to help them in running the Jewish community. Then they rounded up other Jews who might have become opposition leaders—teachers, doctors, lawyers, journalists—and so on. The victims were told to bring their books and to assemble at Gestapo headquarters. Among this early group were photographers—I suppose because the killers were afraid of photographic evidence.

When he first heard the announcement, Willy wanted to go, reminded me that he had a diploma from the Handelshochschule, a business school in Berlin. Since he spoke perfect German, perhaps he could make himself useful, like under the Russians. But I told him to forget about it. That was the first time he had trusted my intuition. One of Willy's uncles went. He was never heard from again. None of the men who went ever returned.

On October 12, 1941, after posting placards in public, the Germans ordered the Jews to assemble in the center of town. Thousands of people showed up with all their pathetic belongings. Some even brought their pets! They were loaded onto trucks and driven to the new Jewish cemetery, where they found SS, German police units, and Ukrainian militia waiting. They were first told to undress and to line up in front of previously dug ditches; then they were machine-gunned to death.

Hans Krueger, the commander in charge of the operation, had brought a picnic with him. He picked people off at random and shot them in the head with his service revolver in his right hand while he munched on a sandwich with his left. Later the bodies were covered over with earth by Ukrainian laborers. The killing lasted from 11:00 A.M. to 7:30 P.M. The *Judenrat*, standing stark naked with the rest, was made to watch the proceedings. Shooting was halted by darkness, although it continued for a while under the headlights of trucks.

A few people, including one of Willy's high school girlfriends, escaped by feigning death until nightfall. They managed to dig themselves out from among the bodies in the ditches and to climb over the two-three meter wall of the cemetery. Other Jews like us survived because they had refused to go to the original roundup. Willy told me that after the *Aktion*, Krueger sent his blood-stained tunic to the *Judenrat* for cleaning.

The next morning, after thanking the Offenbergers, we went back to Hela's. We didn't want to overstay our welcome and endanger them. By the time we got home in the evening we had heard about the massacre. When we opened the door there was a party. Hela, wearing my favorite red dress, which was much too tight on her, was surrounded by her Ukrainian friends, who were singing and drinking vodka. I asked Willy to stay in the hall. They would see a man, and there would be trouble. When I walked in, Hela was dumbfounded.

"Madame is still alive?"

"You see, I'm still alive."

"I feel real bad that I'm wearing your dress."

We exchanged looks, she turned away. Then she chased all her Ukrainian friends out of the house, took off the dress, and got right back to work. She washed Sylvio and prepared dinner for us as if nothing had happened. Hela was no angel, but she stood by us when we needed her.

The next day I went to the *Gmina,* the seat of the Jewish council, to find out more about what had happened. The few Jewish acquaintances that I ran into seemed like shadows. They would sidle up, whisper a few words, and quickly move on. I found it all very bizarre. No one grieved or showed any emotion whatsoever. People would mention that their wives or husbands or children or parents had been shot, but they did so without expression, almost as if it were distant news. I was no different. I too spoke in the same impersonal tone of voice. My body was chilled. Half the time I was trembling, and my vocal cords seemed paralyzed.

At first, Willy stayed home because he was afraid of being recognized. Later he was able to get hold of a railroad worker's uniform, including an official-looking cap, that allowed him to get out at dusk. On one of his walks he had seen a small crowd surrounding two elderly religious Jews, still dressed in their long black *kaftans,* being humiliated by German troopers.

The two old men were on their hands and knees while two grinning Germans were straddling their backs as if they were riding horses. A race was on, and the old Jews, their beards mostly cut off or pulled off, were being whipped about their bloody faces and buttocks to "gallop" as fast as they could. Other troopers, laughing and shouting, were placing bets as to which of the two "riders" would come in first.

Willy tore himself from the crowd and ran blindly home. He told me the story without looking at me, as if he were addressing the air. I could sense his rage and grief. But when I asked him what we should do, he replied simply, "I don't know."

For a while Willy thought that we could save ourselves by getting converted like the Offenbergers. He went to a priest for help. The priest, an elderly man, totally bald, dressed in a black cassock with a heavy cross dangling from his neck, was very cheerful about the whole thing. He told Willy that it might take six months of heart-felt study and dedication to get converted. When Willy pointed out that he didn't have six months, the priest shrugged and announced that it was impossible. As Willy left, the good man urged him to take an apple from a bowl on his desk.

Willy didn't realize that conversion wouldn't have helped anyway. The Offenbergers, whom we had envied for their foresight, were later murdered with all the others when the Jews of Stanisławów were shipped off to the Bełzec extermination camp. But that came later.

Soon after the massacre of October 12, the Germans blocked off a few streets and ordered the surviving Jews to move into a ghetto. The Carpens, friends of ours who owned a bakery, came to visit and proposed that our two families look together for a place to stay. I agreed. I liked them because, although they had been reduced to being humble bakers, they were charming, good looking, and had a great sense of humor. He looked like Leslie Howard, the actor in *Gone with the Wind*. I always preferred Clark Gable, but Leslie Howard was sweet.

"Let's do it, Willy," I pleaded. "We must, and it will be nice living together." I tried to make it seem almost cozy to cheer us all up.

But Willy, who had been silent while we were discussing plans, would have none of it: "Never!" he shouted. "I'm not going into any ghetto. If they're going to kill me, let them kill me here!"

"But you're endangering yourself, Willy," said Carpen.

"No, you are. Don't you understand that in the ghetto we'll all be killed? Outside we have a slim chance." The Carpens left shaking their heads.

The night we were supposed to move into the ghetto, Willy and I stayed up to discuss what to do. We figured that our time at Hela's was running out. Every day she reported that friends were asking her about her strange guests. We had a child, which under the circumstances made things more difficult. We had very little money, only some junk to barter—an old typewriter, Willy's bicycle, a sewing machine, a few good dresses and suits. Meanwhile, we were all condemned to death simply for being Jews. We had to find some way of passing as "Aryans," and we had to get out of Stanisławów, but how? Toward morning Willy and I decided that our only chance was the Zamojskis. When we finally went to bed that night we slept restlessly, listening to strange sounds from the street and the creak of floorboards on the stairs.

We had met the Zamojskis by chance one evening a few months before the war at the Unionka, a cafe and "dancing." The place was crowded and smoke-filled. An orchestra was playing a set of *chardash* Gypsy music, and then it switched to tangos and fox-trots so that people could dance. The proprietor, who knew us, apologized, but there were no empty tables. Would we mind sitting with another couple? He then led us to a corner table where we met the Zamojskis.

Jan Zamojski stood up, clicked his heels, and pulled out a chair. He was tall, bony, and sandy-haired, wore glasses, and was dressed in a somewhat worn double-breasted tailor-made flannel suit. Janina Zamojska was rather plain looking. She was a fleshy blond with watery-blue eyes, but she was well educated and well spoken. After the introductions, Willy and I realized that we had been seated next to descendants of Polish aristocrats who bore an illustrious name. The family Zamojski was old-time nobility. They had been state builders and prime ministers. In Poland the name was as famous as that of Copernicus, Mickiewic, and Radziwill. When we introduced ourselves as "Mendelsohn," Jan and Janina Zamojska did not let on that it made a difference, but they plainly realized that, charming or not, we were Jews.

The two couples danced, exchanged partners, chatted, and flirted. Even Janina and I hit it off when we discovered that we both had little boys nearly the same age. I was especially pleased to make their acquaintance. To speak frankly, I found most of the people I had met in Stanisławów before the war dull and boring. They were rather primitive, even the Jews. I missed Warsaw—its cafes, theaters, films, and nightlife. Now, by pure chance, Willy and I had met another young, urbane couple, named Zamojski no less. Willy, ever the cynic, remarked later, when we got to know them better, that Jan Zamojski was a clerk in the town's administration, though he may have been well educated and had a famous name. The Zamojskis of Stanisławów had no castles, no horses, and no lands. But I was beaming!

We met quite frequently before the war and during the Soviet occupation. We didn't invite each other home—Jews and gentiles didn't do such things—but we agreed to meet at the Unionka or at some other restaurant. By the time the Germans came, we were not exactly close friends, but we were acquaintances who were fond of each other.

One afternoon, a few weeks after the formation of the ghetto, I decided to go to the Zamojskis to ask for help. When I knocked, Janina opened the door and seemed startled to see me, but she quickly recovered. This was the first time that either one of us had visited the other at home.

"Nacia! How nice. Come in."

I was relieved by the cordial reception. She hadn't thrown me out or called me a lousy Jew. Still, I was disappointed by their rather shabby apartment. In my mind I had built up the Zamojskis as rich and powerful and had hoped for something more grand than a nondescript living room, a kitchen, and a bedroom with a few portraits of the family hanging on the walls.

Bogusław Zamojski, their little tow-headed, blue-eyed kid, was playing with blocks on the floor while Jan Zamojski came out of the kitchen smiling and wiping his hands on a towel. They served tea and some home-made cookies. After the usual banalities, I came quickly to the point.

"You know what's been happening under the Germans. The Jews are sentenced to death. Willy, Sylvio, and I are in hiding. We don't know what to do. I've come to ask for your help. You're our last chance."

Jan Zamojski looked sympathetic but confused. "Us? How can we help you?"

"You could let us have your papers of identification, especially your birth certificates. Willy, Sylvio, and I would leave Stanisławów and make a life for ourselves somewhere else. Meanwhile, you could go to church and get new birth certificates. You could tell the priest that you had lost your documents or that the Soviets had confiscated them. It's our only chance." I had rehearsed that speech with Willy, but now I realized how bizarre the proposal must sound.

Jan and Janina listened silently, observing me over the rim of their tea cups. When I finished, Janina stood up, picked up her little boy, and signaled Jan to accompany her. The three Zamojskis disappeared into the bedroom. I could hear the little boy protesting being put to bed. Then I heard some whispering. Finally Jan and Janina came out to face me in the living room. They looked uncomfortable and embarrassed standing in front of me, while I was seated.

"I'm sorry," said Jan, his eyes downcast. "We realize what a difficult situation you're in, but so are we all. We can't just hand over our birth certificates. If the Germans got wind of it, we'd all be killed." He paused, allowing that thought to sink in. "As you can see from where we live," he gestured vaguely to take in their flat, "we are in very difficult straits. After the Russians and the Germans got through with us, we've got nothing left. We have no money and live from day to day." Here he paused again, while my heart skipped a beat. "Willy comes from a well-to-do family. There must be some money left. Perhaps for twenty thousand zloty, about $5,000, we could let you have the documents."

"It's true," added Janina with finality. "We could get new birth certificates at the church. In the meanwhile, of course, you'd have to leave Stanisławów."

"So it's a simple business proposition!" exclaimed Willy with anger. "Our lives for twenty thousand zloty. And where are we supposed to find this treasure? Maybe we can sell the bicycle and the sewing machine, we'll throw my suits and your dresses into the bargain, and then we'll have about five hundred zloty! What the hell are we supposed to do, take Sylvio by his sweaty little hand while he drags his potty behind him and start marching down the road in winter?"

I started to cry. The Zamojskis were our last chance. Now that was gone. We were sentenced to death. We didn't know why, and we didn't know where to turn next.

That night I couldn't sleep. I had taken drops of valerian, hoping that they would help settle my nerves, but all they did was increase my restlessness. The next morning I got up with a desperate plan: I would go back to the Zamojskis. I didn't tell Willy, because I didn't want to disappoint him should my scheme fail, and I was afraid that he would stop me from going. I left in the afternoon, after making a lame excuse that I needed to go shopping.

When I knocked on their door, the Zamojskis were in a good mood. They may have assumed that I was bringing the money and that their economic problems were over. Once again the three of us sat in the living room. Bobi was asleep in the bedroom, and Janina served bitter-tasting ersatz coffee.

"My dear friends," I started, "I spoke to Willy about your proposal. He thinks the price is a bit steep, but he can raise the money. There is no problem from our end. In the meanwhile, I've come to inspect the 'merchandise,' you understand. I need to see what your birth certificates and other documents look like. I hope you don't mind." I smiled. I tried to exude calm and confidence.

The Zamojskis looked disappointed. They exchanged knowing glances, but after a moment's hesitation he said, "You'll have to excuse us for a few minutes." Then they both disappeared into the bedroom. A few minutes later they came out with the documents. There were birth certificates and wedding certificates. These were passes to life. How I envied their being Polish and "Aryan" and not Jewish! But I tried to look as nonchalant as possible as I inspected the merchandise. While the Zamojskis left me alone and busied themselves in the kitchen, I tried to memorize the pertinent information: names, dates, places. I scratched whatever facts I could on the flap of my worn brown leather shoulderbag, breaking a nail in the process.

After a few minutes they returned with a bottle of schnapps and some glasses, which I refused because I needed to keep a clear head. As I left I told them that I'd be back with the money in a few days.

"It's a large sum," I said, "but Willy will manage to raise it. Don't you worry."

When I heard the door of their apartment close behind me, I descended to the ground floor. I sat on their pitch-dark staircase, and by the light of matches I wrote furiously into a child's small lined notebook that I had brought with me just for this purpose. I copied whatever facts I could

remember and make out from the scratches on my pocketbook: Jan Ferdynand Zamojski, Bogusław Marian Zamojski, Janina Victoria Zamojska,
born in Lwów on such and such a date, baptized in Stanisławów at the
Church of so and so. Good.

The next morning around eleven, again I gave Willy a lame excuse
about needing to go out to barter for food. I wore pale rose lipstick that
suited me, I covered my hair in a blue silk babushka in a rose flower pattern, I pulled on a pair of prewar fur-lined black leather winter boots, and
I wore my black woolen coat, which was starting to look ratty, belted at
the waist. I did the best I could to look presentable. I knew I looked like
a hundred Polish young women all boiled into one, and I spoke the Polish of the upper classes. Thus armed I proceeded to the church where all
the Zamojskis had been baptized.

The tall black wrought iron gates of the church were open. I felt gid-
dy as I proceeded toward the priest's outer office. The place was very busy
with clerks and parishioners; nevertheless, a young man stood up and gave
me his seat. Polish men are very polite, especially when it comes to a
pretty woman.

"Perhaps, Madame would like a teensy smoke?" The clerk offered
me a cigarette. He used the cute and polite form of the diminutive when
speaking to me. The thought that, despite everything, I still had my appeal gave me confidence.

I sat down, lit up, grateful for the cigarette, and realized to my surprise that I was as calm as a rock. I decided to treat the whole experience
like a performance at the Adria. I recalled fat Moskowitz and how he had
tried to kiss me, and I smiled to myself.

Finally I was ushered into the priest's study. He was an elderly man,
perhaps seventy, tall, totally bald, dressed in a black cassock, a huge cross
dangling from his neck. He had been standing, paging through a book, but
he sat down behind his desk without offering me a seat. I realized with a
start that he was the same priest who had refused to give Willy the conversion documents. In front of me was the bowl of apples that he had once
offered Willy. But when I looked again, I thought he had a plain but sympathetic face and a cheerful disposition; suddenly, I was prepared to like
him.

"How can I help you, Madame?" he asked.

I smiled and answered him in the most disarming way I could, "But
Father, don't you remember me?"

The good father looked bewildered. There is a Yiddish expression that
goes *Haben den Fisch am Schwantz*, holding the fish by its tail. I knew
he couldn't possibly remember me. So I repeated the question: "Father,
don't you remember me?"

"There's been so many people here today. It's hard to remember everyone."

"I'm Countess Zamojska! Janina Zamojska!"

For a moment he looked like he was going to faint. He stood up and started bustling about. The Zamojski name had produced its magic.

"My dear countess! Your Excellency! Please have a seat! How about some tea or a little glass of wine?"

"No, thank you. I never drink in the morning." For some reason I thought of Willy back at Hela's and what he might make of this scene. "My dear Father, I've come here to ask you for a huge favor . . . Before they left the Russians confiscated all our documents. They were about to arrest us and deport us, but then the Germans came. The Russians, the Germans, may the cholera take them both away! In any case we don't have a single piece of identification. Should the Gestapo ask for our papers, we have nothing to show them, and we're likely to be in a lot of trouble. Perhaps, dear Father, you can help me in this matter. I was baptized here, so was my husband, so was my little boy. I need birth certificates for the three of us." I needed his help, but I didn't want to look pitiful, so I gave him my most radiant smile.

"There is no problem, my dear countess," he said. "Let me just jot down a few details."

He took a pad of paper and a pen and began to question me: "Your full name. Your date of birth. Your place of birth. Your mother's name. Your father's name. Your husband's full name. His date of birth. His place of birth. His father's name. His mother's name. Your son's name. His date of birth. His place of birth . . ."

I had been a quick study back at the Adria. I was prepared, and I never faltered.

He rose and excused himself. "Why don't you just wait a few minutes and have a cigarette. My clerk will type out the birth certificates for you, and I'll keep a copy. They might be of use at a later date."

I thought I had stepped through the screen into a movie. At any moment the director would come into the room and tell me that I was acting in a silly comedy and that I should go home. I also thought how impressed Willy would be with my chutzpah.

A few minutes later the good father returned with the documents. I glanced at them and stuck them nonchalantly in my purse.

As I got up to leave, the priest came from behind his desk and kissed my hand. "We'll be in touch." I smiled and waved gaily at him as I left.

On the way home, I stopped every few minutes to look into my purse to make sure that the documents were still there. I felt I'd burst like a balloon. I had pulled it off! Now we had a slim chance.

When I got home, I took Willy aside. "Willusiu, darling," I whispered, "I've got the papers."

"What?" He almost shouted. "What papers?"

"Willy dear, here's your new birth certificate. You're now 'Count Jan Ferdynand Zamojski.' I'm 'Countess Janina Zamojska.' You can call me 'Nina' from now on. And Sylvio is little 'Count Bogusław 'Bobi' Zamojski.'"

Willy took the documents to the window and for a few minutes studied them carefully. Then he hugged me gently to him, and like a small child I started to bawl.

From now on we were Jan, Janina, and Bobi Zamojski. Sylvio was four years old and had learned his name, but Willy and I tried to impress on him how important it was that he be "Bobi Zamojski" instead of "Sylvio Mendelsohn." He was a smart little kid and must have sensed that we were living in dangerous times. I don't know how, but he soon responded to being called "Bobi," and it was just as well that in time he forgot he had ever been "Sylvio."

Now the time had come to clear out. But we had no money. You couldn't get a taxi or a car. You couldn't take the train; you needed documents to travel. The birth certificates were a start, but to take the train you needed a *Kennkarte,* an identity card provided by the Germans. Jan thought it was too risky to apply for it in Stanisławów, where Zamojskis and Mendelsohns were likely to be known. Besides, the train station was surrounded by young Polish and Ukrainian blackmailers on the lookout for Jews. They were much better at spotting Jews than the Germans were, and if they caught them they'd strip them of everything before turning them over to the Gestapo. We couldn't take the chance.

The day after getting the false papers, calling myself "Nina," I went to a busy garage hoping to arrange something. I wandered in among the cars and trucks, the drivers, and the mechanics until I saw a nice-looking young guy with thick unruly sandy hair and sharp features washing down a large enclosed Mercedes truck. I raised the collar of my shabby woolen black coat, undid my blue and rose babushka, shook out my hair, and lit a cigarette. Then I sauntered over to the truck, the way I had seen Marlena Dietrich do it in *The Blue Angel.*

"Hi! What's your name?" I asked the young guy in Polish.

"Stash," he said.

"My name is Janina, but you can call me 'Nina.'"

"Okay, Nina. What can I do for you?"

"Look, I've got a problem. The Russians took my husband away. I don't have a *grosz,* and I have a little boy. I'm all alone with no one to help me. I'd like to get to Kraków, where I have an aunt."

Stash gave me a second look. "You're in luck. On Thursday I'm off to Kraków. I'm supposed to haul the furniture, the rugs, the lamps, the pictures, all the junk Commander Krueger swiped from the rich Jews. I just have to make one stop to see my brother in Lwów. It'll be all right. I'll take you with me."

When I had explained how to get to our place, Stash added, "Now, Nina, you know there's a 'condition,' but you've probably figured that out for yourself already."

"Sure," I said with a broad smile. "I'm looking forward to it. You won't be disappointed."

When I got home, I explained to Jan about Stash and the truck without mentioning Stash's "condition." Jan was so jealous and possessive; he was skeptical but he had no choice.

The night before Stash was supposed to arrive, Hela helped us pack, including a bicycle, a typewriter, a sewing machine, some prewar suits and dresses, a large blue down-filled comforter, and other stuff we might use for barter.

On Thursday afternoon—he had been delayed by a flat—Stash and his truck pulled up in front of the house. I ran out and sat next to him in the passenger seat and kissed him, while Hela opened up the back of the truck and Jan climbed aboard.

The young trucker was in great spirits. He pulled out a bottle of vodka and offered it to me. I took a swig. He took a swig. Soon the both of us were a bit sloshed. To make sure that Stash would give Willy enough time to find a hiding place in the back of the truck, I put my arms around him, and we made out.

A nice-looking *chłop,* a peasant, I thought. He's thrilled that a good-looking educated woman is willing to sleep with him. Is he in for a surprise!

Once I saw in the rearview mirror that Jan was inside, I disentangled myself from Stash and went to look for Sylvio, whom I had to be careful to call "Bobi." The child had been riding his little red tricycle, a gift from his grandfather. When I had called him to get ready because the truck had come, he had made sure to drag his bike with him and then to sit on it.

"We can't take it," I said impatiently, "just what we need!" and dragged him screaming to the truck. I didn't have the time or patience to explain that I couldn't take the chance of opening the back of the truck just so that we could take his little red tricycle with us. Stash looked annoyed, and I got worried that he'd change his mind about taking us to Kraków. It was only when the engine turned over and the truck started to roll that Bobi calmed down somewhat.

Meanwhile, Jan later told me, in the back of the truck he found six people sitting on boxes. They were all Poles and Ukrainians. Most looked like peasants. The two women among them had long red woolen dresses. There were no Jews among them, and no one as far as he could tell had recognized him. Apparently they too had made arrangements with Stash to go to Kraków. Instead of sitting with them, Jan crawled further inside, and, finding a mattress, he stretched out deep in the bowels of the truck. As we started to move, he could hear the conversation of his fellow passengers.

"They shot two lousy Jews behind the factory."

"They drove a truck over a whole bunch of them behind city hall."

They spoke in whispers. Someone laughed. After a while he stopped listening and shut his eyes.

Everything in that truck—all the furniture, lamps, pictures, clothes, bedding—were things stolen from the Jews that Krueger had murdered. Among this loot was the Mendelsohn furniture, including some of our own stuff. Under it all, covered by our huge blue comforter, Jan was stretched out asleep.

About an hour out of town, the truck ran into a roadblock manned by Special Order Police and Gestapo. Stash and I, holding Bobi asleep in my arms, had to get out. In late November the weather was getting cold, and the Germans were stomping their feet and pounding their chests to keep their circulation going. While Stash showed his papers to one of the Germans, I walked up to the officer in charge. I decided that when dealing with Germans you had to be assertive. Politeness and humility would simply rouse their suspicions.

"Why are you holding us up? You think we're Jews? I have a little boy. He and I are freezing. Can't you hurry it up?" I spoke in broken German, hoping that the little Yiddish I knew would not interfere, but I had made myself clear, and the more I got into the part, the more honest outrage I felt. They're like mad dogs, I thought. When dealing with them you have to be firm or they'll tear you apart.

The guy in charge looked embarrassed. "*Nein, nein. Sie sind eine Polin.* You're Polish. I can see that." And then he added, "I know that you're not Jewish because you look like beautiful Holy Mary Mother of God with little baby Jesus in her arms!"

I was speechless. They didn't even ask to see my papers!

Meanwhile, one of the policemen had opened the back of the truck and poked desultorily in it. He didn't bother with the Poles and Ukrainians in back. Jews were what they were after, but Jews they didn't find, and they waved us on.

As we approached Lwów, I started getting worried about the "payment" I owed Stash. Just then the truck pulled up in front of a small kiosk where you could purchase hot tea and sandwiches. While Stash disappeared to the bathroom, I suppose, and the other passengers were congregated around the kiosk, I climbed to the back of the truck and spoke to Jan in hushed tones. Quickly I explained the situation, and we cooked up a scheme. When the truck reached Lwów, Jan would try to jump out without being seen, make his way to the front of the truck, and pose as my long-lost brother who was meeting me by sheer chance. It was ludicrous—a drawing-room comedy—but what else was there to do?

We got to Lwów. Stash parked the truck, Jan got out without being seen, and he and I made a great show of running into each other by chance.

"Jan, could it be you?"

"Ninochka, my little sister—after all these years!"

Stash's relatives, amazed at the good luck of brother and sister meeting by chance right in front of their house, served us bread with cheese and hot milk. Then they showed us to our room—a little cell of a place— two beds side by side, each covered by a grimy gray comforter.

Jan and I assumed that we had solved the problem of Stash by having me sleep with Bobi in one bed, while Jan lay down in the other. But Stash would not be so easily dismissed. A few minutes later he came in. He had plastered his thick mop of hair with water. Wearing fresh flannel pajamas, he climbed into bed next to me. The guy was already passionate and getting more amorous, when Jan climbed into bed next to him and whispered in his ear that he always slept with his own sister! Immediately Stash cooled off and jumped out of bed.

"I'll go sleep with my brother," he whispered, closing the door.

After we had tucked Bobi in for the night, Jan and I fell into each other's arms. It was probably sheer hysteria, but we were shaking so hard that we had trouble standing up straight from laughing.

The next morning Stash took us to Kraków as he had promised, apparently without suspecting anything. As payment he got the sewing machine and the typewriter. Meanwhile, we needed to find a place to stay and some way to make money. We needed lots of money to play the role of "The Noble Zamojskis."

Bobi

I don't recall ever having been called "Sylvio Mendelsohn" or starting life as "Bobi Zamojski." Both of these identities seem foreign and strange to me now. However, I do remember having my bike taken from me. The truck had arrived, my mother was sitting up with the driver, while my father climbed in back and disappeared. Meanwhile, I rode my red tricycle, a present from my grandfather, Julius, which I loved.

Behind Hela's yard a bumpy path led to the top of a hill through a field of tall sunflowers. I'd drag my bike up there and ride it down, my legs stretched out in glee. Often kids from the neighborhood would join in, riding the handlebars or perched behind me. Laughing, clutching at each other, we'd careen down through the patch of flowers toward the house.

When *mamusia* called me to get ready because the truck had come, I made sure to drag my red bike along and then to sit on it so that no one would forget to take it. As soon as the truck was packed, *mamusia* kissed Hela good-bye, then she picked me up. Hela gave me a quick peck on the cheek, while I tried to hang on to the handlebars of my bike.

"We can't take it," my mother explained impatiently, "just what we need!" She peeled my fingers off the handlebars and dragged me to the waiting truck. Then I began to bawl. I had a real tantrum—one of those fits of rage and grief where you cry so hard that you stop breathing, which scares you even more, so that you try to scream even harder, but you can't. You just wind up gasping for air, choking, and turning blue. I wanted that bike above everything else.

The doors slammed shut, and the truck took off with us but without it. While bawling and wriggling off my mother's lap on the front seat, I looked out of the side window and saw Hela waving and receding from us. Next to her lay my red bike. It had been turned over in all the fuss.

4   *Colonel Kruk*

Willy

In December 1941, we were in Kraków, the capital of Nazi-occupied Poland. We knew that the Germans were victorious on all fronts and that they were killing Jews. What we didn't know was that already in Chelmno they had experimented with gassing people to death and cremating their bodies and that the other five death camps, including Auschwitz and Treblinka, were either in the planning stage or were nearly completed.

Meanwhile we were out on the street. A light snow was falling. We had some of our junk in boxes around us, including my old bicycle. We had hardly any money and no place to stay. We were Jews on the run, but I felt as if I had been let out of prison. I was sure that I could make a living somehow. I had done business in Kraków, so I was afraid that there were people who knew me from before the war, but I was certain that we had a much better chance of passing ourselves off as Zamojskis in a big city than in my hometown.

I waved down a horse-drawn cart stacked high with hay and traded in a couple of my suits for a lift. The peasant driving the cart took us to a rooming house in Dębniki, a shabby working-class neighborhood across a small river. When I knocked, an immensely fat Polish woman wearing an apron and a babushka answered the door.

"Excuse me, are you Pani Pachowicz?" I asked.

"Yes," she answered. "I'm the landlady here."

"Pani Pachowicz, I am Jan Zamojski," I said and showed her our birth certificates. "This is my family. We have been traveling for two days, and we're completely exhausted. You'll do a good deed, and the Blessed Virgin will reward you, if you rent us a room."

"I have to consult with my daughter, Marie," she replied.

"Did you see the size of her *tuches!*" Nina whispered and poked me in the ribs. "It's like something out of a circus!"

What a moment to notice such things! Sometimes Nina acts like a child. I shushed her just as Pani Pachowicz came back with her daughter.

Marie was an old maid, worked as a stenographer. "A pleasant woman, but ugly—face like a fish," Nina said later.

Marie listened to our story and said, "Of course we'll help you. How could we not?"

"We'd be swine not to help you!" added Mrs. Pachowicz. "We don't have luxurious rooms. The only thing we have is a small triangular-shaped corner room—three walls, hardly any furniture because the damned Germans took all our best stuff. But why don't you take it."

"Auntie! I'm going to call you 'Auntie.'" I gave her a big hug and kissed her fat cheeks. "You're such a warm-hearted and gorgeous woman that from now on, we're family, as far as I am concerned." Pani Pachowicz blushed, shook with laughter, and hid her face in her apron.

"I see my husband has got himself another girlfriend," said Nina to Marie, and the two women exchanged knowing glances.

They took us to a strange-looking windowless corner room with three walls. It was really a large closet or storage place, but it had a double bed, and out of a wicker basket we made a place for Bobi to sleep.

"You've got to do us a favor," I said to the landlady before heading for bed. "We're just too exhausted to go to the police to get our *kartka zameldowania*, residence permit. Here are our birth certificates. See if you can walk down and get the police permits for us. Okay?"

"Sure," said Pani Pachowicz, still blushing. "I'll get them for you while you rest."

I figured the less I had to do with police of any kind, the better off we were. The Polish police had the reputation of spotting Jewish men. They'd have you drop your pants, and if you were circumcised, they'd turn you over to the Germans. I couldn't take the chance.

Then we lay down and slept for eighteen hours, exhausted from the journey, the fear, the hunger, and the cold.

Later in the morning of the next day, Pani Pachowicz—her first name was Sofia—a huge grin on her face, came up with a tray brimming with eggs, ham, butter, cheese, bread, yogurt, hot tea for us, and milk for the child. Next to the still warm rolls lay the Polish police residence permits. And next to them was a bottle of vodka.

She presented us with all that food. "I have good news," she said with a grin. "While you slept, I heard the BBC broadcast on our hidden radio: the Americans have declared war on Hitler!"

"What?!"

Nina and I jumped out of bed and began to hug Pani Pachowicz all over again. If America was in the war, the Germans were finished. It would be all over in a few months. We clicked glasses of vodka to the Americans and to the freedom of Poland.

I asked her about the lodging and the rent, explaining that I was temporarily out of funds, as they say.

"You'll owe me for the rent, but you don't owe anything for the food. I've got plenty. We'll share; it's wartime." And for a while she fed us three times daily without our having to pay a thing. She was a good, generous woman, but I wondered if she was kind because we appeared to be Polish and our name was Zamojski. Would she have been that hospitable and enthusiastic had she known we were Jews?

We had "Aryan" birth certificates, wedding certificates, and a Polish police residence permit, but we still didn't have the *Kennkarte,* the official German identity card. Without it you risked being arrested, interrogated, and unmasked as a Jew. Here again we ran into some luck. It turned out that the *Kennkarten* were being distributed alphabetically starting with *A*. By December 1941, the Germans had finally gotten to Z, at just about the time we got to Kraków. This explained why the Polish police had been satisfied with only our birth certificates and had not asked for our identity cards when we first arrived. After a week, however, it was essential to get the *Kennkarten.*

I went down to the office where the identity cards were being distributed, anxious that things should go without a hitch and that the clerk distributing the documents would not ask me too many dumb questions. I joined a long line and got into a conversation with a toothless old guy, a Pole, who worked as a janitor at a local school. When I asked him if he knew the procedure, he explained that you needed your birth certificate and a witness. I asked the old guy if he would be my witness for twenty zloty. The fellow said sure.

When I got home, Nina was relieved when I showed her our new documents. Next, we needed money; we couldn't live off Mrs. Pachowicz's generosity indefinitely.

A couple of days later, reading the papers, I noticed an ad from the telephone company. They were looking for sales agents to sell space in the yellow pages. When I went down to the phone company's office, they were impressed by my name and my command of German. I landed the job. I was given a list of businesses in the Kraków area and a sheet showing the price for each type of ad. The smallest went for twenty zloty and the largest for a hundred.

Before going on my first assignment, I debated whether to speak Polish or German and decided on German because I spoke Polish with an accent that might arouse suspicions. After a day's work things had gone extraordinarily well—almost too well. Every potential customer had looked terrified and had eagerly signed on for an ad. I wondered what the hell was going on. Then it dawned on me that my customers were taking me for a German official!

Aha! I said to myself. With the money I had made from the first week's sales plus the bicycle, I bought myself an ankle-length black leather coat and a green German fedora hunting hat with a razor brush. I tried to look as German and menacing as I could. Whenever I walked into an office or a business, rather than ask what ads were wanted, I simply ordered my "customers" to purchase whatever I decided was appropriate.

"Please sign here," I'd command in German. They always signed on the dotted line. Soon I was making a lot of money. To celebrate I bought Nina a box of Swiss chocolates on the black market—an insane luxury in wartime Poland.

Those first few months in Kraków were both exhilarating and terrifying. One day I walked into an office supply business where the owner recognized me as "Willy Melson."

"Willy, what are you doing selling ads for the yellow pages, and why are you speaking German?" the guy laughed.

"I've got to make a living," I answered sheepishly in Polish. "You know how it is."

I was damn lucky the guy didn't know I was a Jew and that he took the whole thing as a clever wartime scheme, which of course it was. Had he called the police, it would have been all over.

I also knew the telephone ad business was going to run out in time and that I had to cook up a new *Geschäft*, a deal, to keep going. I got hold of a Kraków and a Warsaw telephone directory. Each evening Nina and I would write out postcards to German-controlled businesses, inquiring if they needed representatives in Kraków.

One day I got a reply from Herr Herbert Bonneberger, a German businessman who said that he had plastic aprons and raincoats for sale. If I would send him twenty-five zloty, he'd send me some samples. At first I was very skeptical—plastic aprons and raincoats, when things were so scarce that you couldn't even buy a plastic comb! But a week later a package came in the mail. Inside was a long commercial plastic apron, an ankle-length raincoat, and a letter explaining that, depending on how well I did, I could become Bonneberger's representative in Kraków. I was in business!

Dressed in my black leather coat and green fedora, carrying a package with some aprons and raincoats, I would descend on an enterprise. I wasn't selling ads anymore. From the manager I would demand to see the workers and the staff.

"Aha. I see you have fifty-five people working for you. Do they have aprons? I see they do not. You will order one hundred aprons and sixty raincoats, in case some get worn out. Cost: 40 zloty for each apron and 120 zloty per raincoat. Sign here please. *Ja, bitte schön, unterschreiben Sie hier.* Yes, please sign right here."

We were getting rich. We had horse meat to eat at least three times a week—an unheard-of luxury during the war. Pani Pachowicz and her daughter were delighted as they joined us for dinner.

One day, about six in the evening, I stood in front of the offices of a company called Spolem, located in the center of Kraków. Before the war it had been a Polish organization of about eight thousand stores that had been united under one roof in order to compete with and eliminate Jewish-owned enterprises in villages throughout the country. Now it was run by a German administration that had almost nothing to distribute to its customers. If I could persuade them to buy Bonneberger's aprons and raincoats, I would have all of Poland and parts of the Ukraine as a customer base. It was risky, but it could be big.

Although it was 6:30 in the evening and the offices were closed, I insisted to the German guard at the gate that I had to see Herr Siegel, the director. It was official business.

Herr Siegel turned out to be a young, slight, blond, friendly fellow from Hamburg who was working late that night. "Come in," he said wearily. "Sit down. What would you like to buy? I have nothing to sell but some textiles and alcohol, and even that's getting scarce."

"Buy? I don't want to buy anything. I want to sell you some plastic aprons and raincoats."

Siegel looked startled. He examined the samples and tried out a raincoat. "How can you sell these?" he asked. "You need ration points to get textiles."

I explained that Bonneberger had got around that rule by claiming that plastic products were chemicals for which you didn't need rations. I didn't tell Siegel that one of Bonneberger's German rivals tried the same scheme and got shot for being a war profiteer.

"Don't worry, I can deliver," I said.

"How many?" asked Siegel.

"How many do you need?"

"Five to six thousand a month."

Up to that point I had been able to "sell" at most fifty aprons and raincoats to my unwilling customers. This was another matter altogether, and I wasn't sure that Bonneberger could deliver, but I didn't blink.

"Five, six thousand? We can get you any quantity you need."

"What's the price?" asked Siegel.

"Forty for the apron and 120 for the raincoat." I knew that Bonneberger's costs were 25 per apron and 100 per raincoat.

"That's a bit steep," said Siegel.

"Herr Siegel," I said. "I'm only a salesman. My commission is 5 percent, but 5 percent of six thousand aprons and raincoats can add up to a lot of money. With this money I can do whatever I like. I can buy my wife a gold cigarette case or, if I had a girlfriend on the side, I could buy her some jewelry. If you want to squeeze me, you can squeeze me. But why should you? If you give me an order for six thousand aprons at 40 zloty and six thousand raincoats at 120, I'll share my commission with you."

Siegel looked mildly surprised and outraged. Came up with all sorts of objections, blah, blah, blah.

"Look, it's late," I interrupted him. "We're both tired. Why don't you sleep on it and meet me at the Cafe Phoenix downtown for lunch tomorrow at noon. Meanwhile, consider my offer. I'll do whatever you think is correct."

With that I stood up. We shook hands. I patted him on the shoulder. He was a young man doing his best, and I left. Not for a moment did Siegel question who I was. He might have taken me for a *Volksdeutsche,* a Pole of German descent. Nor did I act deferential because Siegel was a German official. On the contrary, I felt I could patronize him. As far as I was concerned it was business between two wheeler-dealers, and I was in the driver's seat because I had something he wanted. Meanwhile, I completely forgot the danger I was running.

That evening I explained the situation to Nina. We had been able to save some twelve thousand zloty from the phone business, which she kept on her in cash. The next morning I took five thousand from Nina, placed it in an envelope, and then went for lunch with Herr Siegel.

I got there at noon sharp, ordered some ersatz black coffee, and waited. At 12:15, about the time that I expected, Siegel showed up.

"Herr Siegel, how nice to see you again." Before he could even pull up a chair, I held him by the arm. "I'll make it very short. You don't know me, and I don't know you, but I would like to establish some trust between us. Here is five thousand zloty. This is yours."

With a quick glance around the room, Siegel took the envelope with the money and slipped it into the side pocket of his black wool jacket. Later, over lunch, he placed an order for six thousand aprons at 40 zloty and six thousand raincoats at 120 zloty. And that was only for the first month. On this one deal Bonneberger was going to make over two hundred thousand and I over ten thousand zloty, and this was just the beginning!

After receiving a cable from me, Bonneberger came the next day. He was a true *Volksdeutsche,* a bear of a man, stout, well over six feet tall, and dressed in a fur coat for the winter. He wanted to see for himself what was going on.

We met at the railroad station, where I explained the deal to him. We had much to celebrate. Later, over a few beers, we linked our arms, drank the *Bruderschaft,* and started calling each other "Jan" and "Herbert." The next day Bonneberger opened up a bank account in Kraków, giving me the unlimited right to draw on it at will.

Beautiful, I thought. But there was one more thing. We couldn't continue living with Pani Pachowicz and her daughter, Marie. Our name was too prominent and the money I was making—although people didn't know the details—was bound to draw attention. Ironically, to play the role of the rich aristocratic Zamojskis it would be easier and safer to live among the Germans in a German neighborhood. The Poles were more likely to spot flaws in the masquerade and denounce us to the Gestapo.

During the war there were three ways to survive: You hid in a closet of somebody's house, you hid on a farm in a hole in the ground, or you tried to live out in the open. With my command of German, with my name, "Count Zamojski," with my chutzpah, I chose to live in the open. Right under their noses. So close that they couldn't see who I really was. Otherwise, the Gestapo knew everything. They would soon find out that I was dealing with Siegel and Bonneberger. They would get suspicious if I tried to sneak around or if I lived in an apartment too modest for my position. I was a Polish count, a successful businessman, possibly a *Volksdeutsche.* There was no way that I could hide or live modestly. I had to live up to my name and position. And so I did. Very, very consciously I chose this way to survive.

A friend of mine from before the war, Glowinsky, lived in a closet for three years on the Aryan side in Warsaw with his wife and child. At night he came out, and he was lucky because he survived. As for me, I made it a point to be known, to be seen. That was the magic trick: *to be seen but not to be noticed.* And I carried it off.

Of course every day, every hour, every minute I was afraid that someone in Kraków would recognize me and denounce us all. So what could I do about it? Not a damn thing.

"Herbert," I said to Bonneberger, "I need one last favor from you. My family and I live in a dump. The best apartments are in the German quarter. I want to rent such a place in your name because where we live now is an embarrassment to me and to you."

"Fine," he said. "Sure."

So, fine. I went to the *Wohnungsamt*, the bureau that supplied Germans with apartments, and I saw a long line of Germans waiting to be assigned a place. Suddenly a fat German came up and asked if I would be interested in an apartment. "Can you pay five thousand zloty?" I said sure.

He went with me and showed me a first-class apartment. Herr Roetger—that was his name—had a construction company that had finished a new building, but there were extra apartments to sell. So he sold me an apartment over the official price. This was illegal, of course. I bought the apartment in Bonneberger's name. Then I said, "Listen, I also need a telephone." Through him I also got a telephone. Such things were nearly impossible to get during the war, but through Roetger I got a phone.

Meanwhile Nina knew from nothing. I didn't tell her anything because I wanted to surprise her. It was a beautiful place, 97 Juljusz Lee Street. There were four rooms painted in a light beige color, with a big bathroom. It wasn't furnished, so I drew on Bonneberger's and my new account and ordered brand new furniture. It was all contemporary light blond wood to match the beige walls.

A couple of days later I told her: "I'd like to show you something."

When she saw the apartment for the first time Nina's reaction was panic. "You're crazy! I wouldn't move in here for a king's ransom. I'm afraid to live here among all these Germans. Here we'll be killed for sure."

"Take it easy, nothing will happen." I explained my theory that we're better off living with Germans than Poles, who were more likely to see through us.

Now we had to move from the Polish section to the German side. It was early evening, near the time of the curfew. We hired a *droshki*. Nina told me, "Don't stand in front of the house calling attention to yourself." But I was such an idiot, I wanted to help the driver. I was carrying packages and stuff, when out of nowhere a Polish policeman appeared. He seemed annoyed.

"What's going on? Don't you know there is a curfew?"

I told him that I was moving. It was very logical that he should have asked me for my papers and brought me to the station, which was very near. There, all they had to do was have me drop my pants and it would have been all over. But no, he let me go. Such near misses happened every day, sometimes twice a day. No matter how smoothly things seemed on the surface, we were constantly on edge.

By the way, in this apartment we also had a maid. A maid! In the middle of the Nazi occupation we were moving into an apartment on the German side, we had new furniture, a phone, and the maid was the last detail in the Count Zamojski show!

One morning, soon after we had moved in, Nina and I were finishing breakfast, Bobi was playing on the floor, and the maid was cleaning up in the kitchen. Suddenly there was a loud banging on the door. Nina, who was the closest, opened it, and in barged a Gestapo officer. He wore a black uniform and the cap with the death-head insignia. Carried two pistols on him. "What the hell?" I said, but he ignored me completely.

"I'm Colonel Kruk, your next-door neighbor," he said to Nina in German. "Starting tomorrow morning, you're going to clean my place. The first things that need to be done are the floors and the windows. My wife is coming in a week. I want the place to be spotless."

I felt the blood drain from my face. I was trembling I was so mad. "Colonel Kruk," I said, "I am Count Zamojski. My wife is not a maid, and she's not going to be your servant. You will be civil the next time you speak to her. Is that understood?"

Kruk turned to me dumbfounded. "What did you just say? What tone are you using with me?"

"Just as you hear it," I said coldly.

He turned on his heels and left, slamming the door behind him.

"Jan, you're totally insane," Nina said trembling. "We've got to fix the situation."

She was right, of course, but I couldn't act "Count Zamojski" one minute and then behave like a frightened little man the next. But I'm no fool. That evening when we heard Kruk come back, I grabbed a bottle of cognac and banged loudly on his door. When he appeared, wearing jodhpurs and an undershirt over his scrawny chest, I waved the bottle of cognac in front of him and invited myself in to have a drink. Kruk mumbled something like, "Come in."

That evening Nina and I sat with him, toasting each other and going through the bottle. After that we became great "friends."

Kruk used to drop by our place every evening after "work." His mission, plain and simple, was to murder Jews. He'd brag: "Today I got rid of twenty Jews. Tomorrow I have another batch to hang."

Often he'd come in late at night or early in the morning. When Bobi was still awake, Kruk especially liked to play with the child. He said that Bobi reminded him of his own little boy whom he had left in Hamburg. He'd bounce Bobi on his knees and let him play with his Gestapo cap. The child would put on Kruk's huge cap over his little head so that his face and ears would disappear, and then he'd march around the room giving the "Heil Hitler" salute like a little Gestapo midget. Kruk found it all very amusing.

One day he asked Nina if it would be okay to bring some of his colleagues to dinner. What to do? The guy is our neighbor . . . a Gestapo officer. So I said, "Ja! Of course. With pleasure."

A few days later the maid and Nina prepared a feast. That night as Kruk and his cronies were sitting around the dinner table, most of their conversation was about killing Jews. They were all bragging about it. This one had hung thirty people that day. The other had one hundred shot. A third drowned a whole crowd of Jews. That was the main theme of the evening. Meanwhile we're eating, drinking, laughing. Nina had made a Hungarian goulash. They loved her and her cooking. We couldn't get rid of them. They were happy and contented—just the kind of people you'd see in a Munich beerhall. When they saw me bring in the cognac after dinner, they cheered and clapped. Nina and I were a big hit and so was Bobi. They were normal, ordinary Germans having a great time. When they left, Nina and I avoided looking at each other. That night we went to bed without exchanging a word.

The pressure of making money and of dealing with "little surprises" never let up. Bonneberger told me, "You must sell more plastic aprons because I cannot get raincoats." I had to keep Bonneberger happy because everything depended on him. So to whom could I sell? To Siegel, I already sold the maximum. I needed a new buyer. I heard about an *Abteilung*, a department for forest workers in the *Generalgouvernment*. This was the name for the area of occupied Poland that the Germans had not annexed into the Third Reich. Also at this time Bonneberger told me that he had whole suits made of plastic. So I had the bright idea of selling the plastic suits to the forest workers of the *Generalgouvernment*.

The offices of the *Generalgouvernement* were in a beautiful building in Kraków, but at first I was afraid to walk in. One day Nina and I went by, and I said to her, "What the hell! Let's go." I walked in and demanded to speak with the manager of the forest workers' division, *Forst Abteilung*. His name was Herr Terman—I forgot his first name—a very elegant elderly man wearing a monocle. His wife's name was Greta. She must have been twenty or thirty years younger than him—a big, busty, blond, bombshell of a woman. They had recently arrived from Berlin. He had been an exporter of egg crates. It was a big business, and he was designated supervisor of the forest workers in the *Generalgouvernement*. He and I hit it off right away, and Greta gave me the eye.

So I invited the Termans over one night for dinner. Nina and Greta were two of a kind and went off giggling to the kitchen. Terman and I started on the cognac early. For dinner we had *Schweinebraten*, pork sausages, and the four of us kept on drinking well into the night. When Terman got drunk, he became melancholy and nostalgic and started calling me his *Bruder Jan!* Then out of nowhere, he turned to Nina.

"Nina, tell me the truth. Isn't Jan Jewish? Zamojski can't be your real name."

I felt myself go numb, but Nina kept her wits about her. "What are you saying? That I would marry a Jew?" She laughed and made a joke out of it, but I noticed that Greta wasn't laughing.

Slurring his words, Terman continued, "Don't get me wrong. I like Jews. Greta and I had many Jewish friends in Berlin before the war. Jan strikes me as a typical Jewish businessman."

"Forget it Terman," I said. "We're trying to have a good time here."

"Sure," agreed Greta. "Why raise such a depressing subject? We're having such a good time!"

"Fine," said Terman, "but if you ever need my help, let me know."

"I need you to order some plastic suits from me. Lots of them," I laughed.

The next day, when I saw him again in the office, he kept referring to me as *mein Bruder Jan* and placed a huge order for plastic suits for his forest workers. I made a lot of money on the deal, and Bonneberger was happy. Meanwhile, I tried to put out of my mind what Terman had said about my being a Jew.

I had the Spolem account, I had the forest workers, but I had to keep going to pay off Siegel, Hauptmann Gottfried, another crucial contact, and all the others . . . I had to make money to survive. Day and night, I was on the phone working from my apartment trying to drum up business.

One day I heard that in the Warsaw ghetto was a factory making workers' clothing out of bedsheets that had been colored with blue dye. It was dangerous to call the ghetto, but I felt invulnerable, and I figured I'd throw the ghetto a little business to keep them going. So I called the Warsaw ghetto, reached the factory making workers' clothes, and told them that I was interested in placing an order. They asked for my address and told me that they'd send a representative with some samples.

A few days later I got a telephone call from the Gestapo to come to their headquarters—the same place where Kruk worked. It turned out that their offices were practically around the corner, two blocks from our apartment. What should I do? Should I go? Should I flee? I didn't know. I figured that if they wanted to arrest me they would have come for me, not telephoned. I decided to go.

Without introductions or preliminaries, the Gestapo official started out by shouting at me, "You placed an ad for workers' clothes, and you called the ghetto in Warsaw. Don't you know that's a black market ad?"

"What are you accusing me of?" I shouted back at him in German. "I represent Handelshaus Bonneberger. I am working with Herr Siegel at Spolem, with Herr Terman of the *Forst Abteilung*. Here, call them if you wish!" I grabbed the phone on his desk and handed it to him. I gave him a piece of my mind. I really let him have it. He looked shocked and apologized. No Pole had ever spoken to him like that before. The Gestapo apologized to me! I stormed out, mad as hell . . . I really was mad. You can't fake such things. Under their uniforms they were just ridiculous, cowardly little people who thought that they had become the masters of the world. You had to shout them down, otherwise they would kill you.

I thought I had solved the Gestapo problem, but then a few days later I got another call from them, telling me to stay put. They were sending some people over.

I told Nina, "Get ready. The Gestapo is coming over soon. They want to ask us a few questions."

I watched as Nina put on some fresh lipstick and a black silk dress to make a good impression. Bobi was with the maid, helping her to bake cookies. Meanwhile Nina and I waited for them to come to interrogate us. We must have sat there for an hour quietly waiting for them to come. I didn't know what got into me, but I just felt exhausted by the whole thing and couldn't think straight anymore. A few minutes later it dawned on me—the danger we were running.

"Ninka, we must be crazy to sit here waiting for the Gestapo. They'll just arrest us. Grab the child, we've got to get out of here!" I almost shouted. We told the maid that we were going to visit some friends and we'd be back in a few days.

I can't recall how or where, and I don't even remember their last name, but we had met a young Polish couple in Kraków, Henryk and Zosia, whom we liked, and they seemed to like us too. They told us to visit them whenever we wished, and that's where we headed. We took Bobi by the hand and made our way to their place through the dark and the curfew. When we got to their place, I explained that we needed a place to stay. They didn't ask why, and they welcomed us with open arms, gave us dinner, and actually gave up their bedroom, while they slept on the floor.

The next day, as Zosia and Nina were washing the dishes, Nina took off her ring with the Zamojski crest on it—it was a prop we had made especially for us—and she put it aside on the counter. Zosia then picked it up, examined it closely.

"Dear Nina, please don't be insulted," she sighed, "but we know that you're both Jewish. You don't need to pretend and to wear that ring in front of us."

"How did you come to that conclusion?" Nina asked without agreeing or denying anything.

"We sense it. We can tell. But we have nothing against your staying with us if you wish. We're socialists. Before the war, my husband was in jail for his beliefs. We'll help you as best we can. In our house you don't have to wear that ring . . . to make believe that you're Polish aristocrats."

We stayed with them a few days. We didn't explicitly say that we were Jews, but we didn't protest when they offered to show us how to behave in church. We learned when to kneel and when to stand up and how to take the holy sacraments.

When we got home, I asked the maid, "Did someone come?"

She said, "No. Nobody came." Later we figured that maybe it had been a mistake.

A few days later an elderly gentleman came by to visit us: His name was Zamojski! Blah, blah, blah. Heard that a branch of his family was in town. Wanted to say hello. Asked us about his uncle and cousins in Lwów. And I said very little. Tried to be noncommittal. I gave him some money. He left. Later, some Zamojski "cousins" got in touch with us—apparently our mail had been delivered to them by mistake! Every day it seemed there was a little surprise like that which needed to be dealt with. It was like sailing a small boat in a storm. You never knew where the next wave would come from that would take you over the side.

Bobi

Kruk liked to play with me, when he'd drop by after "work." He used to place his huge Gestapo cap over my head, which made it disappear, and bounce me on his knees. "Off we go on a gallop!" he'd shout, and I'd scream with delight. He found it especially hilarious when I'd wear his cap and march around the living room like a decapitated midget. I'd give the Hitler salute, "Heil Hitler!" and Kruk would clap in appreciation.

One day Kruk tried to come to my aid in his inimitable way. Behind our house was a construction site where, when the workers went home, my friends and I played until dark. The unfinished buildings were connected by wooden planks that ran across pits and gulleys and linked building to building and room to room. The smell of freshly poured cement hung over the place and got into our clothes and our hair. One of our favorite games was to play tag, in which you'd have to run across these planks while balancing yourself and taking care not to fall. Another game was king-of-the-mountain, in which you'd scramble up a pile of dirt, and whoever could fight off the rest and prevent getting pushed off the "mountain" would be declared "king." I'd get pushed off a lot, because I was the youngest and the smallest, but it was fun even when you rolled down the hill.

One evening in the early spring we were playing a rough game of king-of-the-mountain, when for some reason I was left standing on top. I was king, probably because the bigger boys had overlooked me for a moment. But then I saw Władek, another little kid about my age, his head shaved to prevent lice, making his way up the hill. When he reached me, I gave him a good shove and he rolled down head-over-heels into a pile of bricks. When he got up he was sobbing and bleeding from cuts and bruises.

"I'll get you for this," he shouted up at me. But I just laughed, feeling proud of my victory. I was the king!

That evening at dusk, as I turned the corner of our building, he threw a large rock straight at my face. I had just enough time to turn my head slightly so that the rock hit me in the side of the head. After I got up I couldn't see for the blood that was streaming into my eyes.

When I got home I could see that *mamusia* was terribly shocked by the sight of all the blood, which scared me even more. She lay me down on the couch, and without thinking, I guess, she ran next door to Colonel Kruk's for help. He came out wearing his undershirt, hatless, his hair in a mess, buttoning the fly of his black riding pants. After looking over the wound and pronouncing me safe, he stormed back to his apartment and came out waving his revolver. He threatened to kill Władek for having thrown that rock.

"Those goddamned, lousy Poles must be taught a lesson!" he shrieked. It took all of *mamusia*'s charm and persuasion to calm him down.

I thought Kruk was weird and scary, even though he was nice to me. I learned to be a little charmer and clown around him because I sensed that it was expected of me, though I didn't know why. As for Kruk's shooting Władek, I was too dazed to care one way or the other.

5   *Wanda and Tadzo*

Nina

By the time the Germans had invaded Stanisławów, Tadzo was back in Warsaw, living on the Aryan side. He had good papers; his *Kennkarte* did not have the deadly *J* for *Jude* stamped into it. He was blond and blue-eyed, and his name was Ponczek, which is not a Jewish name. Also, like me, he spoke Polish without an accent, so he could pass as an "Aryan." Once he was in Warsaw, he went back to the ghetto to look up our parents, and he tried to help them as best he could. Later, by the spring of 1942, we made contact with him, and he came to live with us in Kraków.

When he arrived from Warsaw, Tadzo told me that my father looked like a starving beggar. His clothes were torn, and he went barefoot. My mother still tried to keep up appearances. She wore makeup everyday, just the way I would have done, but when she saw Tadzo back in the ghetto she fell apart. She could not accompany him to the gate when he left, but somehow my father held himself together and went with Tadzo near to the entrance of the wall to say good-bye.

My father said, "Tadzo, my dear, we're saying good-bye to each other probably for the last time, but I am happy that you and Nacia have a chance to survive."

My mother, with her goyish looks and her non-Jewish-sounding name, also could have escaped, but when Tadzo asked her to come with him she refused to leave her husband. I've never understood her. She was such a *coquette* and a pleasure seeker. She had carried on an affair with Abram Juwiler for years, right under her husband's nose, yet when it came to it, she refused to leave my father alone to die. Did she love him after all or was she doing penance for having betrayed him?

As for my father, of blessed memory, his looks would have given him away—his nose, his Yiddish accent. It's not the Germans who would have recognized him as a Jew, it's the Poles. The Polish blackmailers and hooligans would have spotted him had he tried to escape. They used to stop people in the street and point out, "There is a Jew!" or "That one is a Jew!" They'd get hold of a German officer and urge him to arrest a man on the street if he looked Jewish.

When they reached the gate of the ghetto, Tadzo pulled my father into an alley and gave him his own shoes and jacket to wear. At first, my father refused to take the clothes, but then when Tadzo insisted, he said, "This is a great *mitzvah,* the deed of a righteous person."

The funny thing is that they never got along when Tadzo was growing up. My father wanted him to be observant, but Tadzo refused. He'd eat ham and smoke on Yom Kippur. At home before the war there were horrible shouting matches at the dinner table about Judaism, about being truly Polish. And there in an alley near the entrance to the ghetto, Tadzo gave his father his own shoes to wear! I am sorry for the tears, but I weep whenever I think of my mother staying with my father through it all, and I weep when I think of that delicate man waving to his son for the last time.

When he first came to live with us in Kraków, Tadzo would not leave the house because his nerves were shot, and he feared being discovered. For a while he was very shaky, but in the evenings the maid would cook up some food, and I would bring it to him. Jan would play chess with him to get his mind off his Warsaw ghetto experience.

By the spring of 1942, we heard rumors—Jan had contacts in the Polish underworld—that Jews were not only being shot, as in Stanisławów, but that they were being deported to camps where they were gassed and their bodies burned. For the first time we heard of places like Auschwitz, Majdanek, and especially Treblinka. They would pack Jews onto long trains of cattle cars that would bring them to one of the camps. These cars would be so stuffed that many people suffocated or died on the way. Once the trains reached their destination, people would be pulled and chased out by SS men snapping their whips and releasing giant snarling dogs. The people would be stripped of all their possessions, including the clothes they wore, and, naked, they would be driven with whips and clubs into the gas chambers.

Then in July 1942 we heard that there was a major deportation of Jews out of the Warsaw ghetto to Treblinka and certain death. Tadzo wanted to go back to Warsaw to try to save our parents. Despite my protests—I was terrified that they would both be killed—Jan decided to go with him.

They took the train to Warsaw and stayed in a pension on the Aryan side. There was this high wall, barbed wire, broken glass. They tried to get in, but it was too late. The Jews were being deported, parts of the ghetto were burning, and the entrance was closed. They wouldn't let you in, even if you had the right papers, but Tadzo tried anyway.

Tadzo was going to go in with false papers, changes of clothes for my parents, and money to try to bribe the guards at the gate. Meanwhile, Jan was to wait for him on the Aryan side. He also had money on him and a gold cigarette case. The plan was that Jan would take a seat on the tram that ran by the ghetto and wait for the three of them to come out. The tram was crowded. Many of the passengers were hanging out of the windows to get a better view of the burning ghetto. The second time the tram went by, Tadzo hopped on. He was alone. He had not been able to get in, and they had failed in getting my parents out.

When they got back to Kraków, neither wanted to talk about it. Tadzo locked himself in his room. Jan said very little, but when we were alone, and I embraced him, he began to speak.

"I did it for you," he said. "I hate to see you suffer. We were too cautious. We had the money. We could have gotten them out earlier. This trip was all for nothing."

Then he looked away, his shoulders sagged. He was so bitter and discouraged. "There was a very pretty blond Polish lady sitting in front of me on the tram," he added almost as an afterthought. "When we passed by the ghetto, she turned to me and said, 'At least Hitler is doing one good thing: He's delousing Warsaw by getting rid of the Jews.'"

A couple of months after Jan and Tadzo returned from their trip to the Warsaw ghetto, there was a ring at the door of our apartment in Kraków. When I opened it there stood an elegant, handsome man. He was middle-aged, already turning gray, perhaps in his forties. Pan Kronski, it seemed, was the Polish Aryan representative of the firm in the ghetto whose ad Willy had seen earlier. They were using bed linen dyed blue to manufacture workers' clothes. Apparently that business was still in existence, despite the deportations in July. We asked him to come in, served him lunch. We had a very pleasant meal, good conversation. Kronski stayed three days—slept, ate, joked around with us, and played chess with Jan and Tadzo.

Jan and he talked business, and Jan told him that he was interested in the product that Kronski was selling. Jan wanted the ghetto enterprise to succeed because he thought as long as Jews worked they would not be killed. After the third day Kronski left for Warsaw. He was supposed to send us some samples. A few days later, however, while Jan and Tadzo were playing chess and Bobi and I were playing with a toy railroad on the floor, there was another ring at the door. Wanda walked in. What a gorgeous girl!

She was a stunning young woman. For wartime, she was very well dressed—she had on a silk dress with a black-and-white flower print, and she wore a turban made of the same material. She had black hair and dark eyes and wore long dramatic earrings. A gorgeous kid!

"Pan and Pani Zamojski?" she asked.

I smiled. "Yes. May we help you?"

"Oh, I'm so glad to find you in. Pan Kronski, my cousin, suggested that I speak to you. He told me that he had never met such a warm and welcoming couple as you are. 'People like Count and Countess Zamojski and Pan Ponczek are unique in the world,' he told me."

She paused, took a deep breath, and continued, "That's why I came straight to you. I have come from Warsaw. I'm a cosmetician, but I can't find a place to stay. Do you think you could help me?"

I laughed at her being so nervous and out of breath. "Why don't you freshen up, have a bite, and stay with us until you find a place of your own."

So she did. And meanwhile Tadzo fell head-over-heels in love with her. Couldn't sleep at night thinking of her.

Tadzo fell in love with her, but to tell the truth, I fell in love with her too. For the first time in months, I found myself laughing. She was so beautiful, funny, and charming. She also had a good voice and was very musical. She and I would spend hours singing together: "He'll never return, Save your tears," and various tangos, like, "If not today, then darling tomorrow you'll be mine. I don't lack strength for the battle for your lips and heart." Such nonsense! But we had fun together. I loved her company. In a few days we became very close, Wanda and all of us. There was only one thing that put me off about her. Every time she was frustrated—say she had a run in her stockings—she'd curse, "Those goddamn lousy Jews!" I didn't dare to correct her. I'd just smile and turn away.

She had been with us for about a week when she asked, "Dear Jan, my mother and my sister, Irenka, are back in Warsaw. We'd like to stay together. Could you help?"

"Of course. They can live with us here." Jan has a very good heart and a generous nature. A few days later Pani Marylka and Irenka arrived.

Wanda's mother wore a black dress decorated with lace. She had her graying hair swept up behind her—as was the fashion of the day—and from her neck hung a large silver cross—a typical Polish aristocratic lady. Accompanying her was her daughter, Irenka, who was tall, red-headed, and good looking. Although by then Wanda had found a small room of her own, they all moved in with us. They left their clothes at Wanda's, but most every day, and even at night, they stayed, ate, and slept at our place.

After the three women had been living with us for a few weeks, Tadzo came to our bedroom one morning, sat on our bed, and said, "You know that I love Wanda. She's not Jewish, but I still want to marry her. What do you think?"

"What a dumb question!" Jan answered. "Today we're alive, tomorrow we might all be dead, and you're worried about her not being Jewish? You love her? Marry her tomorrow! The two of you can stay with us." Tadzo was delighted and relieved.

One Friday evening we were all together in the living room. I was curled up on the couch. Wanda sat by my head and Pani Marylka was at my feet. Irenka and Jan were sitting on another couch. We were all chatting, while Tadzo was solving chess problems on a board on the dining room table, and Bobi was playing with blocks on the floor. The maid came in with some appetizers.

Just then Pani Marylka looked up and said in a nostalgic tone of voice, "It's Friday night... I have so many wonderful memories of prewar Friday nights."

I don't know what got into me, because at this point I said something really stupid and dangerous: "On Friday nights I loved to eat carp in gelatin with buttered noodles, washed down with a bit of sweet wine."

We were all so tense that no one smiled or said a word. No one indicated in any way that they had understood what that meant: That we were Jews, and that I was telling the three women that I understood that they were Jews as well.

Pani Marylka and Wanda used to bathe Bobi regularly. They must have seen that he was circumcised, but somehow it didn't connect with them then. Only when I mentioned that Friday night dish did it dawn on them that we were Jewish, and by their reaction we understood that they were as well. But no one said another word about it. We didn't pull out a bottle of wine and drink "*L'chaim!*" to life, or anything like that. We knew, we understood, but we did not discuss it.

Only Pani Marylka quietly said, "I see."

Jan stared at me as if he wanted to murder me on the spot. Pani Marylka looked over at Wanda, but she remained blank. However, a few days later, Pani Marylka came over to me in the kitchen and said, "I suspected that you're Jewish because you speak Polish so perfectly that only a Jew could speak that way. I thought to myself, Perhaps Zamojski is not Jewish. He obviously has a German accent, but his wife might be."

Imagine! She thought that I might be Jewish, but not Jan, who looks more Jewish than I do!

When they had realized the truth, even Tadzo and Wanda didn't speak to each other about it, not even in secret. They were planning to get married and were sleeping together, but they did not discuss their Jewishness! The only thing was that when Tadzo sat on our bed to ask us about marrying Wanda he said that she said to him that she was not a pure Aryan, that her grandmother or her great-grandmother had been Jewish. Some nonsense like that!

We were Count and Countess Zamojski. We celebrated Christmas. We put up Christmas decorations. Every Sunday we went to church. Jan and I sang songs that we didn't understand. We made the sign of the cross, but didn't know what it meant. We didn't know whether to kneel on the right or the left knee. We took the holy sacraments and hoped that we wouldn't gag, but somehow we pulled it off. For a few months Wanda and her family fooled us, but we fooled them too! What a comedy: Two Jewish families living one on top of the other, each thinking that the other was Polish Catholic!

Once we realized that they were Jewish too we felt happy and relieved. We hated Wanda's insulting talk about the "lousy Jews." Now we understood why she said it.

On the day of Wanda's and Tadzo's wedding we all went to church to register them, and the priest asked us for particulars. Tadzo and Wanda have good minds, and they should have been able to get through it in good order, but then at one point the priest asked Tadzo in what church he had been baptized. His mind went blank, but so did mine, and so did everyone's. I couldn't think of any church. I couldn't even invent a name. There was what seemed like a five-minute silence. Then Pani Marylka saved the situation, "St. Joseph's," she said.

When we left the church and got into the *droshki* for the ride home we started to laugh, and then we started to laugh so hysterically that people stopped in the street to stare. We laughed so hard that I peed in my pants.

We planned a big wedding feast for the young couple. Among our guests were Hauptmann Gottfried, a big shot in *Die Werke des Generalgouvernment*. He was chief inspector of all the factories in occupied Poland. Jan let him make a lot of money by selling him raincoats below the black market price, which he resold and then became very rich. Gottfried was a correct but corrupt former Austrian army officer. He became an essential contact for us later when we desperately needed him. Although he was married, he came with his girlfriend, a tall, stunning blond. Bonneberger and Herr Siegel from Spolem came. There was Herr Terman and his wife, Greta. Fat Herr Roetger, the fellow who had sold Jan our apartment, and his wife, and, of course, Colonel Kruk and his wife. She had finally come from Hamburg with their little boy.

By the way, Frau Kruk had volunteered to cook the meal. She was an excellent chef who had worked for a German nobleman before the war, and the meal was scrumptious. They were all there, our German "friends," to celebrate the wedding of Wanda and Tadzo, two Jewish kids from Warsaw!

The next day, I got up early. The apartment was still in a mess, because the maid had not yet come in. I found Irenka in the kitchen, starting to clean up. She washed and I dried, and that's when I asked her about Kronski.

After her father had been killed in Lodz, Irenka, Pani Marylka, and Wanda fled to Warsaw. There they had moved in with Kronski, whom Irenka knew from before the war. He was no longer a young man, but he had fallen in love with her. He was living on the Aryan side and supported the three women as best he could. She was grateful to him, but she didn't find him attractive and refused to have an affair with him. Meanwhile, he was part of the Warsaw Jewish underground that counterfeited papers for people trying to survive on the Aryan side. During the deportations from the Warsaw ghetto, it was Kronski who put them in contact with the Zamojskis.

One day Kronski was trapped inside the ghetto, arrested, and sent to Treblinka, but he wasn't killed immediately. For a short period he

*was put on a work detail. Some of his friends decided on a daring rescue
operation and got Irenka involved. They knew that his unit passed by
the Treblinka railroad station every day at about the same time. The
station was about two and a half miles from the camp. The plan was
for her to go to the station with a change of clothes and some money
and wait for him. He was supposed to detach himself from the column
of prisoners, quickly change his clothes, and together they would board
the next train for Warsaw.*

    *Irenka did as was planned. She took a regular train to the Treblinka
station. Most of the day she sat waiting on a bench with Kronski's
change of clothes in a satchel on her knees. But Kronski's detail never
showed up, no one came, no one even bothered her. When she returned
to Warsaw, she was told by Kronski's comrades that he had been killed
the day before.*

Bobi

There was nothing very funny about Uncle Tadzo when he got back from
Warsaw. Thin, tall, and stooped as he was, he had lost more weight and
had developed a spasm in his left side that left him reeling at times and
gasping for a seat. Gone were his jokes and stories.

    Now that he was back, he refused to play with me and spent endless
hours lying on the couch reading from his precious Edgar Allan Poe. I
kept pestering him to play with me or tell me a story. Finally he gave
in and read me a story about how a wicked man buried his friend alive
behind a wall. *In pace requiescat,* it ended.

    "What does that mean?" I asked.

    "Rest in peace," he said.

    I didn't get it.

    I was glad when Wanda came to live with us, because soon she and
Tadzo were with each other constantly, and his mood perked up quite a
bit. He lost his limp, and he stopped lying around on the couch reading
his depressing stories.

    When I first met her, Wanda was a pretty teenager. She wore a white
carnation in her hair and said that she had come from Warsaw. Would
my parents mind if she stayed with us for a few days while she looked
for a job as a beautician? She had a wide grin, which made you smile
right back, and she had pensive brown eyes, which when they looked
into yours, made you feel calm and sweet. When she held my hand, I
knew that I had found a friend.

    On nights when she didn't go home, until she and Tadzo kept company, she slept in my bed, head-to-toe with me. In the morning, I'd crawl up where she'd be drowsing and nestle in her arms for a few minutes before she went to work at the beautician's. My head resting in the crook of her left shoulder and her breast, my left arm across her belly, I felt tipsy from the smell of her body mingling with that of lilac from her cheap wartime perfume.

"Don't look, Bogusiu," she'd warn me as she dressed. "Hide your eyes under the covers."

And from under the covers I would watch her breasts jiggle as she pulled a sweater over her head, but she hid her privates from me. Why? What was the big secret? My explorations came to a sudden end one night, however, and I almost got thrown out of bed when I brought a flashlight with me and shone it under the covers when I thought Wanda was asleep!

Pani Marylka was taller than Wanda, although not as tall as Irenka. She wore her gray hair upswept in the back like my mother. She loved rings and bangles and long necklaces, which she'd wind in piles around her neck, and she always wore a large silver cross. Her favorite pastime was playing cards—any kind of cards, from poker to solitaire. She knew her cards so well that she could continue a running conversation even as she played.

One afternoon she was sitting by the kitchen table, telling fortunes and drinking tea. Without missing a throw of the cards, she tilted her head and waved me to her. She then explained the significance of her arrangement.

"I threw these down for you," she whispered in my ear as if it were a secret. "You'll live ever so long, and you'll be happy."

"Why? How can you tell?"

"Are you questioning my judgment?" She was indignant. "Can't you see that the queen of spades is up against the ten of hearts?"

"So what?"

"It means, my dear Count Bobi," she answered formally, "that you will love a dark-haired lady and that she will love you back forever."

Little did she know that the dark-haired lady she spoke about was her daughter, Wanda.

At times Pani Marylka would get depressed. She'd sleep late and say little. When she'd wake, neither her cards nor her novels could pull her out of her dark mood. Holding me to her, she'd stare blankly out of the window.

"What's wrong?" I'd ask, trying to get her to be cheerful again.

"Oh, you know," she'd say in a tired voice, waving her hand at the street below, "it's just everything . . ."

One day she and I went downtown to go shopping for soap and other stuff—not that there was much to buy. As we left the grocer's shop, I could see a commotion in the street. People from both ends were running toward us, while at each corner, we could see that army trucks had blocked off each street and German soldiers were grabbing people off the sidewalks like chickens from a yard and shoving them into their trucks.

Pani Marylka grabbed my hand and ran back into the store from where we had come. Without asking questions, the clerk rushed us to the back room, where we were safe.

"Jews or 'ours' for forced labor," he said matter of factly. "They send them off to Germany somewhere."

Pani Marylka nodded. "Mary, Mother of God," she whispered as she crossed herself.

After an hour, when things came back to normal, we made our way back home.

It was a nightly ritual for Pani Marylka and her daughters to bathe me. As I rose from the tub and felt their hands soap me down, I felt a sweet lassitude. Bewildered by my feelings, in order not to call attention to my excitement, I pushed my *ptaszek* between my thighs, making believe that it had disappeared.

"That's what girls look like," I grinned.

"What do you know about it," the women laughed as they wrapped me in a towel, while I squirmed to get away from their tickling.

Later, when I was warm and cozy under a giant white *pierzany*, down-filled comforter, Pani Marylka sat by the side of my bed to tell me a story.

"What's a soul?" I asked.

She adjusted her glasses and looked down at me speculatively. "A soul is something in you that makes you feel that you're you."

"I don't get it."

"When you say 'I' what do you mean?"

"You mean who am I?"

"Yes."

"Bogusław Marian Zamojski, but people call me Bogusiu or Bobi."

"How do you know?"

"I just do. And you know it too."

"Well, the thing in you that tells you you're such and such, Bogusław, Bogusiu, Bobi, etc., etc. is your soul."

"I see," I said dubiously. "Does everybody have a soul?"

"No," she said, taking off her glasses.

"You mean there are people without souls?"

"Yes."

"Who?"

"The Germans."

"All Germans?"

"All."

"And what happens when you die, does your soul die too?"

"No. Your soul lives on and on."

"Where does it go?"

"It goes above the sky, and it looks down to see where it might come again."

"And where does it come down?"

"Oh, sometimes it finds a newborn baby that it likes especially, and it sets up residence there."

"Can it live in animals?"

"Sure."

"In grass?"

"I'm not sure."

"But not the Germans."

"No. The Germans had souls, but recently all their souls fled in fright of them."

"What about my grandparents?"

When I mentioned my grandparents, Pani Marylka looked startled. "What do you know about them?"

"I heard Mom and Tadzo say that they died in Warsaw."

"No, no. You're wrong. Those were some other people they were talking about. Grandma and Grandpa Zamojski lived and died in Lwów. Don't forget that."

"And then what happened?"

"Their souls flew up to the sky after they died."

"Where do you think they might be now?"

"Looking for somebody to live in."

"Could they come and live in me?"

"Quite possibly. Your grandfather might want to come to live in you." Pani Marylka brushed the hair from my brow as if to lighten the effort of my concentration. "I'd be on the lookout for a dream, because that's when souls like to come back best of all. A dream or a daydream."

When she left and the room got dark, I thought about what Pani Marylka had said about my grandparents. She said that they had died in

Lwów, but I would have sworn that I had heard my mother and Tadzo speaking about my grandparents in Warsaw. What was going on? Later, before falling asleep, I had a vision of thousands of millions of souls circling high above the sky like birds waiting to come back to earth.

———————————

On another occasion, Tadzo sat at the side of my bed and told me a story that I had a harder time believing than the story about souls. He told me that the world is round, like a ball.

"You mean we're living on a ball?"

"Yes, a ball."

"But how can that be? When you stand in the street or in the field behind the house you can see that things are flat. You're not standing on any ball."

"That's because the world is very big, and when you stand in one place you think that all around you things are flat, but off in the distance the world becomes curved."

"So what if you kept walking, what would you reach?"

Tadzo crinkled his brow and said, "If you started walking from here, you'd reach an ocean. It's called the Atlantic Ocean."

"What's that?"

"It's a huge body of water."

"You mean like a lake?"

"Like a lake, but so huge that you can't see to the other shore.

It seemed the world was full of mysteries: *ptaszeks* I wasn't allowed to show to anyone, secret trips to Warsaw to save my grandparents who had died in Lwów I wasn't supposed to know about, souls above the sky trying to find a place below on earth, the earth not flat but round like a ball, bodies of water so vast you couldn't see to the other shore.

"Who lives on the other side of the ocean?"

"They're called Americans."

"Americans? Do they walk upside down?"

"No, to them it seems that they're walking right side up, and we're walking upside down."

"So how come they don't fall off the earth?" I asked.

"A force called gravity keeps them and us from falling off."

I didn't get it.

6   *The Honeymoon*

Willy

The newlyweds decided to go on their honeymoon to Rabka and Lanckorona, two vacation spots south of Kraków. Always the point was to appear as normal as possible. So, the day after the wedding, the honeymooners brought their skis, and we saw them off at the train station. We laughed and acted carefree as we said good-bye. A few days later I got a call from Wanda saying that they were having a great time, blah, blah, blah, why don't we join them. What with the strange telephone calls from the Gestapo, I thought, Why not? It was the perfect excuse for getting out of Kraków for a time. I took Nina and Bobi, and we joined Tadzo and Wanda for a skiing vacation. Meanwhile, Pani Marylka and Irenka stayed behind in Wanda's room.

I registered at a comfortable boardinghouse, and if you could pay for it, the food was good. I love to ski. I had learned the sport in Switzerland when I was a child, but I had seldom had the chance to strap on skis since then. Now in the middle of the war, surrounded by Germans on the slopes, I was skiing again! While I was away, Nina, Tadzo, Wanda, and Bobi took long walks or sat by the fire in the lobby.

On the third day, I decided to put off skiing until the afternoon. We were all having lunch, when suddenly I realized that the hotel was surrounded by the Gestapo. Some Pole at the hotel had obviously figured out that one of us was Jewish and had betrayed us. We couldn't run. Had we tried, they would have killed us on the spot. The three of us went up to our room, and Tadzo and Wanda went up to their room, which was directly above our own.

In our nicely decorated room on the second floor, Nina and I sat in our ski clothes on the couch with the false papers in hand, waiting to be interrogated and arrested. Meanwhile Bobi was playing with a toy train on the carpet in front of us. A few minutes later we heard the clomping of heavy boots on the stairs. There was a loud banging on the door.

"The door is open. Come in!" I said in German.

Three Gestapo types barged in. They were wearing winter coats with huge fur collars—gray coats with Persian lamb collars.

"*Sind sie Zamojski?*"

"*Ja.*"

"*Stehen sie auf!* Stand up!"

We stood up. They examined our documents and our faces. They closely looked at my nose and my ears; they peered into my eyes to determine if I had Jewish features. Meanwhile, I tried to remain calm. I spoke to them in German and even tried out a few stupid jokes: "If you get any closer, we'll be dancing!"

They didn't crack a smile, but I could sense that they began to relax. Two of them went upstairs to Tadzo and Wanda's room, leaving one of them behind. This fellow now turned on Nina.

"What is your name?"

She smiled and answered calmly, "Janina Victoria Zamojska."

"When were you born?"

"March 2, 1914"

"Where?"

"Lwów."

"This is your child?"

"Yes."

"What is his name?"

"Bogusław Marian Zamojski."

"When was he born?"

"July 7 . . . no, I mean, excuse me, December 27, 1937."

"How can that be?" he said, looking up from the documents. "A mother doesn't know how old her son is?"

Nina looked like she was going to cry. "I'm sorry that I made a mistake, I'm just very tense."

Nina had made a mistake! She had responded with Bobi's true birth date, which was July 7, 1937, when our papers said that Bogusław was born on December 27, 1937. I figured, this was the end. All they had to do was to take down my or the child's trousers to see that we were Jews.

The Gestapo officer started shouting at Nina, accused her of lying. At this point I was so tense and desperate that I lost control. I placed myself between Nina and him and started shouting back: "I'm Count Zamojski! Speak respectfully to my wife! What is it that you want? Why are you mistreating us?"

Then I did something that was totally insane. I shoved him so hard that the fellow stumbled backward and had to hold on to his cap! He reached for his revolver. I expected him to kill us on the spot. Even if we could pass as "Aryans," for a Pole to behave this way with the Gestapo meant certain death. But, although he was pale with rage, he left his gun holstered. He shoved our papers into his black leather briefcase and made for the door.

"You will sit here until I return," he ordered. He then slammed and locked the door behind him as he left.

I was totally drained. I was sure that they were going to come back to kill us. Had to be. I sat with Nina on the couch, holding her hand. Bobi was strangely quiet sitting next to her. What a pretty woman, I thought. And Bobi, a cute kid. Too bad they'll have to die. I felt my mother near me, and I said to Nina, more to comfort her than because I believed it, "No matter what happens, after our death we'll all be reunited in another world."

"Jan, darling, we are in 'another world,'" she said, arching her brows.

We had sat for more than an hour, when Bobi wiggled off the couch and said that he needed to go peepee. "I'm going to have an accident!" he whimpered, pulling on his little dick. I looked at Nina, and she looked at me. We debated whether or not to get Bobi's potty. If they came in while he was peeing, they'd see his penis, and that would be the end of it. But the child persisted. Nina took down his pants and told him to hurry. Just as she got through buckling his suspenders, we heard them in the hall. The door flew open. Our interrogator friend barged in.

"Are you acquainted with Ponczek?" he asked.

I hesitated, "Ponczek? Yes, he has worked for me." I didn't know what to say, because I didn't know what Tadzo had told them. The Gestapo officer started to shout again.

"Ponczek said that he's related to you. Something smells bad here!"

I didn't answer. By this time the fight had completely gone out of me. He turned on his heels and stormed out. Again we sat waiting for them. A while later they came back. This time they were polite. They handed us back our papers.

"All is in order!" They saluted, turned on their heels, and left.

All I could figure was that they must have called Stanisławów and checked up on our birth certificates with the priest from whom Nina got our papers. Apparently he told them that they were genuine. As for Wanda and Tadzo, they spoke good German and explained that they were new-lyweds on vacation. The Gestapo hardly asked them any questions. They sat around joking with the two of them and flirting with Wanda, while Nina and I sat in our room waiting to die.

That was our little skiing vacation in Rabka.

A couple of days after we left Rabka and got back to Kraków, Tadzo and Wanda continued their honeymoon trip and went by train to Lanck-orona, another resort. Nina and I and the child were home. It was in the late evening. I was drinking a cognac with our "good friend" Kruk. As usual he had stopped off at our place after "work." The phone rang.

"This is the police station of Lanckorona. Are you acquainted with a Pan Ponczek?" A Polish cop was on the line.

"Yes."

"Do you know that he is Jewish?"

"What?!"

"One moment, somebody wants to talk to you."

It was Wanda on the phone. I could hardly make out what she was saying because the connection was bad, and she was crying.

"The police are accusing Tadzo of being Jewish because he is circum-cised. They don't believe that he was orphaned and adopted by a Jewish couple who did that to him. You must do something!" Then the phone went dead.

I felt the blood drain from me. I looked at Ninka. Her parents were already dead. Now her brother was arrested. Meanwhile Kruk asked me what's wrong.

"Oh, nothing, just some business unpleasantness." Finally he left.

"Ninka," I said, "Tadzo and Wanda have been arrested."

Nina stuck her fist in her mouth and looked at me wild-eyed.

I knew Kryzstof, a guy in the underworld who had converted a lot of my zloty into dollars. I had hidden the money in condoms that I buried in large jars of strawberry and cherry jam. The jars were suspended by a rope from a window in the toilet that faced a dark inner shaft of our build-ing. I also had some gold. I had a gold cigarette case that must have weighed a kilo. The night that Wanda called, I went to see Kryzstof. I explained that the police in Lanckorona had made a bad mistake. I gave him the gold cigarette case and told him that I'd give him the rest of my dollars if he could get Tadzo and Wanda out.

Kryzstof was a small thin guy with a mop of lanky black hair and a pencil-line mustache. He had been a student of philosophy before the war. Now he was a counterfeiter, crook, and money changer. We understood each other perfectly; though, until then he didn't suspect that I might be a Jew. He said okay. He'd see what he could do. Apparently he succeeded because the next evening, Tadzo and Wanda showed up. They looked shaky and exhausted, and over dinner Tadzo told us what had happened to them.

After they nearly got arrested in Rabka, Wanda and Tadzo decided to continue with their honeymoon to Lanckorona, where they knew of a good pension. Returning to Kraków after Rabka might have seemed as if they had panicked, and they wanted to appear as "normal" as possible.

It was snowing heavily when they got to Lanckorona in the late afternoon. The pension was near the railroad station, their room was warm and comfortable, and they were glad to be off the train. After checking in and leaving their bags in their room they went to register at the local police station—something they had to do.

The police chief took one look at their documents, at their faces, at Wanda's black hair and brown eyes and declared, "You are Jews, of course."

They were stunned. For a moment neither one knew what to say. Then they denied they were Jews, but before they could convince anybody, the cops had Tadzo drop his pants and saw that he was circumcised. They were then placed in separate cells and told that it was too late to hand them over to the Germans, but in the morning they'd be taken to the Gestapo.

"Why are you doing this?" Tadzo asked. "We're all Poles."

The police chief was a squat middle-aged man with an almost square close-cropped head. He stopped at the entrance of Tadzo's cell. He was so furious he could hardly spit it out.

"You're no Pole, you Judas! Don't you ever say you're a Pole! You're a fucking Jew-Communist. You people fell all over each other to kiss the Russians' boots. The Germans are going to teach you a lesson, and you can kiss my ass!"

Tadzo wanted to argue the point about the Russians, but the Polish policeman wouldn't listen and slammed the cell door behind him.

Tadzo figured that was the end of the road for Wanda and him. As he lay on his prison cot, he thought about his father and the fights they had had about religion before the war. For the first time in years he said the Shma— "Hear O Israel, the Lord our God, the Lord is One" —and fell asleep. A few hours later he was awakened by shouting and laughing coming from the direction of the front door. Peering through the bars of his cell, he could see that it was a party of drunken German soldiers. They had burst into the station to have some fun by taunting the Polish police.

Without thinking much about it, Tadzo began to shout for help in German, which by then he spoke quite well. Soon a young drunk German trooper, wearing wire-rimmed glasses, stuck his head into his cell and asked him what he wanted.

"I want out. That damn idiot police chief has thrown me and my wife in jail. It's all a mistake. You, my friend, have come just in time to right a terrible wrong."

The young trooper tried to focus on Tadzo without much success.

"Why are you in there?"

"You won't believe this. This is really incredible! That idiot out there takes me for a Jew—and my wife too!"

The German, shaking his head to clear his vision, tried to focus even harder. "No kidding! What a swine! What a fool!" He stumbled back toward the entrance and the chief's office.

A few minutes later, the trooper came back with a buddy, and the police chief was forced at gunpoint to open Tadzo's cell and then Wanda's. Wanda had the presence of mind to hug the boys who had freed her and to explain to them, also in quite good German, that she and Tadzo were on their honeymoon. Then, when the police chief, in his fractured German, tried to explain that he had captured two devilishly clever Jews, he was slapped around for his troubles.

"Leave these young people alone," he was scolded by the carousing troopers. "It's obvious they're not Jews. What are you up to? Release them. If you don't there will be trouble."

Tadzo and Wanda returned to their pension accompanied by a squad of tipsy German soldiers who were singing and throwing snowballs at each other and at them, and Tadzo and Wanda threw snowballs back!

When they got back to their room, they packed quickly, but then, in a panic, they realized that they had left their precious **Kennkarten** with the police. Without these papers they were liable to be picked up at any time; moreover, there was no train back to Kraków until morning.

After a sleepless half hour debating what to do—by then it was the middle of the night—they decided that there was no help for it but to try to get their identity cards back from the police. This was a serious mistake.

As soon as Tadzo reappeared at the police station, he was arrested again, and a few minutes later Wanda was brought in. This time they were both kicked and beaten before being thrown into their cells. Tadzo felt numb from the beating and dumb for having gone back. Perhaps he and Wanda should have tried to escape on foot even though it was subzero weather. Perhaps they should have approached strangers for help—anything but this. At first he couldn't sleep. He was too hurt and too agitated. All he could do was sit on the edge of his cot, his head in his hands, reciting the Shma and then the kaddish, the prayer for the dead.

He didn't remember falling asleep, but he remembered being awakened in the early morning by another ruckus at the front door of the jail. When he looked out of his cell, he couldn't believe his eyes. The drunk German trooper from the night before, who had helped to free him and Wanda, was back!

This time the German was stone sober. "I thought this would happen to you," he shouted in outrage, wiping his glasses, his face pale and grim under his field cap.

"I know how these Polish policemen work. They're a bunch of idiots; that's why my comrades and I stopped by to see that you and your lovely bride were not harassed."

"I don't know what to say," Tadzo replied, truly dumbfounded. "You're a great guy."

After having been freed again by the now sober Germans, this time Wanda and he did not forget to take their Kennkarten *and their wallets. Without even going back to their room to get their bags, they headed straight to the train station and took the next train back to Kraków. As they were boarding the train they heard someone cry out in Polish, "Jews! Jews!" but they did not bother to look back.*

All the time they were arrested I thought that my contact, Kryzstof, had gotten them out of jail! But no, it was a drunken German who had saved their lives, and my "business partner" had simply pocketed the gold cigarette case I had given him! Now he suspected that we were Jews, *and* he knew that we had dollars stashed away. I was in trouble, and trouble soon appeared.

Early one morning there was a knock on the door.

"Who is it?" I asked. I was barefoot, wearing my pajamas. Nina and the child were asleep. Good thing that Tadzo and the rest of the family were staying at Wanda's.

"Electric company."

When I opened the door, four guys rushed in. They were wearing masks and pointing revolvers at us. They roused Nina, put us up against the wall, and threatened to shoot us. At the start of the holdup they told us that they were Germans, but they spoke with heavy Polish accents. When I heard them speak I just laughed. "Are you kidding? You want to rob us, make some extra cash, be my guests . . . but you're no Germans."

"You're right," one of them said. "We're from the Polish National Army, the underground. Even rich aristocrats like you have to contribute to the war effort."

I didn't say anything. I knew that Kryzstof had sent them and that they didn't belong to any underground. They were just hoods.

"You lousy Jews," one of them said. "Where is the money? Where are the dollars?"

So I said, "Okay, okay, take it easy. The dollars are long gone, but there is other stuff."

I gave them a lot of the valuables that were lying around the house— a few thousand zloty, some suits, some jewelry. They pulled off a ring and Nina's wedding band with such force that I thought they had broken her finger. Meanwhile, while one of them stood guard over us, his buddies ransacked the place for the money, but they didn't find it.

The guy with the gun on us said, "You're probably not a Jew, but your wife is, 'Count Zamojski.'"

"How do you figure that?" I asked.

"Because her brother was arrested up in Lanckorona, and his cock is circumcised."

"Bullshit," I said, but he just laughed.

When the other three guys came back without the dollars, they were mad as hell. Before they'd start beating it out of us, I told them that our friend Colonel Kruk from the Gestapo was about to come in for a visit from "work." "I'd be happy to make introductions," I said. That got them to thinking. They grabbed our stuff and made for the door.

"Say hello to Kryzstof. Maybe we can do some business together again real soon," I said as they left.

"Don't go away. We'll be back," one of the hoods whispered as he closed the door gently behind him.

Kryzstow suspected that we were Jews, earlier the Gestapo—or someone—had made unexplained calls, the business with Lanckorona and Rabka, the "electricians"—even Kruk began to distance himself and to ask strange questions. They began to smell us out, and I felt in my bones— so did Nina—that we were about to be arrested.

We stopped going out, even to the movies. I hardly left the house. Nina went out from time to time but only to do the shopping. The situation became increasingly tense and menacing. Meanwhile, the rest of the family—Tadzo, Wanda, Pani Marylka, and Irenka—had gone back to Warsaw. They were afraid to stay in Kraków any longer.

One morning Nina and I were lying in bed. "Ninka, we've got to leave Poland, not just Kraków, but Poland," I said.

"But that's impossible. You know that only Germans can travel in and out of Poland."

"No, we've got to leave. They'll get us sooner or later. Another week or so, they'll catch up with us. I feel it."

"So do I," she said, resignation in her voice.

"Let's invite Hauptmann Gottfried for dinner. He goes to Prague by train every week, and I've just had a bright idea."

I had met Hauptmann Gottfried through Terman. Gottfried was a tall, middle-aged guy with thinning hair, about ten years older than I was. He was the most high-ranking German I knew; it just so happened that he was the chief inspector of all the factories in the *Generalgouvernment.* Earlier I had invited him and his girlfriend to Tadzo's wedding, and I let him make a lot of money by selling him Bonneberger's plastic raincoats under the market price. I had cultivated him for a moment just like this.

Nina and the maid made a splendid meal—cognac and so on. Gottfried was in a good mood as we started to drink. Nina sang some songs. He relaxed, stretched his legs, asked how we're getting along, blah, blah, blah. Looks like we're doing well, nice apartment. I just smiled and urged him to have another drink. Certain things you can't rush, and I felt that the time was not yet ripe to ask him for a favor.

In the meantime I let him make a little more money, and then I invited him again. At the end of the second dinner, after we had finished a bottle of good French wine and were starting on the cognac, I turned to him. "I'm having some problems in Kraków. It seems I've made a bit too much money, people are jealous, and I need to leave," I said in German.

He didn't say anything, just looked over his glass of cognac at me. I continued. "You have dealings with Czechoslovakia—why don't you take me along? We might be able to do some business in Prague."

He put his glass down, wiped his mouth, and said, "What the hell! Why not? I'll take you with me. You can work for me in Prague."

"When are you off?" I asked.

"Next Thursday."

Next Thursday Hauptmann Gottfried and I went to Prague by train. He had made an *Ausweis,* an official permit, and that's all it took.

Meanwhile, Nina and Bobi were left alone in Kraków. It couldn't be helped.

Bobi

A masked guy pointing a gun at my face was sitting on the edge of the bed and gently shaking me awake. I was so sleepy that I wasn't even scared.

"Is that a real gun?" I asked him half asleep.

"Sure is, kid. Goes 'Bang!' and you fall over dead."

Despite his mask I could see that he was a young guy, a teenager really, not much older than some of the kids I had played with at the construction site.

"I need to go peepee," I said firmly.

"Go ahead, but leave the bathroom door open."

Afterward, I was lined up against the wall with my parents. *Tatusiu* said not to worry and to do as I was told.

After the hoods left, I wanted to inspect my mother's hands because I was scared that when they had pulled off her rings, they might have broken her fingers or maybe even pulled off some of them. After she showed me that she was all right, *tatusiu* and *mamusia* went to the bathroom. My father opened the window to the indoor shaft and pulled up glass jars of jam and preserves.

"They missed all this wonderful strawberry and cherry jam!" he said.

"Why would they want to take our jam?" I asked. "Don't they have any of their own?"

"Our cherry jam is much sweeter," *mamusia* giggled.

"What's so funny about jam?" I asked. I was mad that they were keeping secrets from me.

"Nothing. Nothing," my mother said patting me on the head. "It's not important."

A few weeks later my mother and I left with Captain Gottfried for Prague, a city far away. *Mamusia* told me that I wasn't to speak to anyone during the trip, not even her. She wrapped a bandage around my face and told me to point to it whenever someone spoke to me.

"You've got to make believe that you've got a toothache. Do you understand? We're not supposed to be on this train."

The train ride was long and boring, and I fidgeted a lot. I was told not to stick my arm out of the window because another passing train, or a telephone pole, might chop it off. Then Captain Gottfried said we were coming to a tunnel. What's that? Things got dark and scary, but then we were out of the tunnel and it got light. The train clanged and screeched to a halt. My mother said this is Prague, a new city. When we got off the train, my father rushed up to us and hugged us. To tell the truth I was surprised that he was still alive.

With him was a tall blond woman called Riya. She shook hands with my mother and bent down to kiss me. Why is she being so friendly? I thought. I don't even know her. But I was glad that I was finally able to pull the fake bandage off my face.

Stefania Bathsheva Gromb Ponczek ("Stefcia"). I am uncertain when this photo was taken because there is no date or place written on the original. Neither do I know how my mother was able to obtain it after the war, but she had it framed and kept it by her bedside until she died.

Joel Mendelsohn ("Julius"). Amsterdam, 1936.

Left to right: Stefcia, a friend, and Nacia (Nina) at a Warsaw café in 1933.

My uncle Tadzo (*left*) and his first cousin Tadek Korman in Śródborów, a vacation resort near Warsaw, before the war.

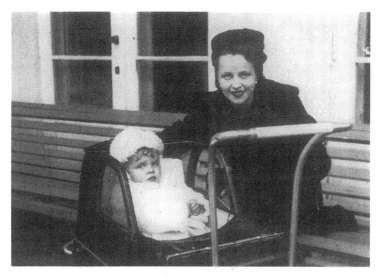

My mother and I in 1938 in Śródborów. I'm wearing the rabbit's fur hat and fur coat mentioned by her at the end of chapter 1.

Tadzo's and Wanda's wedding picture. Kraków, 1942. The next day they left for Rabka and Lanckorona on their honeymoon.

"Countess Janina Zamojska."
Prague, 1944.

"Count Jan Zamojski."
Prague, 1944.

Bobi and Nina strolling in
Brussels in 1945 or 1946.

Left to right: Iren-
ka, Wanda, and
Pani Marylka. This
photo was taken in
Brazil soon after
the war.

Wanda in Brazil soon after the war.

Bobi at Le Rosey
in 1946 or 1947.

Willy, Nina, Richi, Bobi, and Ilona, a friend. Antwerp, November 1947, the day we immigrated to the United States.

Left to right: Richi, Willy, Nina, and Bobi. New York, 1949.

Workers greet Willy at the assembly plant of the State Sewing Machine Corporation in Tokyo in 1950.

Willy tours the plant.

7   *Dina*

Willy

Gottfried took me to the Šroubek, the best hotel in the city, reserved mostly for German big shots. When I registered and they saw the name Zamojski, the Czech manager and the rest of the staff fell all over themselves. "Count Zamojski! Your excellency!" They couldn't do enough for me.

The Zamojskis were famous in Prague. It seems that before the war one of the Zamojskis had helped to fund Sokol, the top sports club in Czechoslovakia, and the Czechs were very grateful. Also the name may have reminded them of the good old days before the war and the German occupation. I got the best suite in the hotel, and after unpacking I called Ninka in Kraków: "Ninka, it's good. It's going to be okay."

Soon after, Hauptmann Gottfried went back to Kraków, and he brought Nina and the child out of Poland with him.

The *Kennkarte*, the ID I had from Kraków, would not have been sufficient for a supposed Pole like me to stay in Prague. It was only because I had excellent connections with high German officials that I wasn't arrested. I had this letter that said I was working for the *Werke* of the *Generalgouvernment*. This was enough. As a Pole I was supposed to work for the Germans in forced labor, but I had affidavits from Bonneberger, from Gottfried, from Terman. I never worked a day in forced labor. I had a document that said that I was *kriegswichtig*, essential to the war effort— a very important document that Gottfried made up for me. I went to the police with my *Kennkarte*, with the Gottfried letter, and I got my *Anmeldungsbescheinigung*, residence permit, from the Czech police.

I was sure that the Gestapo knew about me. They had Gestapo people right in the hotel. If I had arrived alone from Kraków out of the blue, I would have been arrested on the spot, but I arrived with Hauptmann Gottfried, and that made all the difference. I was always looking for the top Germans, not hiding, living out in the open, surrounding myself with German big wheels.

I was in no hurry. I waited a few weeks until Nina came. Then I had this idea to call Siegel at Spolem. I called him from my suite at the Śroubek: "I just arrived with Hauptmann Gottfried. Are you interested in merchandise?"

"Ja. Fantastic! Whatever you have, send me."

I was back in business! In Prague, in contrast to Poland, there was still a lot of stuff to buy. For instance, somebody offered me three thousand combs. So I called Siegel immediately, told him I had access to fifty thousand combs and that he should open a letter of credit with Schenker and Co. under my name. Schenker was a shipping company established all over the world, including Czechoslovakia. A letter of credit meant that I could draw money against the delivery of merchandise.

I started to send all kinds of stuff to Spolem. One day Siegel asked me if I could get some blueing chemical for laundry soap. I found that I could get a whole railroad wagon of it. I made a profit of 5,000 percent on the deal!

Siegel came and visited us in Prague. Hauptmann Gottfried came with his girlfriend many times. They all came. Terman came, and they all got fantastic and very expensive "presents." I mean big bribes from me, of course.

Once I was in Prague, I no longer did business with Bonneberger. I left the apartment in Kraków to Roetger. He said he'd take care of it for me, but instead he took all the furniture, sold it, and kept the money. But it didn't matter—I made so much money in Prague that I didn't care, and what was I supposed to do anyway? Sue him?

At this time a broker introduced me to Riya Villert. She and her husband were very useful to me. She was a businesswoman who offered me merchandise in large quantities for export—shoe paste and so on. She was a big energetic woman who usually got her way. Her husband was completely under her thumb. He probably knew that she and I were sleeping together, but he didn't say a word. Nothing. But we needed him for our business. In fact, for me, at first the main attraction was her husband. He was in the office that investigated black market operations. This was very important, because the kind of business we were in was not so kosher. We bought stuff on the black market and shipped it out to Poland. Riya's husband covered for us. It was a perfect setup.

Riya was in love, but for me it was just a fling. We went to a hotel to talk business. There was a bed . . . she was very willing. She was very strong. She took the initiative. I was not the first. She had a history of such adventures, and her husband looked the other way. At first it wasn't so clear to her that I was a Jew. Later she became suspicious, but if she knew, she didn't care. She wanted me to marry her and to leave Nina. *Weiss ich was?* What do I know? First of all I didn't mind my relationship with her, and second, it was a perfect arrangement. I had an office, a partner, and a husband who could serve as a cover for the business—perfect setup. Although I had this affair with Riya, I never abandoned Nina or the child.

I was constantly on the lookout for merchandise, when one day Riya told me that some guy had sewing machines. Unbelievable, sewing machines during the war! Wow! His name was Baron Kurt von Rabenau. He was a nobleman, just like me! Baron von Rabenau meet Count Zamojski! He had a big wartime business—legal, of course—and was importing sewing machines from Switzerland, which was fantastic. Through Baron von Rabenau, I met his managing director, Rolf Mueller. He was six foot four, blond—typical goy. We became very friendly, and through Rolf I met some other people. We all became friends and formed a kind of social circle.

There was Froemmel, a German who worked for the city administration. He had a great-looking wife, much younger than he, whose name was Mitzi. She had green eyes, red hair, and a great figure and was very vivacious. Everyone wanted to sleep with her, and some did. There was another couple, Naujukat and his girlfriend. He and Rolf were friends from Berlin. And there was a former girlfriend of Naujukat who also belonged to the circle. Most weekends, especially during the summer, we spent at Riya's cottage on a river in the country near the city. During the day we'd swim, and in the evening Nina would sing, play the guitar, and entertain. Sometimes Naujukat would come with one girl and sometimes with another. He changed horses in midstream, slept with this one and that one. It was all very wild.

Soon after I met him, Rolf invited Nina and me to dinner. I was expecting a German woman to greet us at the door, but then I saw Mueller's wife, Dina, who looked like a hundred Jewish women rolled into one! Black hair dyed red and a Jewish nose. She was small, thin, and nervous with a constant smile plastered on her face. She greeted us very warmly at the door, "Jan, Ninoczka! So glad to meet you!"

There was a large party going on. Besides us and the Muellers there were a few German officers, including some SS, with their Czech girl-friends. Riya was there, dominating the room with her rose and pink plumpness, the Froemmels, Baron von Rabenau. They danced and flirt-ed to the syrupy music and throaty tones of Marika Rökk on the phono-graph, "Für eine Nacht voller Seligkeit," "For a Night Filled with Bliss."

We sat at the table with another five, six couples. The maid was serv-ing an outstanding dinner. After dinner, Dina announced that we're all invited to the living room for after-dinner liqueurs. When we got to the living room, Dina turned to Nina and said, "I'd like to play you some records."

About halfway through the evening—while we were drinking and chatting—she put on a record that I recognized immediately. It was a cantor chanting a Jewish prayer! Nina stopped speaking and looked shocked, and then she started to weep and shake. She had to excuse her-self from the table, she was so upset. I tried to cover for her by making some stupid joke, but nobody seemed to notice—or at least they didn't let on that they had noticed Nina's reaction.

Later, when we got home, I let her have it: "Stupid! You almost gave it all away!"

"It was the *El Malei Rachamim*, 'God Full of Compassion,' from the *Yizkor*, Yom Kippur remembrance service," Nina tried to explain. "I couldn't believe what I was hearing! It was so sudden, so unexpected, it caught me completely by surprise."

"Yeah, but you have to be ready for such surprises. You saw that she is Jewish. You should have been on guard."

"Jan"—she called me Jan even when we were alone—"when I heard that music my father's face loomed before me . . . I could not help my-self. I remembered how we'd go to *shul* together before the war, and then I thought of the ghetto . . ."

"The others may not have understood," I said, "but now Dina knows that we're Jews, and if she knows, so does Rolf."

"I know," said Nina, blowing her nose. "A Jew married to a German in the middle of the war—how is it possible?"

I didn't know under what Nazi law it was possible for Dina to stay married to Rolf, but for a while she was lucky, and so was Freddy, her *mischling*, half-Jewish, little boy. Apparently as long as Rolf would have them, they were safe in Prague. But we felt less safe than before that din-ner party at Dina's.

I had been in Prague for almost a year. In the meantime I had found an apartment with a maid near the Muellers. It so happened that the apartment overlooked an ancient Jewish cemetery—what an irony!—but good apartments were scarce during the war, so I took it. I also thought it would be safer for us and better for Nina and me if she took the child and rented another apartment in Poděbrady. The town was near enough to Prague so that I could visit on weekends, and it was a spa, which made it relaxing.

The winter of 1944, Riya wanted to go on a skiing vacation to Austria, but I insisted that Nina and Bobi go too. Riya went to Innsbruck, while the three of us first went to Vienna. I showed Nina and the child the Prater, the amusement park, and the three of us went to the circus together. The next day we met Riya in Innsbruck, high in the alps.

It was evening. A heavy snowfall covered the ground, and more snow was falling. From the station we hired a horse-drawn sleigh to take us to our hotel. Our destination was high up in the mountains, a long distance from the station. It was very cold and dark. There was a snowstorm, and the driver gave us some fur blankets. He started off, but then he lost his way. At one point he got out of the sleigh and started to poke holes in the snow with his staff to make sure that we wouldn't sink. I thought, This is crazy. This is the end. We've escaped from the Gestapo, now we're going to die in a stupid snowstorm!

It was so cold that Nina, Riya, and Bobi started to cry. I had to get behind the sled to push, while fearing that we'd all freeze to death.

To make the story even more interesting, it turned out that this driver happened to be a Ukrainian from Krakovce, a village near Stanisławów, from where the Mendelsohn factory recruited its workers! I was afraid that he'd recognize me, but apparently he didn't or, at first, he didn't let on that he did.

Hours later we saw a light. It was the hotel. Thank God we made it. No frostbite. But we could have died there very easily, because of the snow and the cold, not because of the Germans.

Ten days later we went back to Prague, and Rolf Mueller told me that he wanted to divorce Dina.

In Baron von Rabenau's office there was a young girl, Lisa, who was his secretary—about eighteen years old, a great beauty. And Rolf was crazy about her. He was so jealous that he wouldn't leave me alone with her in the office even for a minute. He told me he went with Lisa to Vienna. He slept with her. It was "heaven," he said—passionate love affair. One day he told me, "You know, Jan, I want to marry the girl . . ."

"Are you crazy? If you divorce Dina, she has to go to a concentration camp with your child," I said. "They'll be killed."

I thought that I had convinced him, but a week later I heard that he had divorced his wife. The whole business probably took him ten seconds. He went to the Gestapo and told them that his conscience didn't permit him to live with a Jew, and that was all. All I could hope for was that he hadn't betrayed us as well.

A week later Nina and I stopped by the Muellers. The doors were locked, and there was no one there. We turned to the janitor, "Did they leave Prague?" I asked. He said that the Gestapo had come to arrest Dina Mueller, but she had escaped. The Gestapo officer who went looking for her was named Bartelt, as I was soon to learn.

When they started to look for her, Bartelt found a photograph album in her apartment and some addresses. And from that he made a list of Dina's friends whom he proceeded to arrest. Among her papers were our photos and addresses. We were all accused of befriending a Jew and helping her to escape. This alone was enough to sentence us all to death.

Meanwhile, with papers provided by our friend Froemmel, Dina escaped to Germany, to friends in Dresden, and there she vanished for a time. It was already near the end of the war, but the Gestapo assigned two grown men, Gestapo inspectors, to search for Dina and her little boy. It was a few months before the end of the war, and they had nothing else to do but hunt for Jews! So stupid!

They arrested everybody, and finally they forced somebody to tell them where Dina was hiding, and Bartelt went to Dresden. She tried to commit suicide by jumping from the third floor of her apartment building, but somehow she lived. Her legs were shattered, and she was brought to the Dresden hospital. Why she and Freddy weren't killed right there, I don't know. A week later—it was in February 1945—Dresden was bombed by the British and the Americans. Thousands of people lost their lives, but their hospital was left standing, and Dina and Freddy survived the bombing. When she had sufficiently recovered, the Gestapo shipped both of them out to Theresienstadt.

Of course once they arrested all of Dina's friends, they arrested me too.

Bobi

I was almost six when we got to Prague. It was a new experience, and I had to learn Czech, a new language. Perhaps that explains why I remember our story so much more clearly from this point. It was almost as if by leaving Kraków, I had left early childhood behind and had become much more aware of everything. For the most part the past of early childhood still appears in finely etched disconnected scenes, but starting in Prague, such scenes started to link up into a more coherent narrative.

The Śroubek had long, cavernous, red-carpeted hallways, and our rooms had high windows covered by heavy crimson drapes. There was a large white-tiled bathroom occupied by a huge bathtub—like an elephant—a toilet, and a bidet. *Mamusia* kept a pot of flowers in the bidet.

When we unpacked, *tatusiu* called to have our lunch sent upstairs. He was in a gay, expansive mood, but he insisted that everyone address him as Count, and he told me that from now on I would really have to behave with greater dignity.

"When a lady walks into the room, you must stand up and offer her your chair, if there is no place for her to sit. When she's introduced to you, you must bow and kiss her hand. Don't just grab her hand like a piece of meat. You must bend down to her hand and kiss it lightly. Don't slobber all over it. Understood?"

"Like this?" I practiced on my mother's hand.

She laughed. "It will do, Bobi. You'll soon become a real Polish cavalier."

"It's not funny."

Tatusiu was not amused, and I would get slapped across the face for making a mistake in deportment. I realized that all of this was important, but I didn't know why. I could see that he took himself very seriously here in Prague. This may account for the general air of reserved respect that hovered over us at the hotel. The Germans may have thought that we were powerful dignitaries to whom one ought to pay careful obeisance, and the Czechs were thrilled by the Zamojski name.

Wherever we went the manager would sidle up, rubbing his hands, and introduce us to his guests: "Count and Countess Zamojski, and this is master Bogusław Marian."

"How charming." Some fat monocled German would lean toward us, not knowing what to make of the scene. German officers were so crisp, so correct, the smell of their high polished black boots mingling with that of the ersatz coffee emanating from the dining room.

In the morning my father went to his office, while my mother and I had breakfast in our room. When it got warm enough my mother would take me down to our swim club on the Vltava, where later we'd meet my father and Riya for lunch. Riya was a big-boned, big-breasted, blond Czech woman who would ordinarily be considered attractive in a loud and earthy way, but she was a woman whom my mother detested and considered nothing but "vulgar and coarse."

After lunch we came back to the hotel, where I was sent up to our suite for my afternoon nap. I hated those naps—empty periods of exile in the middle of the day. I wasn't even tired, yet I had to lie sleeplessly on my bed, waiting for my parents to come back from shopping or wherever they had gone. I lay there studying the intricacies of dust particles reflected in the sunlight streaming in from gaps between the windowsill and the curtains. I longed for Wanda, Tadzo, Pani Marylka, and Irenka. I had no friends or playmates, and I missed them. I was also afraid of Prague because, at the beginning, I didn't speak the language.

Toward evening, I could hear my parents in the hall outside. Feigning sleep, I'd hear them quarreling about Riya. "What do you see in her? A fat ass, is that what you want?"

"Shut up! Shut up! The child will hear you."

"I don't give a damn. He should know that you're placing all of us in danger. She's going to drag us by your circumcised dick straight to the Gestapo."

"Shut up!"

When I'd hear my father slapping my mother and her muffled cry, I'd imagine myself rushing for a huge kitchen knife to plunge through his treacherous heart. Instead, I'd curl up in a ball, too terrified to move.

After a few months at the Šroubek, we moved to an apartment not far from the hotel, right across the street from what turned out to be a Jewish cemetery. That desecrated and abandoned plot of land was segregated from the street by a wall about two meters high, but many of its headstones had been smashed by rock-throwing kids. Now that my mother was busy with furnishing the apartment and dealing with Mrs. Pihlerova, our landlady who doubled as our cook, I was left to my own devices, and, as in Kraków, once the weather got warm, I started to play with the kids on the street.

We were a mixed bunch that included some Czechs, Germans, and

Freddy Mueller and me. Freddy was Dina's son, about my own age. He had curly red hair and owned a pedal-pushing bright red car that was the envy of the whole neighborhood. Neither Freddy nor I, of course, knew that we were Jews.

Our favorite game was "Russian front." We'd choose up sides, with the German kids playing the "good" Germans and the rest of us, including Freddy and me, cast as the "evil" Russians. Invariably the Germans won. Young as we were, we knew that it might be dangerous for our parents should it be known that the "Russian" side insisted on winning the war.

One evening that spring, we had been playing by the riverside, and I was walking home alone. I had already turned the corner of our street when I saw a gang of Hitler *Jugend* teenage boys—there must have been five or six of them—heading in my direction. I was scared because they were bigger and carried daggers on their belts, but I didn't run. I hoped that I could pass them, and they'd leave me alone. As I came abreast of them, they surrounded me and started to jabber at each other in German. I quickly realized that they were looking for Czech kids, no matter how old, to beat up.

"You're a Czech louse, right?" a tall skinny blond kid asked me.

"No, I'm German," I said.

"Let's beat the shit out of the shitty liar," someone said.

"How come you don't speak German?" the skinny kid asked.

"My mother is Czech, but my father is German. We speak Czech at home."

"Bullshit! Bullshit!" another kid piped up and drew back his fist, but my skinny buddy stopped him.

"What's your name then?"

"Hans Mueller. My name is Hans Mueller, but they call me Hansel."

After conferring with his crew for a few seconds, the skinny kid said that I was okay. "Go home and don't wander the streets at dinnertime," he warned. "There are Jews who might kidnap and eat you!"

I ran home out of breath, and when I told my parents the story they praised me for my quick thinking. "Hans Mueller! Hans Mueller!" my father laughed. "Where did you dig that out from?" I had no idea, except that one of the German kids on the block was named Hans, and Freddy Mueller was my best friend.

A few days later some of the kids from the block, including Freddy and me and the real Hansel, a stocky German kid with a crew cut, were sitting on the wall of the Jewish cemetery. We were watching horse-drawn carts top heavy with hay rolling ponderously across our street to the fields outside of the city. We had been down to the river to watch men fishing. We had thrown rocks at the remaining headstones in the Jewish cemetery. We had been down to the square to watch another regiment of "valiant" German troops off to the Russian front. By the railroad station we had seen one German trooper come out of a train with his nose missing. Where his nose had been was nothing but a large ugly hole.

"The Russian winter," Hansel had explained. "It's so cold that people's body parts fall off."

I had never realized that German soldiers could lose body parts, but I was pleased.

We were bored—nothing to do.

"I dare you to eat it!" cried Hansel, jumping off the cemetery wall.

"Eat what?"

"This!" Hansel picked up a piece of horse manure and stuck it in his mouth.

"It's delicious. Salty," he cried, doubling over with laughter.

We all jumped down and joined Hansel in his crazy trick. Throwing rocks and horse manure, we chased each other around the block. We pulled out our *ptaszeks* and peed against the cemetery wall. I didn't care who saw it! We climbed the trees like monkeys and jabbered at each other in incomprehensible languages.

Suddenly in the middle of all this fun appeared a stout middle-aged woman who tried to walk briskly past us. Hansel noticed that she was wearing an armband with a yellow Jewish star.

"A Jew! A Jew!" cried Hansel.

Grabbing handfuls of horse manure and whatever garbage we could find to pelt her with, we chased her down the block. At first she tried to run. We screamed and laughed at her comical bounce and waddle as she tried to duck our missiles, but once she got to the end of the block she stopped running. She turned and faced us, which stopped us in our tracks and silenced us. Her face expressed no anger or fear. Instead, her hands on her hips, her head tilted to one side, she fixed us with a puzzled and mocking smile, like someone who had been told a dumb joke that she didn't get. Then she turned the corner and disappeared.

When I came home that evening, *mamusia* asked me what all the excitement was about. I was too ashamed to tell her about eating horse manure. Instead I just told her about our chasing a Jewish woman down the street. I expected my mother to make a joke of it. After all, weren't Jews queer?

Instead, her eyes dilating, my mother went pale with rage. She grabbed me and shook me hard. "Leave them be! Leave them be!" she hissed and then started to cry.

Truly, I was puzzled. I thought that *mamusia* and I were close. What was all the fuss about? It was only a Jew.

———————————

When I think about it now, I feel myself being swept up in a moment of hilarity and fun, while trying to keep up with the other kids in the chase. I recall being scared, exhilarated, empowered, and sorry for the woman all at once. I didn't know what "Jewish" meant, but I knew that it was bad and dangerous. Moreover, the very fact that we were able to humiliate a person because she was a Jew without being punished for it reduced all Jews to something less than human.

I had no hesitation in transferring our hapless Jewish victim from the world of real people into the world of imaginary and evil apparitions like witches, sorcerers, and ghosts. For me such evil apparitions were just as real as the people I knew. To strike out against a Jewish "witch" was to gain control over my fears of a frightening world. That's why I didn't understand my mother's angry reaction: All my friends had thought it right to abuse the Jewish woman, but my mother's fury challenged that notion and left me confused.

What about the Jewish woman whom we had taunted that day? I have no idea who she was and what happened to her. I do know that most Czech Jews were deported to Auschwitz. Very likely she was among them.

———————————

Soon after, to keep me off the street and to give me some education, my parents hired a governess. Miss Berta was an old maid, thin, nervous, compulsive, and a devout Catholic. In addition to giving me lessons in deportment, language, and arithmetic, she took it upon herself to instruct me in religion, a subject in which she found me woefully deficient. Knowing by then that I was to please adults and not complain, I tried my best to follow her instructions.

"What is it that you want to do when you grow up?" She'd bite her lower lip and fix me with her stare.

But I knew how to answer correctly: "I want to become a priest and give my life to Jesus."

"That's right. That's right." I was spared a whack with her ruler for saying something dumb, like, "I want to be a pilot."

In the morning we'd go to mass. After breakfast we spent hours doing arithmetic. I cried into her problems, while she swatted me with a ruler whenever I answered incorrectly. After lunch I would nap for an hour—I actually began to look forward to this respite from her—and then we'd do grammar. Toward evening we'd be back in church for the evening service, and then dinner, prayers to Jesus and to the Virgin, and finally release from Miss Berta in sleep. I dreaded my governess, but sometimes she told me wonderful stories of saints. The story I liked best was that of St. Christopher and baby Jesus.

It would seem that St. Christopher, a powerful, burly, red-headed man, claimed to be the strongest man in the world. One day while crossing a river he saw a small child sitting by the water's edge, afraid to go in. "What's the matter?" asked St. Christopher.

"I'm afraid to cross the river by myself," answered the child.

"Why then I'll take you across," volunteered St. Christopher.

With one swoop he lifted the child onto his enormous shoulders and proceeded to cross the river. No sooner had he reached the middle, where the river was deep and treacherous, then he felt the child grow heavier and heavier. The child grew so heavy that St. Christopher feared that they both would drown if he continued across, and he was sorely tempted to abandon the child to save himself. Despite the unbearable burden, he persevered. Slipping, sliding, and gasping for air, he made it to the other side. As he laid the child down, he noticed a golden halo spreading around its head.

"You have just carried the whole world on your shoulders," said baby Jesus, "and for this I shall love you always."

I wasn't sure whether I loved baby Jesus or I thought myself to be baby Jesus, but I did long for a St. Christopher, gentler and stronger then my father, who would protect me all my days.

One afternoon Miss Berta took me to see a passion play in the old city of Prague. I had never been to the old city, and I was intrigued by the narrow, winding, cobblestoned streets and crooked little alleys leading into walled-in courtyards. After much climbing, we came to a square packed full of people watching a spectacle.

There was a bent and ragged Jesus, his crown of thorns nearly slipping off his head, carrying his cross up to Calvary. All around him were creatures hideously disfigured and bent over in postures of craven fear and violence. With each step these masked creatures would pounce on our Lord and whip him until he fell forward, his cross on top of him. Then, with superhuman effort, he would rise, his cross on his back, and resume his journey. I was fascinated, frightened, and repelled by the scene.

"Who are the creatures torturing Jesus?" I asked.

"Jews," she answered with a grimace. "They betrayed and crucified our Lord."

Jews, I thought. Again, Jews. I disliked Miss Berta and mistrusted her, but I decided that, to be on the safe side, it was just as well not to fall into the Jews' clutches.

––––––––––––

In the fall of 1943, a few months after the Warsaw ghetto revolt, Hauptmann Gottfried managed to bring Tadzo and Wanda from Warsaw to Prague. He had received a huge "present" from my father. I was told that we didn't want to call attention to ourselves at the train station, where people might get suspicious.

"They're Poles," *mamusia* explained. "They're not supposed to be on that train."

When Tadzo and Wanda got off the train, they looked thinner and older than I remembered them. The grown-ups shook hands all around, without the kissing, the hugging, and the shouts of joy that I would have otherwise expected. *Tatusiu* helped Tadzo with the suitcases while Wanda took my hand, and we made our way back to our apartment.

After Tadzo and Wanda unpacked we had lunch. The grown-ups started a conversation while I listened. Although there was much to say, the conversation was very low key, carried out mostly by what seemed to be words, gestures, and looks that were in some kind of private code. Was it my presence that was preventing them from speaking frankly or was it that their experiences were so beyond comprehension that they could not be spoken?

"Well, how was the trip?" *tatusiu* asked.

"Oh, fine. Uneventful," Tadzo answered. "Gottfried seems to know what he's doing."

"Gottfried is getting very well paid for what he's doing. Don't worry about him."

"And over there? It must have been hard for you," said *mamusia.*

"You can't imagine what went on toward the end," said Tadzo, looking deeply into his borscht. "And how has it been here?"

"We've been very lucky so far," replied *tatusiu.*

"Extremely lucky," *mamusia* chipped in.

"Bobi looks good," said Tadzo.

"The difference between here and there is the difference between the north star and the earth," said Wanda, interrupting and not making sense.

"Was it that bad?" *mamusia* asked.

"At the end they burned it all down," said Tadzo. "Some of our Polish 'allies' celebrated when they heard the news."

"Inside the walls it was burning, outside they had a carousel playing. While some of 'ours' were set on fire like torches and leaped from burning buildings, some of 'theirs' cheered and applauded," Wanda added. "It was all part of the show."

"Where was the carousel? Who was on fire jumping from burning buildings? Who cheered and applauded?" I asked.

When I looked toward Wanda I was startled. I had expected a straight answer, but instead I saw that her head was tilted in a quizzical manner, her eyebrows were arched, and, instead of answering my question, she gave me a mocking smile, like the Jewish woman my friends and I had chased down the street. Our eyes locked for a moment, and then she turned toward *tatusiu*.

"I think it's time for your nap," *mamusia* said.

"I know you're worried about your mother and Irenka," said *tatusiu* to Wanda. "I'll try to get them out with Gottfried as soon as I can. I don't want to rush him. He's not aware of who he's bringing out. Do you understand?" Wanda looked down and nodded.

"Bobi, I told you to go to your room. It's way past your nap time," *mamusia* insisted.

I left the table reluctantly. I was relieved that Tadzo and Wanda were with us again. I hadn't realized how much I had missed them, but I was worried about Pani Marylka and Irenka, and I was confused by what I had heard. The earth . . . the north star . . . people leaping from burning buildings while others applauded . . . Wanda giving me strange looks. What did it mean?

A few months later, Pani Marylka and Irenka were brought to Prague from Warsaw by Hauptmann Gottfried, just as my father had promised.

The winter of 1944–45, my parents and I together with Riya went to Vienna on vacation. Riya went on to Innsbruck, where later we were to meet her for skiing, but in the meantime the three of us were left alone in Vienna for a few days. My father had some business in town while my mother and I went to the Prater, the amusement park.

The day was clean and crisp. Running, laughing, out of breath, *mamusia* and I played hide-and-seek under a tunnel of overarching chestnut trees leading to the amusement park. Our footsteps were cushioned by a thick blanket of fallen multicolored leaves. Once in a while, we picked up chestnuts. I was delighted by their hard, shiny brown surfaces.

In the distance we could hear the honky-tonk of the amusement park. Soon we were engulfed in a milling, shoving crowd of children and youths, and everywhere we saw the multicolored flashing lights of rides and games of chance. For the first time I rode a rearing black stallion on the carousel. I was terrified when I lost my mother in the hall of mirrors. But the greatest thrill of all was to steer my own little red electric car and bump it into others while avoiding being bumped by them. As I whizzed around the track, extricating myself from tricky situations, I glanced up to see my mother wave to me in a calm and reassuring manner. She was smiling her golden smile, totally absorbed in me and in the moment. When I got out of my car my feet tingled from the electricity in the floor. Later, over lunch, she told me she was pregnant.

"It's war and so on, Bobi. But I've decided to have a child. There is a brother or sister waiting for you in my tummy." I was thrilled, but I wondered how it got there.

In the afternoon my father joined us in our hotel room. Our happy mood must have infected him too because no sooner had he unpacked then he invited us out to dinner and to the circus. There we sat, the three of us, watching the show. Out came the dancing bears, the acrobats, the lions and their tamers. Out came the clowns, the midgets, and the prancing horses. I glanced up at the darkly handsome face of my father and the blond, sunny, Polish face of my mother. Their faces were made soft by the dim yellow lights of the circus tent, and for a brief moment I felt lighthearted and happy. The show released us from some deadly preoccupation that had been dogging us ever since I could remember.

The next morning we took the train to Innsbruck, high in the Austrian Alps. When we arrived in the evening, thick snow was falling, Riya was waiting for us at the station, and the brief moment of family happiness had vanished.

When we got to our hotel, my parents had another one of their violent quarrels. "Why did you bring her here?" my mother sobbed. "She'll denounce us. She'll kill us. She's been talking to the sleigh driver. He's from Stanisławów. I'm sure he knows who we are . . ."

"Shut up! Shut up! Watch out what you're saying in front of the child." My father stomped out to spend the night with Riya, leaving my mother to cry herself to sleep and leaving me to comfort her in our elegant and spacious quarters.

After we had been in Innsbruck for a week, *mamusia* woke me in the middle of the night. "Call your father," she said. "I'm sick."

When my eyes adjusted to the bright lights in our room, I could see splotches of blood on her bed and bloody tracks leading to the bathroom. By the time I got *tatusiu* from Riya's room, my mother had straightened out a bit and was sitting, pale but composed, by the window. She looked up at *tatusiu* when we entered and said with finality, "It's gone." I was surprised by how hard and brittle she seemed, an aspect of her I had not seen before.

He sat gingerly on the edge of my bed. I moved to a corner of the room.

"I'm leaving for Prague tomorrow," she said.

"I'll come with you," he said. It seemed to me I heard a note of tenderness in his voice.

"You can stay here with your whore if you like."

"You don't understand," *tatusiu* said, as if to a recalcitrant child. "She knows."

"Knows what?"

"Everything, for God's sake."

"You told her?"

"She figured it out, and our friend the sleigh driver told her the rest."

"Well then," my mother asked, "what's the difference where we stay? We're finished either way."

"Not as long as I stay with her."

"I'm going. You can do as you please."

"What about Bobi?"

"Bobi will come with me, of course."

"Ninka," my father said, using the affectionate diminutive, but one look at her taut, pale face convinced him to say nothing further. He got up and left. Since I didn't know what to say, my mother started.

"The blood you saw was the start of a baby your father and I made in Prague."

"Where is the baby now?" I asked, fascinated.

"Actually there was no baby, just the seed. You understand? Like planting a sunflower or a lilac bush, you need seeds. Well the seed didn't want to grow in me. It died and flushed itself out last night."

"Are you going to die?"

"No, I'm not going to die and neither are you if we can help it."

"But she knows."

"Who knows what?"

"*Tatusiu* said she knows."

"He meant that Riya knows something about us. It's a secret that happened before the war. Don't concern yourself about it. She's nothing but a dumb cow."

"Are you going back then?"

"Yes. You heard what I told your father. You can come with me or stay with them. As you please."

"I'm going with you," I said without hesitation.

"As you wish."

When we got back to Prague, my mother left my father "with his whore" and took me to our hotel room in Poděbrady. In effect my parents were separated. Soon after our return from Vienna, we heard that Dina Mueller had been arrested, and a few days after that, my mother got a call from Pihlerova, our landlady and cook in Prague. She said that she was coming to Poděbrady to see us.

When Pihlerova came, *mamusia* and I were alone in the room. She was middle-aged, lumpy, and clumsy, and it took her some time to extricate herself from her coat. Wiping her upper lip, which was covered by a thin black mustache, she faced us. It was clear by her pose and ingratiating pleasantries that she had some dramatic news to tell us. Looking down at the floor she said, "I have some bad news for you, Countess."

"Jan has been arrested," said my mother softly.

"Yes."

"How did it happen?"

"Day before yesterday, three men came to your flat. It must have been, I don't know, about five in the morning. Woke everybody up. 'What do you want?' says I, opening the door. 'Shut your mouth,' they say. 'This is Gestapo. Where is Zamojski?' Then they get the count. He was mad, but they slapped him around and took him away."

"Obviously, there's been some misunderstanding," said my mother almost in a whisper.

"Of course there has, of course. I called my son right off and told him about it, and he said there must be some misunderstanding."

At the mention of her son, who was in the Czech police, my mother turned an inquiring face to Pihlerova.

"And what were your son's impressions?"

"As I said, he thinks there has been some misunderstanding, and he told me to come to see you and tell you about it."

"That's nice of him."

Here Pihlerova looked away with what seemed like embarrassment. "He also told me that you shouldn't try to get back to your flat just yet. It may be dangerous. In the meantime, he and his wife will move in to look after your things." It was obvious even to me that Pihlerova's son had grabbed our stuff, but my mother didn't let on.

"That's extremely good of you. I'm sure that we'll be able to clear things up in no time. In the meantime feel free to use our things—better you than the Gestapo."

After some more pleasantries, Pihlerova rose and squirmed back into her coat. "Be brave," she said to my mother, and then, opening the door with one hand, she pinched my cheek with the other. "You're the man in the family now."

When the door slammed shut, my mother went back to sit on her bed. She had the wide-eyed dumb look of someone who had just witnessed a bloody car accident. For a moment she said nothing, and then with her mouth hanging open in an idiotic grimace she whimpered, "They've got him, Bobi, they've got him."

With that I started to cry. Without my father, how would we live?

8   *The Arrest*

Nina

Soon after Dina's arrest, Jan came to visit me in Poděbrady. He didn't even mention Riya, and neither did I. He said we had to get out of the country and explained that, when we had been in Vienna on vacation, he had met people who had connections. Apparently if you had the money you could get papers to Switzerland. He was planning to leave for Vienna from Prague the next morning to see what he could do. Meanwhile, I was to wait with Bobi for his call and follow him later. In the evening he returned to Prague to spend the night, but instead of leaving for Vienna the next morning, he was arrested.

After Jan's arrest I didn't know what to do or who to turn to. I was all alone with Bobi. Earlier when they heard that the Gestapo was searching for Dina, the rest of the family—Tadzo, Wanda, Pani Marylka, and Irenka—had gone into hiding without telling me where. I was glad not to know because, if I were arrested and tortured, I didn't want to betray them. To steady my nerves I started chain-smoking and became ill from nicotine poisoning. I was sick. I could hardly eat—couldn't swallow food. After everything we'd been through together, it just didn't seem worthwhile to go on living without Jan.

Suddenly Pani Marylka appeared, showing great courage. She didn't say where they had moved to, and I didn't ask. She nursed me to some kind of health, fed me tea, applesauce, barley soup. But after two weeks she told me that the rest of the family was leaving Poděbrady. "I wish you'd come with us," she said, "but I know that you won't leave Jan." She was right.

After she left, I hardly stepped out of our hotel room. Bobi and I would lie in bed together—the mere presence of his small boy's body was a comfort to me—but I was too frightened and depressed to move.

One day I got a summons that I was supposed to appear at Gestapo headquarters and that I should bring all necessary documents with me. The date came and went. I figured that they'd arrest me anyway, no matter what I did, and I was too ill to travel.

Then something in me rebelled. A few days after the summons I decided, what the hell, I'll go to the Gestapo before they come to me! Once I had made a decision to act, I forced myself to eat better—I didn't want to appear like a living corpse in front of them. Now the question was, What to do about Bobi? Who could I leave him with? I couldn't leave him alone, because if I were arrested, how would he live? To take him with me to the Gestapo would be the end of the three of us, because he was circumcised.

It was an unusually warm day in winter when I went to the park with Bobi to let him play outdoors a bit. I sat on a bench while he made a snowman and urged me to join him. I smiled and nodded absently, but I didn't move from the bench. I was chain smoking, one cigarette after another— Czech cigarettes wrapped in newspaper, a hundred cigarettes a day.

While I sat smoking and watching my boy, a stout woman sat next to me on the bench. She looked like a lumpy peasant with a pleasant face, but she was expensively dressed. "What a cute kid you've got. You should be so grateful to have such a beautiful child," she said turning to me.

"I am. And what about you, do you have children?"

"If I had kids, I wouldn't be here. I'm not from here. I come to Poděbrady from time to time to see a doctor and to take the waters at the spa. My husband told me that if I don't get pregnant next year, he'll divorce me. He wants children that badly, and I can't have any."

To my surprise, she began to cry. As Mrs. Wesely—that was her name—was speaking, something dawned on me. Maybe her willingness to bare her heart to me allowed me to do the same to her.

"My husband has been arrested by the Germans," I blurted out. "I must go to Prague to look for a lawyer." I took her hand and said as earnestly as I could, "Take care of my boy for two or three months. Don't tell me where you live. Just tell me how you live. Do you live in an apartment? In a house?"

She looked stunned, but didn't withdraw her hand. "We live on a farm. We own horses, cattle, and pigs. We bake our own bread, cure our own hams and sausages. We are well off, but we have no children. Are you serious or are you kidding?"

"I couldn't be more serious." She hugged me and began to kiss me on the cheeks. I guess for her it was a miracle that she was being given a child, even if it was on loan. "When are you leaving?" I asked.

"Tonight at midnight I have a train."

"I can give you some money for Bogusiu's expenses."

"Don't insult me. It's you who are doing me a tremendous favor. I have all the food and all the money I need."

Before she could tell me, I warned her, "Don't tell me where you're taking him."

"Yes, but how will you get him back?"

"The war will soon be over. When it's over, I'll try to get on the radio and make contact with you that way. You do have a radio, don't you? I'll say 'Dear Mrs. Wesely, this is Janina Zamojska. I live in Prague at such and such an address. At such and such a phone number.' And you'll be able to reach me."

We agreed to meet at the train station and shook hands on it. I didn't tell her anything about our being Jewish—in Czechoslovakia there were antisemites—it wouldn't have helped. I spent the rest of the day shopping with Bobi and bought him some skis he had always wanted, also mittens, and a warm red woolen hat with earmuffs. We packed, had dinner at the hotel, and then I brought him back to the train station to wait for Mrs. Wesely.

While waiting for her, I told him I wanted him to behave like a gentleman and stressed that he should never show his *ptaszek* to anyone. "It's extremely bad manners," I emphasized.

"I know! I know! You told me that a million times." He was plainly annoyed, but I was worried about what would happen to him and didn't know how to prepare him for the journey.

At about eleven she came. We chatted for a few minutes and then her train rumbled in. She was in a holiday mood as she took Bobi's hand to take him away. When they started to climb the steps up to their wagon, I grabbed him to me, hugged and kissed him. He seemed bewildered, but when I reminded him about his new skis, he smiled and seemed glad. Then I slipped some chocolates into his coat pocket, as a surprise for later on.

When the wagon door shut behind him, I felt as if a huge weight had been lifted from my back. I was relieved, because I knew that no matter what happened to Jan and me, Bobi would live. Mrs. Wesely seemed like a kindly person. Even if later she realized that he was circumcised and a

Jew, she and her husband were unlikely to turn him over to the Germans and have him killed. The locomotive tooted loudly, the huge wheels turned, smoke billowed, the train picked up speed, I waved, and Bobi disappeared from view.

Now I could turn my full attention to the question, How to save Jan? I went to the hairdresser and had a makeover, made myself into a platinum blond to look even more goyish, manicure, pedicure. Came out looking like a human being again—a *mensch*. I knew only too well that looks count a lot with men.

The next day I went to the Gestapo. In my overnight bag I carried my black lace underwear—I figured I had to be prepared to sleep with somebody in order to save us—rose-colored bedroom slippers, a tube of Gibbs toothpaste, my toothbrush, a silk robe—all the things a woman needs in prison or a concentration camp! I left for Prague by train first thing in the morning, at seven.

In the train compartment with me was a gang of workmen who were passing a huge bottle of vodka between them. I was only too grateful to join them in swigging from the common bottle. In addition I had a few cigarettes. That was my breakfast.

When I got to Prague, I remembered that Jan had a German business acquaintance whose name was Naujukat. He was a Berliner, and his girlfriend was a Czech model—beautiful girl. Naujukat was a shady operator, a playboy, a complete cynic. He thought that Hitler was a madman. He made sure to avoid the army, and he managed to make a lot of money on the black market—that kind of guy. I recalled that he liked Willy, and I also remembered that he had once told us, "If you ever need a favor, don't hesitate to call on me."

When I entered Naujukat's apartment in the morning, he and his girl were just getting out of bed. He was fine-boned, thin, unshaven, wearing a green silk bathrobe with a crest of an eagle over the heart. They were glad to see me. We spoke about the Dina affair, and he told me that Froemmel was dead and that Mitzi Froemmel had been arrested.

The story was that after Froemmel had been arrested for aiding Dina, Mitzi had gone to the Gestapo to try to save her husband. Colonel Bartelt, the arresting officer, had dragged her to the toilet by the nape of her neck. He nearly drowned her by shoving her head in the toilet bowl in order to wipe the makeup off her face. Later he had Froemmel beaten to death. On his death certificate they had stamped "RU," *Rückkehr unerwünscht*—return unwanted.

"Why did you come?" Naujukat asked me.

"Look here, you're a friend of Jan's. He's also been arrested by the Gestapo. Help me out."

I had on me a heavy gold bracelet that Jan had bought for me for just such an occasion, and I handed over the bracelet to his girl.

He turned to me, looking chagrined. "Unfortunately, I can't help you. After what happened to Dina, Froemmel, and Mitzi—forget it. It's much too dangerous." He picked up his girlfriend's wrist and examined the bracelet I had given her, then he looked up. "In the past I could have helped. I had a few contacts, knew a few guys, but now is not the time. If I get involved, they'll arrest me too. But I can see that you're exhausted. If you need a place to stay, you can stay with us."

I was grateful for the offer, but I noticed that Naujukat's girl didn't return the bracelet, and neither did he, and under the circumstances I didn't ask for it back.

Then I recalled that Jan had another couple of friends with connections to the Gestapo. They were two brothers, also operators. In fact not only did they have contacts at the Gestapo but one of the brothers was suspected of being a Gestapo agent. I went to their place later that morning. When they heard my story they grabbed me by the hair and threw me bodily out of their apartment. After that I bought myself some cognac because I was shaking from fright, and I needed it to keep myself together. I had a few swigs, vomited, and called Gestapo headquarters.

––––––––––––––

Gestapo headquarters was in a massive dark gray stone building, a short walk from the opera house. Before the war it had been a bank owned by a Czech Jew. There were giant SS banners hanging at the entrance, and through the iron doors you could see the Nazi flag. At a checkpoint you were searched and had to show your papers. The elevator was a small cage with doors that folded like an accordion. When you got to your floor, you walked down a long and wide corridor until you reached Colonel Bartelt's office. There you had to wait your turn until they called you in.

While I sat on a bench waiting to be called two Gestapo officers sat next to me and started to banter and flirt with me. They offered me a cigarette, and finally one of them asked me, "What are you doing here? You're a beautiful woman. What are you doing on this floor where they deal with Jewish affairs?"

"Of course I'm no Jew. I'm here because I have got some business to settle for friends."

Finally they left. They had wanted to take me out. All during the war it seems I had great success with them.

As I sat there in the corridor waiting to be called into Bartelt's office, quietly to myself I said the *Shma:* "*Shma Israel, Adonai Elohenu, Adonai Echad.*" "Hear O Israel, the Lord Our God, the Lord is One." I prayed to my parents: "Dear Mommy and Daddy, wherever you are, help me now. Soften their hearts. Help me to save Jan." I repeated that prayer over and over again until my name was called. I was so agitated, running a fever—felt red as a beet.

When my name was called I was shown into Bartelt's outer office, where there was a stout gray-haired secretary. I explained to her that I was Countess Zamojska and that I had received a notice from their office to show up earlier, but I had been ill. "May I see Colonel Bartelt now?"

"I think so," she said.

She went into his office, but left me waiting another hour, probably to break me down further. No one called me in. I smoked cigarette after cigarette. My heart was jumping in my breast. Finally she appeared and said, "Follow me."

I followed her into Bartelt's office. I was wearing my Persian lamb coat draped on my shoulders and a Persian lamb hat. I carried my overnight bag and tried to look like a wealthy countess prepared to go on a short excursion, to the country perhaps. I knew that everyone who walked through that office trembled and wept, but not me. I wasn't going to let on for a moment how I truly felt. I was not going to plead and look frightened. I flashed a huge diamond ring that I was wearing in front of the secretary and later in front of Bartelt. I thought that perhaps I could use it as a bribe.

Bartelt was about fifty, maybe older, brown-haired, clean-shaven, of medium height—no Adonis, but presentable. He sat, his head bowed to the paper, writing something. While I stood before him, I said to myself, If he keeps this up, I'm lost. So I interrupted him: "Colonel Bartelt. I am a woman whom you can't get to know unless you look her straight in the face."

"I am not looking at you because I'm furious. I ordered you to come a week earlier. You came at your own convenience. My dear lady, what do you think this is? A hairdresser's salon? This is Gestapo headquarters." He said all this without glancing up at me.

"Colonel Bartelt, please be so kind as to look up at me," I said as sharply as I could.

Only then did he raise his damn snout and finally looked up. "Why didn't you come as I ordered?"

I answered truthfully, "Because I was scared that you would arrest me too, and I detest the Gestapo. To come to you is like taking poison, like going to see rabid dogs." I don't believe that anyone had ever spoken to him like that. He looked shocked. I continued, "Rabid dogs are preferable to the Gestapo." I was a bit tipsy, but the liquor gave me courage. In fact, at that point I stopped giving a damn. I figured they were going to arrest me and kill me anyway. Why be polite? I told him what I thought. Almost.

He was furious and half rose in his chair: "How dare you speak to me like that."

"I'm telling you what I think," I said and shrugged.

He leaned back, "You realize that you are going to be arrested together with your husband."

"That's why I am here—to get arrested. But Herr Bartelt, before you arrest me, bring me a chair. I'm a lady. I'm not used to standing in front of a man while he is sitting down."

"This is not a coffee shop."

"I realize only too well that this is no coffee shop, but I expect you to act like a gentleman."

He looked annoyed, but he stood up, crossed the room, and offered me a chair. Before I sat down, I turned my back on him and said, "Please hang up my coat, it's much too hot for me in here." Bartelt had to reach over to take my coat and drape it over my chair. I sat down, and I looked through my bag for a cigarette, but I realized that I was out.

"Do you smoke?"

"No."

"Would you mind getting me some cigarettes?"

He went over to the door and called one of his colleagues. "Kurt," he shouted, "there is a charming woman in my office. Get us some cigarettes and a bottle of cognac." In walked Kurt, who clicked his shiny black boots and handed me a pack of cigarettes, while Bartelt leaned over and lit one for me.

I took a long drag. "Do you want to see my documents?"

"Not really."

We sat there in silence for a few moments while I smoked and he examined me. Then I looked him straight in the eye and said, "Colonel Bartelt, you like me, and I can tell that you're attracted to me. Help me out."

I didn't plead for Jan's life. That wouldn't have been smart. I wanted him to bring it up. I wanted him to set Jan free, but I wanted to convince him that I was interested in him too, not just in Jan. Pleading for Jan without paying attention to him would have spoiled the moment.

"Sure, but you'll have to sleep with me"—straightforward like that.

"Of course, I'm looking forward to it!"

I was pretty clever. I pulled my black lace panties *mit dem koronkes,* with a white frilly border, out of my bag and I tossed them onto the desk in front of him to show him that I was ready for anything. He looked startled, but then he picked up my underwear and started to laugh. He clutched his stomach and doubled over with laughter.

"Well, I see it's getting late. Let me take you out to dinner."

I said to myself, This is not so good. I really was in no mood to go to bed with him. "You know that I have a little boy waiting for me in Poděbrady. I had no one to leave him with. I must go home to him now. But I promise you, if you call me, I'll come—just not today. I wouldn't enjoy going out with you tonight knowing that my little boy is alone waiting for me."

"Okay. I'll walk you to the train."

"No, I'd rather not. I have many friends in Prague. If they see me walking down the street with you they might think that I work for the Gestapo. I don't want that." Then I rose. "I'm going to leave now, but should you want to get in touch with me, just call, and I'll come to see you."

I handed him my number in Poděbrady, and he said, "All right." He rose, clicked his heels, bowed, and kissed my hand, and I left.

Not a word about Dina or why Jan had been arrested. Nothing.

When he had arrested Jan, Bartelt had taken the keys to our Prague apartment. Before I left his office, he gave me back my keys. He said, "You probably have valuable things in the apartment. You may want to stop by to make sure that everything is in order." Not to be believed!

After I left Bartelt's office, I took a taxi to the train. I was half drunk and half crazy. I had no intention of going back to our apartment in Prague. I just wanted to get home. I was exhausted and totally drained. I felt like going to bed, pulling the covers over my head, and going to sleep for a hundred years.

When I sat in the train compartment, and the train started to move, I closed my eyes and thought, What just happened? Was that real or was I hallucinating? I picked up my bag and pulled out the keys he had given me back. It was no dream. I had not been hallucinating.

And in the train I saw the same bunch of laborers who had come down with me that morning, going home from Prague to Poděbrady. Once again they pulled out a flask of vodka, and again they passed it around the compartment, and again I joined them and took a long swig. The liquor warmed me from head to toe. I was nearly drunk, but I was still alive.

Bartelt had said that he would call me in a few days. Later in my room in Poděbrady I started to unwind and feel better. I knew that he wanted to sleep with me, but I also sensed that he liked me as a person.

When I had told him that I thought that the Gestapo were a bunch of rabid dogs who frightened me, I spoke in such a naive way, like a little girl. He called in his secretary and asked her, "Am I crazy or what? Look at this woman, what do you make of her?"

So the secretary, an older gray-haired lady, looked me over and said, "I think she is a very nice young woman." I could see that he was very pleased with her response.

I didn't dare to tell anyone what had happened. No one would have believed me. In fact when he said that he'd call me in Poděbrady I asked him not to say that he was from Gestapo headquarters. He should announce himself only as Herr Bartelt to the phone operator, otherwise someone might have thought that I was working for the Gestapo in some way.

Back in Poděbrady I woke up early in the morning to have breakfast and to take a short walk. The rest of the day I spent in my room waiting for Bartelt's call. I thought about what was happening to Jan in prison. Each day was like a year . . .

A week went by. Another week. Three weeks. Nothing. No call. Something was very wrong. I started to think that my trip had been useless. But I kept sitting by the phone. I read books, stared out of the window, walked around the room. Finally, one day the phone rang. It was a woman speaking: "Hello. This is Frau Bartelt. We met in my husband's office a few weeks ago. I am his secretary."

I recalled the older woman who had shown me into Bartelt's office. That was his secretary? Now she was on the phone. What did she want from me?

"My husband told me about you, and we want to help. Unfortunately he's had a very bad cold, and he can't speak to you right now. He asked me to tell you to stay put. Don't go to headquarters just now. Things are a bit dangerous. Do you understand? Just hold tight and wait for our call. We'll tell you when to come."

Frau Bartelt called *me* to warn *me* not to go to the Gestapo because *I might get arrested!* Who would believe it?

I lost my faith in God when my parents were killed, but still sometimes I do believe in higher powers, in something, some spirit that looks out for me. Have I been chosen by God for a purpose that I don't understand?

So I reconciled myself to an even longer wait. I kept taking walks during the early morning and sitting by the phone during the day. I spoke to no one. Tadzo and Wanda were in hiding. It would only endanger them if they got in touch with me. Bobi was with the Weselys on their farm.

A few weeks after Frau Bartelt's call, while I was in the bathtub, the phone rang again. I leapt out without even drying off. It was Bartelt. "My dear lady, come to my office tomorrow at six in the evening. Most everyone will be gone. We'll be the only ones there. Bring a basket of food with you, some cocoa, because your husband has lost thirty kilos in jail. He looks awful, but tomorrow you'll see him again."

Not a word about our sleeping together. Nothing.

I felt drained and stone sober the next day when I made my way back to Gestapo headquarters. I got to Bartelt's office at six, just as he had asked. I saw that he'd laid out a small round table. It was covered by a white tablecloth. On top was a pot of real coffee brewing, a plate of pastries, a bottle of cognac, and some wine glasses. There was a small couch in his office. He asked me to sit down, handed me a cup of coffee and some pastries, later a drink. He sat down next to me and embraced me and kissed me on the cheek—on the cheek!—as if he were an older relative.

A moment later, the doors of his office sprang open, and between two Gestapo guards, Jan entered the room.

He looked like a walking corpse. A skeleton. He was unshaven. He had a huge black eye. His hair was long, uncombed, matted, and falling over his ears. He wore a prison uniform of white and gray stripes that hung on his frame. I could see that he was in shock—he was shaking so badly. He looked wildly about the room, but didn't recognize me. I said to him as tenderly as I could, "Jan, darling, it's me."

But he didn't acknowledge me. Instead, he stared at Bartelt and started to shout. "Colonel Bartelt, why am I being held? I am no Jew. I am innocent. I demand to be released. I feel sick. Why should my wife be left alone with my boy? I've always loved German culture." He went on and on, making no sense.

Bartelt turned to me and said calmly, "Don't worry about it. All our 'guests' wind up a bit insane."

He dismissed the two guards and told Jan to quiet down and to get a bite to eat. Jan, looking bewildered, sat down at the table, while I came up behind him, kissed his ears, and whispered, "Jan, get a hold of yourself. I'm going to get you out of here." At which point he glanced up at me, calmed down somewhat, and realized that I was in the room. Unfortunately, as soon as he started to eat he became ill. The food that had been laid out was much too rich for him. He had to excuse himself to go to the toilet. Then they took him away again.

Bartelt turned to me and said, "Go home now. I'm not going with you. Wait for my call."

The next day the phone rang. It was Riya! She had called to tell me that she had heard from some Czech police that Jan had been killed. He had been tortured and made to lie on broken glass. There he had bled to death. I asked her calmly when it happened. She said last week. Then she added, "I've closed our joint bank account. Don't even think about trying to get your money out." I knew she was lying because I had seen Jan the day before. As for the money, she could keep it. She was simply being cruel, turning the knife. I was trembling with anger and was tempted to tell her what I knew, but I simply said, "You're a *cholereh*," and I hung up.

A few weeks later Bartelt called again. "Janina, come before six in the morning tomorrow, before the office opens. Bring some warm clothes for your husband. He's being released. Take him home and good luck to you."

The next morning I took the five o'clock train to Prague. I arrived at Gestapo headquarters, which was closed, but there was Bartelt, waiting for me at the main gate.

"I'm delighted to see you again. In an hour, they'll be bringing your husband from Pankrac prison."

Jan arrived, we embraced. He looked awful. I whispered to him, "We're going home."

Bartelt gave me a package and said, "Janina, you probably haven't had a real cup of coffee during the war. Here's a kilo of coffee and some sardines. Take your husband home. I'm glad that I was able to help."

It's strange, but Bartelt never said a word about why Jan had been arrested. He never accused him of being a Jew—neither him nor me. Only once did he raise the question obliquely. Apparently Riya had called him and denounced Jan as a Jew. I told him that she had been Jan's lover, that she wanted him dead to keep his money. Bartelt said, "*Ich verstehe*, I understand." And that was all. Then he never raised the issue again. It would have been so simple for him to find out about Jan's being a Jew. All he had to do was take down his pants. I don't know. Perhaps, so close to the end of the war, he didn't want to know.

I brought Jan back to Poděbrady. I took him to a sanatorium and got him some medical help. He was in very bad shape. He had been beaten up. He had turned white from anemia. He was depressed. For hours he sat by the window and hardly moved. Sometimes I'd find him weeping. I tried to get him to talk about his experiences, but at first he refused and then slowly his story came out.

The morning of his arrest two men came, Bartelt and another guy. They were from the Judische Abteilung, *the Department for Jewish Affairs at the Gestapo. Bartelt was the arresting officer. Jan tried chutzpah to intimidate and shout them down like he had done in Kraków once before, but this time it didn't work.*

Bartelt asked him a routine question: "Are you Jewish?"

Jan sprang up, "Of course I am not Jewish! What do you take me for? My name is Zamojski. You are insulting me!" He wore his monogrammed ring and everything. Maybe that helped. They didn't bother taking down his pants to check. Why, no one knows. Of course, they were arresting him not necessarily because he was a Jew, but because he had been a friend of a Jew who had escaped. They had arrested everybody in Dina's circle. Now it was his turn.

Pankrac prison was about a half hour's drive away. They brought him down to the cellar, where first he saw a group of Jews sitting on the floor. Huge crosses had been painted on their backs. From time to time some Gestapo officer would come over and strike them in the head or abuse them in some other way. Jan refused to elaborate. Nearby sat the Czech prisoners, but they were left alone. Willy was placed with the Czechs and tried not to see or to hear the torments of the Jews who were later shipped out to some camp—Auschwitz, probably.

He sat on the floor for hours with the other Czechs. At ten or eleven o'clock at night they had the men undress to take showers. Jan tried to hide that he was circumcised. A Tyrolean guard at the door of the showers inspected all the prisoners. Perhaps he didn't notice. Maybe he didn't understand about circumcision. Anyway, he let Jan go.

After the showers, he was assigned a small cell, nine by ten feet, which he shared with a Czech peasant. That first night he lay down on the straw on the floor and fell into a deep sleep.

"Never before or since did I have such wonderful dreams," he told me. "Everything was sharply defined, in bright lifelike colors. I saw you

the way you looked back in Warsaw. You were so lovely, and I longed to touch you, but I couldn't. Later you were standing by a phone waiting for me to call, but every time I tried to reach for a phone of my own, it would dissolve in my hands. The dreams turned into nightmares . . ."

Now prison life started. Imagine, prison—to be locked up in a tiny cell—for a person like Jan, who feels confined in a large apartment. At eight o'clock in the morning they brought them out to a courtyard for fifteen minutes of exercise. Then they gave them bread and some soup. Then at two o'clock they brought them out again, and that was it. What do you do all day in a tiny cell in prison? Jan tried to fight down panic attacks. He was afraid of going out of his mind. He tried to keep his sanity by doing various chores. His cellmate's pants were torn, so Jan found a nail and traded some bread for thread with another prisoner.

One night they brought in a Belgian engineer who had been spying for the British in Bulgaria. He helped to direct the Allied bombing. They had tortured him, but they couldn't get him to talk because his daughter had also been arrested, and he wanted to protect her. He was half dead, lying on the floor. Jan tried to nurse him to health, and when the Belgian recovered somewhat, the two of them played chess with pieces of junk they had found in the cell.

Jan tends to be impulsive and headstrong. One day when the men were taken out for their daily exercise, he came across a young Gestapo officer who amused himself by cracking his whip at them as they marched around the courtyard. Jan didn't say anything, but he looked at him with hatred and contempt. That was enough. Later that day the Gestapo man came into Jan's cell.

The walls were covered with all kinds of scribbling. The Gestapo man pointed to some graffiti, "Who did this?"

Jan didn't want the others to take the blame, so he said, "That's mine." Whereupon the Gestapo man beat him senseless and closed both his eyes. From then on in, the German would find ways to torment him.

When I asked Jan, "Were you ever tortured?" he said no. But his experience was torture enough.

Jan is a proud man, who had known abuse as a child. He had once told me, even before we were married, that when his mother had died and he had been left alone in Switzerland, he had been beaten mercilessly by his teachers. He had sworn to himself even then that when he grew up, he would never allow anyone to strike him again. The sense that he was being abused by the young Gestapo man, and that he could do nothing about it, was almost worse than the physical pain.

When he told me the story of the beatings he wept with rage and punched the wall of our bedroom. I had to hold his thin body to mine so that he would not hurt himself again.

Every day they shipped people to some camp. Every day he was prepared to go. Others went, but he stayed. He didn't know what was happening. The only thing he knew was that after a few weeks, he received a package with fresh underwear and a tube of Gibbs toothpaste. The brand name was the one that he and I used. It was my way of telling him that I was still alive.

One afternoon he got called: "Jan Zamojski!" He thought, Four o'clock? This is completely irregular. Maybe they want to torture me.

They took him back to Prague by car, a half hour's trip. It had been more than a week since he had received any packages.

"Has my wife been arrested?" he asked the guard siting next to him. "She's dead," the German replied.

When they brought him into Bartelt's office, there was a table full of beautiful food. Bartelt was standing next to it and so was I, but Jan didn't recognize me, in part because he couldn't see, and in part because he was a bit crazy.

He was in such bad shape that had Bobi been home he would not have recognized his father, but Jan was alive and that's all I cared about.

One day, while Jan was still recovering, I stood by the window of our room. It was my turn to be depressed.

"Jan, how will we get Bogusiu back?" The war wasn't over yet. I couldn't broadcast by radio that I was looking for my child.

Jan tried to calm me down. "Nina, you'll get Bogusiu back. As soon as the war is over, we'll get him back by radio or through the papers."

While the two of us were standing looking down at the street, suddenly I saw Mrs. Wesely go by! I recognized her coat, her babushka, the way she waddled. Like a madwoman I rushed downstairs, Jan after me. I ran after her and grabbed her by the arm. "Mrs. Wesely, it's me! When did you get here?"

"Yesterday."

"Where is my son?"

"My dear lady, your boy is doing just fine," she said as she freed herself from my grasp. "He's put on weight. He's learned to ride horses. He loves our sausages. We love him very much, and he loves us too."

"Mrs. Wesely, you don't understand. Bogusław is my son. I want him back. What shall I do?" And I started to cry.

After a bit she said, "I understand. I'm going home tomorrow. I'll send him back to you."

She was a generous and kindly woman. I'll never forget her. A week later Jan and I went to the train station to wait for Bobi. When he stepped off, he looked suntanned and well. We hugged and kissed, and then he asked, "Who is that man?" pointing at Jan. His father had lost so much weight—and was wearing a black eye patch—that Bobi didn't recognize him.

"That is your daddy!" I said smiling from ear to ear.

Then the three of us went home, and for the first time in ages I was happy again.

———————————

Over the years I've often thought about my little adventure with Colonel Bartelt. Had he asked me to sleep with him I would have done it, no questions asked. To sleep with someone, even a Gestapo officer, in order to save Jan's and Bobi's lives would have been a small price to pay, and I was ready for it when I walked into his office. *Vas banque*, I thought. This is war. I am a fighter, and this is what I must do.

However, had I slept with him, I am sure that my mission would have failed. Maybe it was my looks, maybe my title, but somehow I got him to act the "gallant-German-officer" to my "countess-in-distress." By treating me with respect and releasing my husband, he showed his magnanimity—a kind of power. Had I slept with him, it would have broken the spell. In his eyes I would have become just another terrified woman willing to do anything to save herself and her husband. I am sure there were many such that crossed his office. His reaction might have become contemptuous and cruel. In fact, since Frau Bartelt was also his secretary, I doubt that she would have called to warn me had I slept with her husband. To put it simply, I was ready for it, but I am glad that Bartelt and I stayed out of bed!

When he and I discussed it, Jan's explanation for why he had been spared by Bartelt was more straightforward: "I suppose that one of the reasons he released me," he said, "is that they had found Dina, and so they didn't need me anymore." Then he continued with anger and barely suppressed contempt: "The whole reason was Dina. To find Dina Mueller they arrested twenty people and killed some of them. What an outfit! What a waste of time! Instead of being on the Russian front defending their country, they were chasing Dina with her little son! They had whole wagon trains filled with Jews going to Auschwitz, instead of using these trains to transport troops for the front and using the Jews to work in their war effort. This was the stupidity that we were up against."

Why Bartelt acted as decently as he did remains a mystery. The mystery deepens when the Jewish question is raised: Riya, Jan's former lover, had denounced him to Bartelt as a circumcised Jew. To verify her story, all Bartelt had to do was have Jan drop his pants. Yet he never did. If he pursued the Jewish angle with me, it was most reluctantly, almost as if he did not want to know the truth.

Did Bartelt suspect that we were Jews? Neither Jan nor I know the answer. Jan thought that Bartelt must have ceased being a Nazi by the end of the war and the looming German defeat. Yet he was Nazi enough to have hunted Dina and Freddy all the way to Dresden, and he had them deported to a concentration camp. And he was Nazi enough to have Froemmel beaten to death for aiding a terrified woman and her child.

We will never know what made Bartelt act as he did. When the Soviets were already in Prague, I heard that Bartelt and his wife committed suicide.

Bobi

During my father's affair with Riya I had become my mother's little confidant. "Her best friend," she had said. But when my father was arrested, I didn't know what to do or how to help her. It wasn't enough to tell her that she was pretty and that his affair with Riya would pass. Things were much too serious for that. All she did was lie in bed and stare at the ceiling or she'd get up momentarily and smoke her way through a pack of cigarettes. I'd go down to eat alone in the hotel dining room, and then I'd come back with some food, tea with crackers, but she refused.

I felt like a diver who had fallen into a deep and muddy pond, where my movements felt clumsy and deliberate, the visibility was poor, and my air supply was about to run out. But I couldn't let my mother know. I didn't want to make her feel worse by complaining or seeming to need her help. I tried to appear as cheerful and as "normal" as I could. I ate, I played, I chattered away as if nothing had changed. I knew that she wanted me to be all right, so I made sure to appear that way. Apparently it worked, because even after she told me that I was to leave her and go with a total stranger, *mamusia* thought that I was happy.

The day I was supposed to leave with Mrs. Wesely, *mamusia* bought me some toys for the trip and a set of skis and poles, which were too long for me, but I didn't protest. All would be well. I appeared very grateful. After dinner she gave me a lecture.

"You know, of course, you are to behave like a 'gentleman.'" She used the English word. "Always say 'please' and 'thank you.' A smile is always better than a frown. No one looks ugly smiling. Remember that." She licked her fingers and tried to smooth an unruly lock of my hair that had tumbled out of place. "And never ever forget that you're Bogusław Marian Zamojski, the son of Count Jan Zamojski and me. There might be some bad people, like the Gestapo, who might try to convince you otherwise, but don't you let them. Do you understand?"

Why remind me again? What was there to understand? But I didn't ask.

"And the next thing I have to tell you is very, very important. You are not to show your *ptaszek* to anyone. It's very bad manners to do so. Do you understand?"

Again the lecture about my *ptaszek*. I was annoyed. But I tried to look serious and obedient.

"When you're taking a bath in front of people, you're not to take off your shorts? Understood?"

She had said that a million times. Miss Berta had been very impressed by my modesty. But then why were Wanda, Pani Marylka, and Irenka allowed to bathe me and to see my *ptaszek* while others were not? Perhaps because they were family. I didn't ask. "Sure" was all I said.

That night we went to the Poděbrady train station to wait for Mrs. Wesely. The day had been cold and gray. The station was crowded with travelers bundled for the winter. Across the tracks from us stood a troop train full of soldiers I didn't recognize. "Hungarians fleeing from the Russians," my mother explained.

Off in the distance as it got dark you could see a searchlight sweeping back and forth across the sky, trying to spot American bombers. Then Mrs. Wesely arrived. She waddled up to us, a huge grin on her face. She hugged me to her and chatted with my mother until our train arrived. It was pulled by a monstrous steam-driven locomotive that shrieked and whistled and seemed to expire as it pulled up beside us.

My mother gave me a hug and slipped what turned out later to be some chocolate into my coat pocket. "I'm not going up into the train with you," she said. "Don't forget what I told you, and don't worry, we'll all be together quite soon."

Mrs. Wesely and I climbed aboard. She let me have the window seat, from which I could see my mother on the platform. We exchanged mutually incomprehensible signs. Then the train began to move, and *mamusia* ran clumsily beside it like a girl. She had plastered one of her radiant golden smiles on her face. It was her turn to play at "everything-is-all-right," but I knew better. She waved. I waved. Then she disappeared from view.

When I turned to Mrs. Wesely, she too was smiling at me. "All will be well," she said, and then she began to tell me about the farm and all of the wonderful animals that lived on it.

I tried to follow her, but I had fallen ever deeper into my muddy pond, and I could hardly make out her words. Most of me was so deep in the dark pool that I was surprised that she could still see and hear me. The one thing I knew was that I had to smile and appear cheerful. So I did, as if my life depended on it.

The Weselys lived on a large prosperous farm somewhere in the mountains near Brno in Slovakia. Mr. Wesely, a tall, dark-haired, hearty man, picked us up at the station in his red horse-drawn carriage. He had me sit next to him and let me hold the reins on the way back to their farm. When he cracked the whip and the horse started to trot, my mood lifted, and I almost felt gay. Then we arrived at their farm, and I remembered that my father had been arrested and that I might not see my parents again.

At first Mrs. Wesely showered me with affection—even had me sleep with her. Apparently she and Mr. Wesely did not share a bed. But this time, in contrast to my lying with Wanda, I really didn't care what Mrs. Wesely looked like under her nightgown. Besides, she took baths only once a week, and on off days she smelled bad. She'd try to hug me before going to sleep, but I'd just roll over and cling to my side of the bed.

I knew that I should feel grateful to Mr. and Mrs. Wesely for looking after me, but I also suspected that she was trying to take the place of my mother, and I resented her for that. The result was that I was never able to climb out of the dark pond into which I had fallen. I could scarcely hear them when they spoke. I wish I could have cried—it might have brought some relief—but my breathing was so shallow that I couldn't get up the energy for tears. The few times I'd get roused was when she'd try to give me a bath, and then I'd just get mad.

She looked stunned when I refused to take my shorts off in the hot tub that she had drawn for me. "But you're just a little kid. Don't worry, I've seen it all before."

"No!" I practically shouted. "It's extremely bad manners to show your privates. My parents forbid it."

Later, when Mr. Wesely came back from doing the chores, she told him about it, and they both had a good laugh at my expense. But I didn't care. I had promised *mamusia,* and anyway what did these peasants know about good manners? The son of Count Zamojski shows his *ptaszek* to no one!

After a few weeks it was apparent that Mr. and Mrs. Wesely didn't get along, and like my father, Mr. Wesely, who was a strapping handsome man, was having an affair with a woman from Prague who lived nearby. One day when Mrs. Wesely was out, I saw them kissing in the kitchen. When Mr. Wesely saw me he seemed flustered. "It's got to be our little secret," he said. "You don't want to tell anyone." He needn't have worried. I knew all about men cheating on their wives, and I was good at keeping secrets.

Mostly I refused to go outdoors and clung to Mrs. Wesely in the kitchen, but as the weather got warmer I ventured outdoors and met some of the kids from the neighborhood. During the day most of them were still in school, but sometimes we'd play tag in the afternoon.

One evening we had lost track of time and played until dusk. Then as we walked back to our respective homes, the six o'clock church bells started to peal. One of the kids cried out: "If you're not home by six, the witches will kidnap and eat you."

In a panic we ran home through the muddy snow. When I flung myself through the door, the Weselys laughed after I told them about fleeing the witches. There were no witches, they said. But then what about the Jewish woman, a witch for sure, that my friends and I had chased down the street in Prague?

Spring came, and Mrs. Wesely left for her yearly treatment in Poděbrady. When she returned, she said that she had run into my mother and that I'd be going back the next day. She and Mr. Wesely took me to the station. She cried when she said good-bye, but I was hardly aware of her. I was worried about my mother and why she had sent for me. My father was probably dead by now. Why hadn't she been arrested? Was this a trick? Mr. Wesely stayed with me halfway, and then he put me on another train that was to take me all the way to Prague.

"Thanks for keeping our little secret," he said gravely. What was he talking about? Who cared?

When I got off in Prague there was a small crowd at the station. I didn't see my mother. Instead I saw a very thin elderly man flinging himself in my direction. He wore a black eye patch and a black hat that shaded his skull-like face. Gestapo! I thought in a panic as I clutched my bag and fought my way through the crowd. I ran as quickly as I could toward the tea shop, where by previous arrangement I was supposed to meet *mamusia*. As I glanced backward I could see the cadaverous Gestapo agent gaining on me.

In the tea shop, unaware of the danger, my mother was sitting by a table calmly drinking tea. When she saw me she rose to hug me and began to laugh. I thought that she might be crazy or hysterical. I fought off her embrace, clutched her by the hand, and tried to drag her to safety. If we hurried we might be able to lose ourselves in the crowd.

"Bobi! Bobi!" *mamusia* jerked me back. By her expression, I knew that someone was behind me. I spun around just in time to have the Gestapo agent grab me and lift me in his arms.

"It's all right now. It's all right," whispered my father, and it nearly was.

9 *Liberation*

Bobi

By 1945 the Allies had nearly total control of the skies and were able to bomb German cities and industrial plants at will. Even in Prague, which was hardly touched by the bombings, you could hear the distant hum of the American B-24s flying overhead. With other kids I stood by the river squinting into the bright skies, hoping to see the outline of an American plane. First, all you heard was the noise of the engines, then its outline would appear, floating like a shark at the top of the ocean while we lesser beings watched it from the shadows below. The sirens would go off, and we'd scramble for safety. The Germans cursed the American and the British bombers, but I hoped that the planes would pulverize them.

Early in May, while the Russians were rumored to be on the outskirts of the city, my mother and I stood on the balcony of our apartment in Prague. The day was windy, and the sun cast intermittent light on the scene below. Across the street was the desecrated Jewish cemetery. On the corner, in front of the grocery store, some men were lolling about while one of them pulled down its iron grated shutters. My mother left my side to go back inside the apartment, while I watched a German soldier approach the corner and the clump of men.

As he got closer, I saw that he was young, possibly a teenager, one of those Hitler *Jugend* types that they were drafting into the army toward the end. Absentmindedly I admired his uniform and the dagger he wore at his side. As he started to pass the store, the clump of men I had been watching earlier surrounded him and began to club him with heavy bats. Thwack! Thwack! Thwack! I could hear the bats dully striking his body and imagined them breaking his bones. The soldier tried to defend himself by raising his arms to ward off the blows. He ducked and weaved, his motions becoming increasingly jerky and disconnected. Then like a puppet whose master has suddenly stopped pulling its strings, he collapsed in a heap. A car turned the corner. The men took off in every direction. The car slowed down near the prone body of the soldier. A head peered out, then the car accelerated and disappeared. The men from the grocery store reappeared, lifted the body, and laid it gently in the shadows of the cemetery wall.

The dead young German lay directly below me. I felt disconnected from him and from what I had just witnessed as if I was looking at a photo. Then the sun broke through, and the day became as clear as if someone had suddenly switched on the light in a dark bedroom. I looked down into the blood-splattered face of the German. A thin stream of blood was flowing from his open mouth, otherwise he looked like he was snoring in his sleep. Then my mother called me from the kitchen.

"Bogusiu, come quick. They're shooting in the street!" I ran back into the living room.

A minute later, my father rushed in breathless from outside. "There's been an uprising. The partisans expect either the Russians or the Americans at any moment. They're trying to take Prague from the Germans. Get away from the windows!" As he spoke, the shooting became more brisk and seemed to get closer.

He crawled down to the balcony and reported back to us in the kitchen. "The partisans are down below. I can see some Gestapo. They're coming this way!" Ashen-faced, he ran back to the kitchen. We heard the pounding of men on the stairs, then the door of our apartment flew open, and the partisans took up positions in our living room and on the balcony. From the cemetery across the street the Germans were firing on our building and into our apartment.

"Keep down! Keep down! Get your ass out of here!" one of the partisans shouted at us, but prompting we didn't need. We clutched some blankets and a suitcase of food we had prepared and ran down to the basement.

The basement was dark and musty. In one corner was a coal pile. In another old pieces of furniture and empty boxes were stashed away. One entrance led out back to the alley at ground level and the other opened up to the lobby of the building upstairs. By the time we got there, most of the people in the building had already assembled and were sitting around in groups. We recognized most of our Czech and German neighbors. They had kept to themselves and had had very little contact with us or with each other. But now, beset by a raging battle going on above their heads, people exchanged tentative greetings. Smiles appeared. Sandwiches were passed around. A semblance of order was established.

A German doctor—an old man wearing wire-rimmed spectacles with thick lenses—suggested that the battle might go on for days and that we'd better prepare for it. Some of the men went back upstairs during a lull in the shooting to fill up pots and pans and bathtubs with water. Others ventured out into the alley to shut and barricade the side door. We agreed that until the fighting stopped no one else was permitted to enter our stuffy sanctuary.

But the fighting did not stop. Apparently a battle was raging for the Hradčány castle on the hill overlooking Prague. The Americans or the Russians must have joined the fight because we could hear the Boom! Boom! Boom! of exploding cannon shells and other heavy guns. I wanted the shooting to stop so that I could rest, but as the day dragged on into night, the battle raged ever more furiously, until a cannonade started with such intensity that individual explosions merged into one loud roar that took your breath away. The lights went out in our basement, but I was too frightened to say a word. I must have made some kind of sound, perhaps a whimper, because I could feel my father's arms tighten around me.

Later that night I was awakened by the sound of machine gun fire very close to our building. The cannonade had stopped, but the shooting so close to us had an even more ominous sound. People relit their candles and stared with concern at each other. We could hear men running and shouting, first in Czech, then in German, then more shooting, then silence. Then we were startled by the sound of whining outside the back door leading to the alley. At first I thought it might have been a cat, but then the whining turned to moaning, screaming, and pleading for help in Czech. It was a wounded partisan.

"Please! Please! Please!" I whispered, not daring to speak louder. "Can't someone help him?" But no one did.

The next morning, to everyone's relief, the shooting stopped. We decided that someone should go see what was happening. We followed *tatusiu* into the blinding light of a beautiful spring day. Nearby lay the partisan who had died the night before. He was curled up knees to chin like a baby. The doctor removed his glasses and bent over the body. After listening and feeling for signs of life, he waved his spectacles at us and pronounced him quite dead.

Our apartment was a shambles—bullet holes everywhere and in some places splotches of blood. Later that afternoon we could hear a low rumbling coming from the street. We ventured out on the balcony from where we could see some people scattering below while others were congregating on the street corner.

Then we saw the first Russian tanks and trucks. They kept on coming and coming, well into the night and the next morning. On every truck and on the tanks too, in tableaux of pain and exhaustion, sprawled the ragged Russian soldiers. Half of them looked like young street urchins. So this was the mighty Russian army that had so terrified my German playmates, I thought. We joined in the applause. Some people in the crowd threw flowers. I stuck out my chest and felt proud and happy that our side had finally won the war.

The next morning partisans came to our building, rooting out Germans and collaborators. Among the partisans was the janitor who worked in Dina Mueller's building.

"Death to the Nazis, death to the traitors." They came swarming up the stairs. Most of them had been drinking and were in a mood of vengeful hilarity. When they broke into our apartment, they were struck by the plush surroundings—not a good sign for us—but then Dina's former janitor, who must have known about Dina's and my father's arrest by the Gestapo, intervened. He pushed himself forward, grasped my father around the shoulders, and declared, "He's one of us."

I don't know how many Nazis or collaborators they found in our building, but they did manage to round up the elderly German doctor, his wife, and his daughter. Didn't they know that most of the bad Germans had already fled Prague? Apparently they didn't. Now the doctor and his family were dragged into the street, where they were surrounded by a crowd in an ugly mood.

"Hey, you bitch, you whore, you German cunt."

"You fucking motherfucker."

"Hey, you cock-sucking whore."

The women were made to kneel in the street. They were beaten and kicked, and their hair—all of it—was shaved. When they were allowed to stand up again, they looked like two ugly, skinny old men. They stood there blinking in the sunlight, too terrified to weep. Then a young fellow peeled off the doctor's wire-rimmed glasses and ground them with his boots; the sound made a crunching noise. The German screeched out, "But I can't see!" And the crowd laughed and applauded. I didn't join in the approval, but neither did I condemn anyone. I was amazed and relieved that one could do such things to Germans without getting killed.

I was almost eight years old. The Germans were defeated and gone, and I was permitted to wander the city streets on my own. I felt exhilarated by my newfound freedom. I wandered past our street to the river and then to Václavské Náměstí, the center of town. I became part of a milling crowd of shaken, stunned, but happy people, like patients coming out of a hospital after a long illness. The square was full of Russian soldiers, Czechs, and suddenly freed prisoners of war of every stripe. They congregated in small groups, wearing assorted combinations of torn uniforms and civilian clothes. Some of the Russians had brought out accordions, while others squatted on their haunches and danced the *kazak*. Young men flirted, young women laughed, the weather was balmy, and no one was afraid.

One day whispering in the street said that "they" had arrived at the railroad station. Who were "they"? I went to the railroad station, where I saw a parade of strange-looking people. They were dressed in striped uniforms, but they looked like walking corpses. They were all so thin and fragile looking, with their shaven heads. At the head of the procession was a tall bony man carrying the Czech flag. The square was lined with people, but no one applauded. We stood in silence as if at a funeral.

"*Lagers*. Camps," people said. I had no idea what they meant.

The Soviets had beaten the Germans, and that was good, but in a weird way, the situation created a new problem for us, although I was unaware of it at the time. Our identification papers said "Zamojski" but now the NKVD was looking for Polish aristocrats to have them shipped off to the gulag. If we were asked to identify ourselves, how could we explain that we were not what our papers and what our neighbors said we were? It would have been impossible to convince the NKVD that we were a family of Jews named Mendelsohn who had survived the war by impersonating Polish nobility. It was nearly comical, if the implications had not been so dreadful, that the very false papers, the phony birth certificates and the *Kennkarten* that had saved our lives during the Nazi occupation, now threatened us with deportation once we fell under Soviet rule. My parents thought of burning them, but they were the only identification we had, so we soldiered on—me obliviously—as Zamojskis.

Tadzo's experience showed us just how dangerous was our new situation. During the Czech uprising, he and the rest of the family were in hiding in Poděbrady. When the Soviets arrived, they asked everyone to register with the new authority and told Tadzo that a special train had been commissioned to take Polish refugees back to Poland. Tadzo, Wanda, Pani Marylka, and Irenka were ready to take the Soviets' offer and board the train back to Poland. Tadzo especially wanted to get to Warsaw to look for his parents. He hoped against all hope that they might still be alive. However, for some reason Tadzo and the rest were delayed and did not make it to the train on time. Later they heard that the whole convoy was transported to camps inside the Soviet gulag.

Again, as in Stanisławów, by sheer chance Tadzo had avoided becoming a victim of the Soviet concentration camp and labor system. When Jan heard the story later he could only shake his head in disbelief that Tadzo would trust anything the Soviets told him. Unlike Jan, who trusted nothing and no one, Tadzo never became a cynic. Perhaps because he was kind and trustworthy, his first impulse was to believe in people and to take them at face value. It was Tadzo's trust and ingenuousness that endeared him to me, but—had his luck not held out—that trust in others would have killed him.

We knew that General Patton's American army was in Plzeň, a few hours away by car, and that's where we decided to flee. But how to get there? And how to elude the Russians and their secret police? The first step was to get a car or a truck.

A few days after the end of the uprising, when things were still chaotic, Jan noticed, as he was passing the hotel Šroubek, a truck whose engine was still running. There was no one in or near the vehicle. On the spur of the moment, he leisurely hoisted himself into the driver's seat and drove away. We filled the stolen truck with our stuff, including my father's shiny black bicycle, which I coveted. We had some trouble restarting the truck because you needed a handcrank to turn the engine over, but after much sputtering it roared to life, and in the early afternoon we were off to the Americans.

As we hit the open road, we passed the debris of war—the burned-out trucks and tanks, the shelled husks of buildings. Every few miles we could see the straggling lines of refugees moving who knows where, and everywhere we saw Russian troops sprawled by the side of the road like dangerous Boy Scouts on some tiresome hike. By nightfall we saw the warning signs of bonfires in the distance. Then as we got nearer we saw some trucks and tanks blocking the road and around them milling Russian troops.

"That must be the border," said *tatusiu* nervously. After a rapid whispered consultation, my parents decided that my father should stay back in the truck while my mother and I persuaded the Russians to let us through.

Nina adjusted my shirt and put on some lipstick. Then she took my hand, raised her bosom, and tossed her hair, as we sauntered forward in the direction of the Russian guards. I looked up at her face and thought of the determined, devil-may-care look of the lion tamer we had seen in the circus in Vienna. She squeezed my hand to give me courage as we ran toward the roadblock. "*Tovarish! Tovarish!*" she cried out laughing. "I'm Nina Zamojska, the singer. Doesn't anyone here have a guitar? Mine got smashed back in Prague."

The Russian tommy gunners looked at each other incredulously, but then they relaxed and began to joke. "Why did you bring your little boy? Much protection he's going to give you!"

"Protection? Why, he's my accompanist—my dancer."

"And who's the old man in the truck? Does he dance for you too?"

"That's my husband and my manager, so don't you get fresh *smarkacz*, snot nose." She patted a grinning young Mongolian on the cheek, and everybody laughed.

Someone brought out a guitar. Surrounded by Russian soldiers, most in their teens, some of them women, we squatted down in front of the fire, and Nina began to sing old Russian folk songs like "Polenko Pole" and "Stenka Razin." And when they requested it, somehow she dug "Tovarish Stalin" out of her repertoire of Red Army marching songs. As she threw herself into her music, I could see the faces of the young soldiers grow tender with nostalgia or gay with abandon, and I knew that she was a hit. Then the show was interrupted by the arrival of a command car. An officer in a peaked hat stepped out—a young man, not much older than his troops.

"What's going on here?"

"She's Nina Zamojska, an entertainer on her way to Plzeň to sing for the Americans."

"But your papers are not in order," said the officer sternly.

"Who can get proper papers in times like these?" Nina replied smiling, while I bowed and clicked my heels with Prussian deference. The officer looked over his lively, grinning troops.

"Can she sing?"

"She sure can!"

"Then what are you waiting for, you bastards, let them through!"

The glare of the bonfires grew dim behind us and the road began to wind. Then we saw the flickering lights of a town ahead. "Plzeň," *tatusiu* said.

As we came around a bend we saw a pair of headlights directed straight at us up the road. A jeep stopped and two soldiers, revolvers in hand, waved us down. As they entered the arc of our headlights, I saw to my amazement that they were both black. Never had I seen a black person before, though I had heard from my playmates in the street that in Africa were black people—dangerous natives mostly, who attacked European explorers and shipwrecked sailors.

The two young men hoisted themselves on the running boards on each side of the truck and demanded in broken German to see our papers. After much palaver, mostly in sign language, they understood that we were Polish refugees seeking shelter in the American zone.

"Okay, okay," one of them said. The other pointed in the direction of the Russian roadblock. My father nodded.

"You're one lucky son-of-a-bitch," the American said, or at least that's what we understood him to mean.

"Yes! Yes!" my father agreed, grinning from ear to ear.

While one jumped off the running board and headed back to the Jeep, the other reached into his shirt pocket and came up with a pack of Camel cigarettes. Taking one himself, he passed the pack around.

The grown-ups lit up and inhaled the smoke slowly. When my mother tried to give the pack back to the soldier, he shrugged and said, "Oh, no, for you! For you!" He then jumped off and ran back to his Jeep.

For some time thereafter, I felt that Americans were mostly black, insanely generous, wonderfully free, and the most powerful people in the world. Later, when I learned to smoke, I would buy only Camels.

We checked into a hotel in Plzeň, and the next evening my parents went to see an American movie: *Alexander's Ragtime Band.* "It was the last American movie I had seen in Poland before the war," *tatusiu* explained. "And now it's here again! It was like meeting up with an old friend." He sang the tune in broken English, "Du, du, du, dum! Alexander's Ragtime Band!" and tooted away in a young and light-hearted manner I had never seen before.

In the next few days, while my parents were out negotiating with various agencies, especially the United Nations Relief and Rehabilitation Administration, I practiced riding my father's big black bike in a lot adjoining the hotel where we were staying. The seat was much too high for me, but somehow I managed to get the bike started. I fell and scraped my hands and knees many times, but I was determined to learn to ride.

One day when my parents came home, I showed them that I could ride *tatusiu's* big bike. He was amazed at my feat, and my mother was proud of me. Later, as the sun was setting, the three of us went for a walk, hand in hand, around the airfield where the planes that would fly us out of Czechoslovakia were supposed to land. As at the circus in Vienna, I felt safe and whole and wished that the moment would never pass, but it did.

Across the street from our hotel was an American compound. When I wasn't practicing on my father's bike, I tried to hang out with the American GIs. They'd hand me Wrigley's chewing gum or Clark chocolate bars in an absentminded and distracted manner, mostly to get rid of me. They paid no attention, but I relished being among them. Everything they did was grist for my imitation. I learned to chew gum with their mindless abandon, and I learned to walk like they did. Americans slouched, dragged their feet, and wiggled their asses. Unlike the Germans, Americans didn't need to have their backs ramrod straight and their chins pointed to the sky to show their superiority and disdain. They didn't need to walk over people—somehow they walked right past them. By their walk they seemed to be saying: "Ain't I just fine and sexy. And I won the war, but I don't give a shit one way or the other. You guys wanna die for your hallowed ground, keep it. I don't need it. So fuck off."

"Fuck off, kid," they'd say to me. I was convinced that if I practiced walking like them, and if I learned to say "fuck off" just right, I too might become an American just like them. "Fuck off" are the first words I learned in English.

They couldn't get rid of me. And when they weren't looking, I sneaked out back and tried to drive the Jeeps parked in the driveway. One day somebody left the keys in the ignition of his Jeep, I got it started somehow, and it began to roll out into the street. At the last moment the cook jumped in and stopped the car. He cuffed me one and pushed me out, but the driver of the Jeep just laughed when he was told of my attempted getaway.

"Forget it. It's okay!"

"Fuck off" and "It's okay"—I practiced saying it all day.

On the outskirts of Plzeň was the UNRRA compound and a refugee camp set on the site of a former concentration camp for women the Germans called Pilsen-Karlow. We went there one day to speak to the director about getting out of Czechoslovakia by plane. He was the tallest person I had ever seen—a six-foot-six-inch American giant with tousled blond hair and a gentle self-deprecating manner. I sat listening to Jan and Nina explaining our predicament to him while he leaned back in his chair and put his feet up on his desk. "It's okay," he said. "When you're ready, come and stay here with us. Any day we're expecting some planes from France. I'll try to get you on, but you'll have to pass for French people. Can you do that?"

"Of course," Jan explained, "we speak French like natives!"

After we left, Jan was insulted that the director had put his feet up on his desk. Nina thought that he lacked refinement, but I loved it.

When we got back to our hotel in Plzeň, the manager intercepted us, and taking my father aside told him nervously that at that very moment the NKVD were waiting to arrest us in our room upstairs! Jan spun on his heels and directed my mother and me to follow. He hailed a taxi, and we returned as we were to the UNRRA camp. After Jan explained to the giant director what had just happened, the American allowed us to stay in the refugee camp and said that the NKVD had no jurisdiction there. But we weren't so sure.

A few days later, after calling the hotel to check that the coast was clear, Jan went back to retrieve some of our stuff, including a couple of typewriters and the bicycle that he hoped he could use to barter once we got to France.

What had happened? How did the Russians trace us to Plzeň? Apparently, after he had stolen the truck, Jan had written to the NKVD that he had it. He hoped that if someone had questioned him about it, he would have a document of some sort explaining his possession of the truck. But here he had been too clever by half, because once the NKVD found about it, they sent agents to arrest us all.

"Sending that letter was really dumb," Jan said later. Nina and I agreed.

The camp consisted of a number of wooden barracks in which the refugees, wrapped in a couple of blankets, slept on wooden platforms. Everyone got a pot filled with porridge in the morning and soup for lunch and dinner. With the soup we also got some bread. The pot was also used for washing up. We lived like that for about three weeks. Later, when I thought of the women who had been interned there during the war, it occurred to me that to them our existence would have seemed heavenly. As for us, our biggest problem was boredom and anxiety.

Every morning we joined small groups of fellow refugees on the tiny airfield adjoining the camp grounds. There we waited for the planes to come, but day after clear sunny day nothing happened. Not even a speck in the sky appeared. Meanwhile, I saw that my parents were worried that the Russians would return and arrest us.

One morning we woke up to a drenching rain. This would clearly not be the day when the planes would come. Out of a growing lassitude, many of the people in our bunk stayed in bed past the morning porridge. When the rain seemed heaviest, someone burst into our cabin shouting, "They're here!"

When we got on the plane, Jan addressed our fellow passengers. He said he had heard that conditions were much better in Belgium than in France. Would they mind if he spoke to the pilot about taking us to Brussels? Since there was no objection, he went up to the pilot and explained to him that we all wanted to go to Belgium rather than France. The American said, "It's okay by me." I had never been on a plane before. It was exciting when it took off, but then it dipped into a pocket of air, and I threw up.

10 Jews

Bobi

Some weeks after our arrival in Brussels—we had an apartment near the Manneken Pis—my parents told me straight out that I was Jewish. It was a beautiful summer's Sunday morning when they broke the news. I had overslept, and when I woke I could hear my parents whispering. My mother giggled softly, "But you're terrible, Willy. How could you? Just like that!"

Willy? I thought to myself. His name is Jan, why is she calling him "Willy"?

Then I heard my father's impatient voice: "You always complicate things. How long can you keep it from him? He's eight years old. He must have figured out some things for himself already."

There was more whispering, and then they must have heard me shuffling outside their door, because they called me in. My mother was in bed, wearing a pink nightgown, and my father, dressed in his shorts, was leaning against the windowsill.

"Bogusiu, there is something you must know," said *tatusiu*, while he glanced toward my mother. "During the war . . ."

"Yes?"

"Well, during the war . . ." And here my father began to grin broadly, and my mother suppressed a nervous giggle. "Well, during the war people do some strange things, right?"

"Sure." I tried to go along with what seemed to be a joke or at least a funny story.

"Oh, what the hell," said *tatusiu* as he pushed off the windowsill and sat himself at my mother's feet on their bed. "Bogusiu, you're a Jew."

"What?"

"You're a Jew. You're a Jew," he repeated as if he were a teacher and I some dumb student.

"Willy," said my mother, "you're ridiculous." She got out of bed, led me to a chair, and faced me.

"Bobi, what religion are you?"

"I believe in Jesus," I said.

"Right. You think you're a Christian, but what *tatusiu* is driving at is that you only think you're a Christian, but you're really Jewish. During the war we had to pretend we were somebody else."

"I see," I said, not quite getting the point, but trying to be helpful.

"We had to make believe we were somebody else because the Germans were out to kill all the Jews. Do you understand?"

"Of course he understands," added *tatusiu*, giving me a broad grin, his face expressing the wish that I'd get the point and not make too much of a fuss.

"I think I do," I said tentatively, keeping the news at bay, the way one might a dog who wags his tail but is known to bite.

"Brace yourself," continued my father. "Your name is not Bogusław Marian Zamojski."

"Oh?"

"Our real name is Mendelsohn. Forget about Zamojski. Zamojski was a ruse, a trick."

"During the war we pretended to be called Zamojski, but our real name is Mendelsohn," my mother added helpfully.

"Mendelsohn?" I asked in wonder.

"My real name is Natalia, not Janina. Before the war I was called Nacia not Nina."

"And my name is Wolf. People call me Willy. It's not Jan Zamojski," added my father.

"And what's my name?" I asked, without intending to be smart-alecky.

"Sylvio," said my father. "Sylvio. You were named after my mother. Her name was Sara, but she preferred to be called Sylvia."

"Sylvio." It sounded strange—not Polish at all.

"Do you want to be called Sylvio?" *mamusia* asked.

"I don't know."

"We can keep calling you Bogusiu or Bobi. We're all used to it by now. I'm going to keep 'Nina'—there's been enough confusion in our lives."

"Yes, I think I'd like Bobi better."

"You see," said my father expansively as he rose, "the kid is a real trooper—taking it real well."

So I'm Jewish, I thought, without knowing what that meant, except, hadn't we killed Jesus? I looked up at the faces of my parents and realized that their smiles were those of chagrin, not of pleasure. It was almost as if the revelation of our true identity, which they had tried to pass off lightly, as almost a prank, had not been convincing. If it was a joke, it was a joke that had gone too far, and they seemed embarrassed by the result.

As for me, the unintended butt of their prank, I felt confused but also to some extent relieved at finally being included into the secret lore of my parent's lives. So many things suddenly became clear. And for that inclusion, I was willing—for the moment at least—to trade Christian for Jew, Zamojski for Mendelsohn.

Jumping on one leg while trying to get into his slacks, *tatusiu* ended all revelations with a final warning. "Though now you know our real name, Bobi, you gotta remember that our papers still say 'Zamojski.' It'll be a while before we can get them changed. So if anybody asks you, especially the police, say you're Bogusław Zamojski. *Dobze?*"

"Sure. *Dobze.*"

Later that day we went shopping on the Rue Neuf. *Tatusiu* bought me the toy revolver and the toy American helmet that I had longed for. The next morning, wearing my helmet and brandishing my gun, I went down to play in the park. I hid in the bushes and destroyed a whole armored division of Germans by picking off their tanks one by one.

The Shalom was a restaurant and cabaret located on the third floor of a walk-up on Boulevard Anspach. At one time it had been called Johnny's, because the owner had wanted to attract GIs, but it had become a hangout for Jewish refugees, hence the name change. One night, my parents took me along.

The place was crowded with people eating dinner around checkered tablecloths. Nina and Willy were in an expectant mood, their eyes flashing glances everywhere. We stood in the lobby until a tired-looking waiter with dark eyes, pale skin, and large knobby hands showed us to a booth. Finally my father couldn't contain himself any longer. He stood up and embraced the startled elderly man.

"My name is Willy Mendelsohn," he said grinning, "and that is my family." By now my mother was standing too and crying, and everyone else turned inquiring but friendly glances toward us.

"You should stay healthy and live to 120," growled the waiter as he pumped my father's hand and allowed himself to be kissed by my mother. Later he brought us chicken soup, carp, noodles, and sweet red wine.

The little wine I was permitted spread a warm and cozy feeling in me, and I must have dozed off because when I woke with a start, I saw that the room had become even more crowded and thick with cigarette smoke. I sat by myself observing the scene. There were clumps of people, some sitting, some standing, including my parents, who were talking with animation and gesticulating to a couple across the way. There were kids too, my age and younger. Some were sitting with grown-ups, others were sitting or leaning against a wall.

Jews, I thought. All these people are Jews. I was glad to be there, yet I felt strangely distant from them too, like an explorer in the middle of a friendly but exotic tribe.

The table-hopping and milling was interrupted when a pudgy, balding man pulled in a piano and called for "Shulamit." He was soon joined by a heavy-set woman who looked like a gypsy.

"Shulamit, sing 'Tum Balalayka'!" someone shouted. Shulamit had a high, sweet voice. Some of the songs people joined in with gusto. To others they listened in stony silence, and then, when she sang an old Yiddish lullaby, "Meine Yiddishe Mameh," they gave in to their grief and wept.

I tried to find my parents, but they were lost somewhere in the crowd. I felt very distant from the music and the sadness. The words sounded vaguely German to me. I had been surprised that my father seemed to speak Yiddish fluently. Where had he learned it? And even my mother had understood the waiter. But I was a stranger, and I tried to be on my best behavior.

When the singing stopped, people moved even closer together. They hugged and exchanged names and addresses. It was almost dawn when we made our way home. Hoping that it would please them, I turned to *mamusia* and *tatusiu* and said, "I see that Jews can be nice people too." *Tatusiu* took me by the hand and vacuously smiled down at me as if he didn't know what I was talking about.

———————————

My mother resumed telling me stories about our family, but this time she didn't have to disguise them as Zamojski lore, and I started to understand what had happened to us during the war. She told me how she had grown up in Warsaw, how my grandfather Leon ("Leib") loved music, and how one day when his grandmother was ill he traveled all the way to Spain because he had heard that there was a plant grown in Barcelona that would cure tuberculosis. She told me how pretty my grandmother Stefania, "Stefcia," was and how all the gentlemen admired her when they went to the opera. And how my mother had performed at the Adria and how fat Moskowitz had tried to kiss her. She told me how she met my father, Willy, how handsome and debonair he was, and how he had blocked my mother's and my grandmother's way. "Haven't we met somewhere before?" Here my mother would laugh. And how they fell in love, and how later I was born. "You were our love child, Bobi. 'My god,' I said to myself when I saw you the first time, 'this kid is my exact copy!'" And how we moved to Stanisławów, and the Russians, and the Germans, and the Zamojkis, and the false papers. She told me about Tadzo, Wanda, Pani Marylka, and Irenka, and how one Friday night we all found out that we were Jewish. She told me about Riya—"that fat cow!"—about Dina and about *tatusiu*'s arrest, but by then I knew some of the story myself and was able to fill in some blanks and even to remind her of parts she had missed.

Since as a stateless refugee Willy wasn't permitted to work in Belgium, he turned to smuggling watches from Switzerland and tried to get an affidavit that would allow us to immigrate to America. Getting to America had been his childhood dream; now that the war was over his chance had come to act on it. Meanwhile, Nina became pregnant with my younger brother, Richi. At first, Belgium was a happy interlude for my parents, but then Nina began to dwell on the fate of her parents and was determined to find out what had happened to them.

Although Nina was nearly certain that Leib and Stefcia had perished in Treblinka, she still nurtured some hope that they had survived. One sunny day not long after our arrival in Brussels, my mother took me with her to a Jewish agency to inquire about survivors. She had been told most everyone was dead. Still, she had made a list of family and friends she had known before the war and went to check things out.

The agency had set up shop in a decaying little three-story walk-up. For security reasons the building was discreetly unmarked, so we passed it a few times before Nina discovered it. She checked the address, and we began the steep ascent to the top floor. There was a crush of people, some standing in line, some rushing about, and everywhere we heard the staccato of typewriters.

The missing persons office was at the end of the hall. You had to stand in a long line of people making inquiries. "Why don't you wait over there," said *mamusia*, pointing to an alcove near a window, "while I stand in line. It's going to take longer than I thought."

In the alcove were a few chairs, some with ripped upholstery, and a little cocktail table with stacks of magazines piled high. I straddled one of the chairs and looked out on an alley below, where two girls were playing hopscotch. Past them the alley opened into a broad park, where leafy trees swayed ponderously in the midafternoon breeze. I slid into a seat and reached for a magazine. I wanted one with large glossy pictures, since I didn't know how to read French, so I picked up what must have been the Belgian equivalent of *Life*. It was there that I came across my first pile of corpses.

Little voyeur that I was, my first reaction was to examine the bodies for some signs of sex, but to my shocked distaste I realized that I couldn't make out any breasts or buttocks or bushes or any sexual difference at all. The wispy broken cadavers piled on top of each other like wooden logs were surrounded by grinning—*grinning*—German soldiers.

I kept on turning the pages past more and more bodies, past piles of what looked like false teeth—although I doubted my own sight—until I came to the last picture, which had me stumped. A little girl, perhaps my age or a year younger, was standing by a blackboard with what looked like mad squiggles scribbled all over it. She had uncombed bangs extending almost into her eyes, and her little beret was perched precariously on her head. Her look was that of a small, hunted, crazed animal.

Grabbing the magazine, I ran up to my mother; she had made considerable progress in line. "What are you reading?" she asked, glancing down at me. I handed her the evidence.

"Oh!" she exclaimed, quickly snatching the magazine out of my hands. "You really shouldn't be looking at things like that. They're terrible, but they don't concern you." I pulled the magazine back away from her.

"Wait, tell me," I said. "Who is this little girl, and what's happening to her?"

My mother gave me an angry look and turned away. Then she sighed, relented, and read the French caption under the photograph. "She is a little Jewish girl who was separated from her parents during the war and was found wandering the road by some American troops."

"Why are all those mad squiggles and circles and things on the blackboard behind her? What do they mean?"

"They say that she's a mute, and when they asked her to write her name—anything—that was all she could produce."

"I guess she must be crazy," I said.

By then our turn had come, and we stood in front of a desk with a very pretty black-haired girl behind it. Like Wanda when I first met her, she had sparkling black eyes and wore a white carnation in her hair.

"Have you brought the list?" she asked. It would take weeks to trace the names, she said, and even then the agency could not be sure who was dead and who was still alive.

———————

Mamusia and I walked out into the bright summer day.

"I don't know," she said. "It looks much worse than I had imagined."

"What does?" I asked.

She walked along for a while without answering my question. Then she gave me a sidelong glance and said, "Everything. The war. It's a disaster."

During lunch at a sidewalk cafe she told me about the ghetto and that my grandparents had perished at a place called Treblinka. "First they gassed the people and then they burned their bodies in the crematoria. Can you imagine?"

"Were some of the people still alive when they were burned?"

"I wouldn't know."

She told me that in some of the other camps they had found mountains of old suitcases, shoes, dolls, hair.

"Suitcases, shoes?" I asked.

"The dead don't need them."

"Dolls?"

"Dolls that were taken from the children who were to be killed."

"Hair?"

"They shaved the people's hair and shipped it back to Germany."

"Why?"

"I don't know—maybe to weave into some kind of cloth."

I heard what she told me about the "war," as she called it, but I didn't understand what she meant. I looked over at her and she looked away. She seemed embarrassed about having told me such terrible things.

After lunch we went shopping on rue Neuf. A street photographer snapped our picture as we strolled hand-in-hand. My mother looks radiant for the photograph, and I seem to be smiling with pleasure.

———————

Kazik ("Kuba") Stern, my mother's cousin, and his wife, Halinka, both survivors of the Warsaw ghetto, stayed with us in Brussels for a few weeks on their way to Australia. They had been invited by my mother's aunt, Eva Korman, Stefcia's sister, the same person who had urged Nacia to find out about Willy's being a Jew before the war. Kazik was a nice-looking young man with curly brown hair, in his late twenties, who wore high black riding boots polished to a sheen, like the Germans had. It seemed somehow incongruous for a Jew to be wearing such boots after the war.

A few days after he and Halinka had left for Australia, and my father was out on business somewhere, I found my mother sitting alone in the living room. She was examining her hands and her eyeshadow had left streaks on her cheeks, apparently from crying. Was my father having another affair?

"What's wrong?" I asked.

"Nothing. Nothing. You're too young to know such things," she said, vaguely waving her hands in front of her face as if she were trying to dispel an apparition.

"What?"

"Kazik was in the Jewish police in the ghetto."

"He was in the police? There were Jewish policemen in the ghetto?"

"Yes, they helped the Germans to round up their own people. Can you imagine? They thought that they'd save themselves if they did. Of course Kazik had his mother to support and two sisters, one who was retarded. I guess he did it for them . . . not that it helped. They too were deported. He survived by escaping to the Aryan side, where Halinka had found a hiding place. Before they left for Australia he told me . . ."

"What?"

"I can't tell you," she said with finality.

"What?"

"How my parents were murdered. Why did he have to tell me? That really was not necessary. I know that they were killed, but I don't need to know the details of their death. Apparently he was there and saw it all, and now I can see it too."

"You didn't want him to tell you. You didn't want to know."

"No. The knowledge of how they died lies heavy on my heart. I can see their murder. I can feel it. He told me all the details, Bobi. I won't repeat them to you . . . I can't . . . I won't.

"My father had a *ziseh neshomeh*, a 'sweet soul' you say in Yiddish. He was a delicate person. Tadzo and I have some of that from our parents. Kazik should never have told me . . . *From his window facing the street, he saw the Gestapo men laughing and cursing as they dragged my father onto the sidewalk, where they beat him mercilessly. Why did they beat him? Because a Jew is not supposed to be tall. They beat him and kicked him and crushed his skull with the butts of their rifles and their revolvers. Then they trampled his body with their heavy boots. My mother had witnessed the murder. After that she fell apart. Kazik told me that when they rounded up my mother, with all the other women and children, she had lost her mind and no longer knew what was happening to her. She was waving at passersby and singing an aria as they marched her away. 'The masses of people who were being deported, by and large,' he said, 'had become insane.'"*

Whenever she touched on my grandparents, I knew that we were on sacred ground. What had happened to them was beyond pain and death. Their murder was the destruction of all that was kind, delicate, fine, and true in the world, and I knew too that she blamed herself for having abandoned them in the ghetto in order to save herself and me.

When my mother had finished speaking, the bodies I had seen in the photographs at the Jewish agency lost their anonymity. Suddenly I saw Leib's broken body lying in the ghetto street, and I imagined Stefcia lying on one of the piles of twisted cadavers I had seen in the photographs. Thus it was that my mother's story became my own, and I became a Jew.

I wasn't all that well after the war. I had lost weight. Then my hair fell out, and then my hair grew back in. I had never been to school and seemed to be at loose ends. My father decided to do something about it. He had heard that Le Rosey was the best and most exclusive boarding school in Switzerland. The Agha Khan sent his children there and so did the king of Belgium. The smuggling business was good, and Willy decided to send me there as well. Since Nina was preoccupied with the coming birth of my brother, she too thought it was a good idea. The catch was that Le Rosey did not permit Jews, but Willy was not to be dissuaded.

Meanwhile, Tadzo, Wanda, Irenka, and Pani Marylka had joined us in Brussels—they had made it out of Czechoslovakia through Germany. There was a brief interlude when the seven of us were together again, but to my disappointment they seemed preoccupied with leaving us to go to Rio de Janeiro. Alicia, Wanda's and Irenka's sister, had immigrated just as the war started, and now what was left of their family, including Tadzo, wanted to be reunited in Brazil.

It was raining that January morning in 1946 when my father and I got on the train from Brussels to Gstaad in Switzerland, where Le Rosey held its winter session. The night before, *mamusia* and Wanda had sat up stitching name tags on all my clothes: "Bogusław Marian Zamojski," "Bogusław Marian Zamojski," "Bogusław Marian Zamojski," over and over again.

We spent the night in Zurich, where my father had some business to transact with a wholesaler of watches. He got me a new Omega, "for the occasion." On the last leg of our journey, he briefed me on the situation, enlisting my help in the forthcoming deception.

"You understand, don't you," he asked, leaning earnestly across the aisle, "that we're trying to get you into the very best school in Switzerland, perhaps in the whole world?"

I nodded.

"And you remember what they told me about letting Jews in?"

"Yes."

"Well, we're not going to be intimidated that easily, are we? . . . No, of course not," said my father, answering his own question.

"I called Madame Carnalle, the headmistress. I explained that I am Count Zamojski and that I wanted to place you in Le Rosey. She invited us to come straight out. Apparently she knows the English branch of the family. Keep in mind that we have family in London—apparently she's met some of them. Do you understand?" Impressed by my father's passion to get me in and by all the efforts he had made on my behalf, I gravely nodded.

"But everything, everything hinges on not letting on that you're Jewish. You're Count Bogusław Zamojski. Let it go at that. If anyone discovers the truth, not only will you be thrown out of school, but it might have some unpleasant consequences for us with the Belgian authorities. If they found out the truth, it might even hurt our chances of getting to America."

I understood. My parents had been impostors for five years without my even knowing about it. Now it was my duty to wear a mask.

"Did you like going to prep school in Davos when you were a kid?" I asked.

"Like? Davos? Frankly, no. My mother died when I was ten. I had a hard time after that, but that shouldn't bother you. Stand up for your rights. Be forthright. Don't ever snitch, and never refuse a fight. You'll be all right, you'll see."

Soon after, in the midst of a light snowfall, we heaved and shuddered into Gstaad. As we got off the train, we were engulfed by a crowd of cheerful vacationers who had come after the crush of Christmas for the skiing and the international nightlife. Not since the days of the Šroubek and the Nazi upper crust did I see so many pretty women decked out in long furs and men of every nationality laughing eagerly at their own jokes as they carried their ski equipment into the cozy station. Inside we gravitated toward a blazing fireplace. Everything smelled of crushed snow, smoking pine, and hot chocolate.

"Count Zamojski?"

"Yes."

"We are from Le Rosey. Madame Carnalle sent us. Will you follow us, please." Two tall, elegant fellows wearing blue loden coats ushered us out of the waiting room.

"What about the bags?"

"Madame Carnalle asks you to leave the bags at the station. Master Zamojski will be able to get his bags once the interview is successful."

"We're not in yet," my father whispered nervously.

We climbed into a horse-drawn sleigh with the two guys above us in the coachman's seat and started off at a gentle, bell-ringing trot through the narrow streets of Gstaad, toward the winter campus of Le Rosey.

Wrapped in a fur blanket next to my father, who was deep in thought, I looked up at the swirling gray sky, and I opened my mouth to swallow some snowflakes. On the outskirts of town, in sight of the ski slopes with its rope tows and chair lifts, we stopped in front of a clump of chalets.

"Le Rosey," announced one of the guys. "The *directrice* is waiting for you in her office." It had stopped snowing. As I rose to climb out of the sled, I looked down toward the ski slopes and saw dark figures advancing like an army in our direction.

"The boys are coming back from skiing," one of our guides explained.

We followed our guides up two flights of pine-scented stairs and down a long hallway past a row of classrooms, past groups of staring boys dressed identically in ski pants and blue-and-white V-necked ski sweaters.

In the outer office we were greeted by an old woman dressed all in white who introduced herself as Madame Brummel, the English teacher. She rose from behind the typewriter and ushered us into the inner office. "The madame will be right with you," she said.

On one side of the office, a large picture window overlooked the ski slopes and the jagged peaks above them. With its back to the window, facing the door, a massive mahogany desk squatted. Across from the desk were two plush leather sofas and a coffee table in the shape of a large leaf. A maid entered with a tray of tea and pastries. My father and I sat next to each other on one of the sofas. The door opened and a tall red-headed woman in her fifties walked in.

"Monsieur le Conte?"

"Madame."

Madame Carnalle was dressed in a simple black suit with a ruffled white blouse, setting her off like a cameo broach. She extended her hand in a sweeping motion. We rose and kissed her proffered hand with gravity. "No, no, please sit down," she said in French. "Make yourself at home." My father and I sank into the divans. I reached for an eclair.

"I met your cousin this fall," she said to my father.

"Oh?" said my father, just a bit too enthusiastically. "I haven't seen him since before the war."

"Yes, yes. In London. A fine horseman."

"And hunter too," added my father, relaxing into the story.

"Yes, at his summer home. Lovely."

My father having passed his litmus test, and so quickly, Madame Carnalle turned her gaze on me. "And so you are Bogusław Marian?" she asked in English.

"*Je ne comprends pas d'anglais*," I said, giving her my disarming golden smile.

"Yes, well, we'll teach you how to speak English here, my dear. Have no fear," she replied in French, and so in a matter of a few minutes we had both passed once more into the inner sanctum of aristocratic exclusivity. No Dogs or Jews Allowed had been the signs on some stores in Warsaw just before the war, my mother had told me.

Madame Carnalle explained that I would be placed with the juniors—kids my age—and given special tutoring to catch me up. Then my father chatted her up a bit, asking her about her job and the history of the school. They were hitting it off splendidly. I looked past Madame Carnalle out of her picture window. I could see boys carrying their skis over their shoulders like rifles.

"Ah. The boys are back from the slopes," Madame Carnalle said, signifying that the interview was over.

Once we were out of range of her office, I thought my father would turn to me and laugh about the joke we had just pulled. Far from it. As I ran to keep up with his long, determined stride, he said, "Charming woman." "Seems to know what she's doing." He failed to mention that we had never met our "cousins," the London Zamojskis.

While waiting for the sleigh to take him back to the station, he reminisced about his boyhood days in Switzerland, but I could hardly hear him. I had fallen back into the deep dark pond of the Wesely days, where it was hard to breathe and sound penetrated in muffled tones. We had never been close. His affair with Riya and his cruel treatment of my mother had created a wall between us; and yet, as he got in and his sleigh pulled away, I felt as if I had received a blow to the stomach. He too must have felt something, because he turned and waved to me all the way until his sleigh disappeared behind a bend in the road. I turned back toward the school when I couldn't hear the ringing of sleigh bells any longer.

———————————

Passing various groups of boys who waved politely to the headmistress and gave me a once-over, Madame Carnalle brought me to my room. It was modern and brightly lit and smelled of newly glued wallpaper. Everything was in threes: three beds, three closets, three desks. There were books on the shelves, family pictures on the walls, and ski clothes strewn all about. I noticed my empty bags in one of the closets. My clothes had already been unpacked by a maid and placed where they belonged.

"Your roommates are Amin Khan and Franz Pischelle. Franz is at the infirmary, but should be coming out tonight. I've spoken to Amin about your coming. He'll be here soon, and he'll take you to dinner. Don't forget that coats and ties are required for all meals." And with that, she left me to my own devices.

After I inspected some of the family portraits and admired the intricate design of one of my roommate's ski boots, the door flung open and a slim, brown-eyed, curly headed boy about my size and age entered.

"Welcome," he said. "My name is Amin Khan. You are Zamojski." He crossed the room to shake my hand.

"Yes," I said. "My name is Zamojski."

"Never mind, never mind. Go on with what you were doing. You like the boots? Custom made, a gift from my mother." I replaced his boots, and Amin rattled on. "Carnalle told you, of course, that I'm one of your roommates. The other is Pischelle, otherwise known as 'Pissoire' because he still pisses in his bed. Do you understand? Steals things too. Loves to collect watches—look out he doesn't take yours."

I was so fascinated by his looks, by his quick, nervous gestures, and by the staccato rhythm of his speech that I missed much of what he was saying. He turned to me and asked, "Carnalle told us that you're a Polish count, is that right?"

"Right."

"Well, she's very impressed with that sort of thing, you know. It doesn't mean all that much here though. My father is a prince and my mother is an actress. They're divorced, of course."

"Of course." I knew what "divorced" meant. Rolf Mueller had divorced Dina Mueller, and it had killed her.

"Are your parents divorced?"

"No."

"And you're a Catholic."

"Yes," I lied.

"Well I'm a Moslem. My brother, Karim, and I are the only ones here. I get excused from confession on Friday and I have the morning off on Sunday. People are sorry for me about my parents being divorced, but it doesn't matter, you know, because that way I get twice as many visits. After the horse racing season is over my father comes, and my mother comes between films—takes me right out of school, and we go off on trips together. She promised to take me to Paris with her next time and then to Hollywood. Do you want to come?"

"Hollywood? In America, where they make films?"

"Of course."

"Would she really take us?"

"Of course. I'll speak to her about it when she comes."

Amin was clearly a magical being who sprang from magical beings. I couldn't wait to ask his mother if she knew Charlie Chaplin, Tarzan, and the girl who played Margie in the movie by the same name. Just then there was a loud ringing in the hall. I stiffened, thinking we were about to be bombed, when Amin jumped off his bed, laughing. "Don't worry," he said. "It's just the warning bell for dinner. Coats and ties." With that he slipped into his blue-and-white Rosey blazer and ran out, with me following close on his heels.

By the time the last bell for dinner had sounded, we had made it to a large dining hall on the first floor of the chalet. About two hundred boys were in the room. Amin and I stood by our chairs on opposite sides of a table headed by one of the teachers. "These are the juniors," Amin whispered. Twenty heads turned toward me and twenty sets of eyes examined me. Other tables were filled with boys of various ages, all the way up to the seniors, who were about seventeen. On a raised platform was a table separated from the rest, around which stood the older teachers.

"The senior staff," whispered Amin as Madame Carnalle walked in. She climbed the platform and looked down into the upturned faces of her boys.

"Let us pray."

The dining room reverberated with the Lord's Prayer, which Miss Berta had taught me well, and then with a loud "Amen!" and the scraping of chairs as we sat down, but the *directrice* was not finished yet.

"I have some announcements to make," she boomed. She read some schedule changes and class assignments. "Last but not least, I want to introduce to you Master Bogusław Zamojski, whose nickname is 'Bobi' and who joined us this afternoon. Bobi hails from Poland. He has a very interesting background, having lived in Prague and Brussels too. He'll be rooming with Khan and Pischelle." At the mention of Pischelle some of the boys snickered. "Good luck Zamojski," she finished, ignoring them. "Welcome to Le Rosey."

The boys responded with a loud but perfunctory "Welcome!" and then, among a clatter of silver, started off on their lentil soup.

"I'm sure glad you came along," said Amin. "Until now I've been alone with Pissoire. What a drag." But I hardly heard him. I felt like a ghost from another world.

After a dessert of rice pudding and a prayer of thanksgiving, we marched past Madame Carnalle, each boy bending low to kiss her hand. When my turn came I bowed lower than most. I had been taught that in the best circles it is impolite to raise a woman's hand to one's lips. The correct manner is to lower one's lips to her hand.

"I've always wondered," said Amin, "why she doesn't get sores on her hand from all the kissing."

By the time we got back to our room, a delegation of boys was waiting for me. Including Amin, there must have been about ten boys ranging from eight to twelve who had come out to meet me. I exchanged manly handshakes with a few and tried to deal with the questions that flew my way.

"What kind of ski binding do you use?"

"Haven't bought skis yet."

"Get Shrantz to give you the new French style."

"It's a bitch to wrap around your boots though."

"Have you ever skied before?"

"Sure, near Innsbruck."

"Innsbruck—great trails out there. You must be good."

"You're from Poland?"

"Yeah."

"Is that in Russia?"

"No, but Russian troops occupy it now."

"Have you ever seen Russians?"

"Sure. Saw them conquer Prague."

"You were there?"

"Yup."

"You mean you actually saw Russians fighting Germans?"

"Sure did. They fought for a long time—tanks, cannons, machine guns, the works."

"How come you weren't killed?"

"I was in a bunker with some American commandos. Saw everything."

"No shit. *Merde.*" I had obviously gained much prestige, but my ordeal wasn't over yet.

"Have you met Corchoran yet?"

"Corchoran? No."

"Come along then," said Lichty, a rugged-looking Swiss fellow who turned out to be the juniors' best skier. "Saw him in the billiard room."

"Yeah, time for Corky," they all responded, grinning.

"Look out, Zamojski," whispered Amin. "Corchoran is tough." I realized with a rush of panic that I was being led into a fight.

There were some big guys playing billiards, and I almost fainted with fright at the thought of having to fight one of them, but instead I was thrust up in front of a short, stocky kid with a crew cut and a distinctly American accent.

"*Mois, suis Corchoran. On m'appelle Corky.*"

"*Et mois, je m'appelle Bogusław Zamojski. On m'appelle Bobi.*"

No one had told me that I was supposed to fight an American. They had never lost a war. Why was I chosen to test that thesis? There weren't too many preliminaries. Someone pushed me forward into my adversary, and when he didn't react immediately, someone else pushed him forward into me. Suddenly I could feel his squat, chunky body against mine with a lock gripping me about the neck. This was it. Instinctively I made a move that my father had taught me back in Brussels. In case of a head lock, you throw your right arm over your opponent's left, and gripping your right wrist with your left hand, you bear down, using his shoulder as a fulcrum. The contest descended into a test of strength and endurance. Perhaps I had more at stake, for otherwise we were well matched, but to my astonishment and relief I felt him give way. With a groan Corchoran fell to one knee, with me twisting his right arm behind his back. It was all over.

"*Ça va*, Zamojski," he said. "You're okay." That's how Corky and I became friends. After the fight I was followed by a cheerful group back to my room.

I kept to myself, except for Amin and Corky. The less said the better, I reasoned. After all, I had a secret religion, a secret name, and a secret past. Ironically, it may have been the very attempt to establish distance that intrigued some of my friends. They were always after me to tell them about the war. Though they were the sons of the privileged classes—boys who had spent the war years on their estates in England, Ireland, South America, India, or the United States—the war and the fantasy of war was their favorite topic. They wanted to know about death and dying, suffering, humiliation, and heroism. I rose to the occasion, surprising even myself with my invention.

"Before the underground helped us to escape, I saw plenty, I can tell you." There would be five or six boys in my room, listening intently. "Mounds of bodies. People of all ages. Women and children too. They had been gassed, you see, and they were going to be placed in these huge ovens to be cremated."

"You saw that?"

"Sure."

"Women too?"

"Yup. All of them stark naked."

"Naked—you could see their breasts and everything?"

"Everything. Even the hair."

"Were they all Jews?"

"Of course not—Poles, Russians, Frenchmen too."

"No kidding. *Merde alors.* Frenchmen too."

"And how did you escape?"

"I told you already."

"Tell us again."

"The underground. In Poland it was led by an American called Johnny Johnson, who had parachuted down to destroy the camps. He joined the refugees hiding in the woods and organized them into fighting bands. One night, Johnny Johnson himself sneaked into our bunk in the concentration camp and explained to my father that for the sake of free Poland he was going to get us out. And he did."

"Where did he take you?"

"To Innsbruck."

"That's where you learned to ski?"

"Right."

"How could he get you out? Weren't the camps surrounded by armed SS?"

"*Merde,* he wasn't scared of those bastards. He had an American tommy gun and his men were superbly trained commandos. Any of the SS would come near, he'd just rat-a-tat-tat-tat-tat." I made the gun noise and gesture. "They'd fall over like a bunch of pins."

"Yeah, I heard about him," said Corky, getting into my movie. "They gave him a parade up Broadway—that's in New York. After the war, I mean."

And the others nodded sagely.

———————

I found Friday afternoon catechism and confession a trial. Our teacher was a cheerful, pink-cheeked young priest from the village, who looked even more cherubic in front of a classroom than he did in church. He was simple and sweet; he was also a raving hater of Jews. Like Miss Berta, he identified Jews with the Antichrist. Blood guilt, blood sacrifice, and retribution for deicide ran heavy every Friday afternoon:

> So they took Jesus, and He went out bearing his own cross, to the place of a skull, which is called in Hebrew Golgotha. There they crucified Him, and with Him two others. . . . Pilate also wrote a title and put it on the cross; it read, "Jesus of Nazareth, King of the Jews." . . . The chief priests of the Jews then said to Pilate, "Do not write 'King of the Jews' but instead write, 'This man said, "I am King of the Jews."'" Pilate answered, "What I have written, I have written."

"So, you see, once again, according to St. John, the perfidy of the Jews," intoned our young priest with a gentle smile. "Not only did the Jews crucify our Lord, they even quibbled over his name."

Every Sunday all of us Catholics, including Madame Carnalle, would troop down to Gstaad for morning mass. I'd scrunch down in my seat while the service droned on and clouds of incense swirled around me. The church itself was a lovely, airy structure with religious motifs on the walls and the ceiling so eroded by time that one had to concentrate to decipher their pastel colors and abstract shapes. Above me I watched Moses shield his eyes from the presence of God, while Christ rose, born again from the cave of death itself. When my time came to swallow the Son's body transubstantiated into a thin wafer, I would kneel in front of the priest and stick out my tongue with the rest of my friends. It was here that I would feel a momentary chill of the soul. What if I dropped the wafer and therefore Christ himself? What if I choked on him? My true identity would be revealed, and it would be a disaster. "A Jew, a Jew! Praise the Lord, we found Judas in time before he swallowed our Savior! Kill the traitor!"

But Judas was not found out, and an hour later he ran out laughing with the rest of the boys into a clear, sunny winter's morning, strapped on his skis, and took refuge in blissful, silent skiing.

I spent a year and a half at Le Rosey, toward the end much of it in the infirmary for undiagnosable ailments. I had revealed my true identity only once, to Amin, but he didn't know what to make of it and thought I had made it up just to show off.

One day my mother arrived to take me back to Brussels. In the privacy of our train compartment she told me that Wanda, Tadzo, Irenka, and Pani Marylka had left for Brazil.

"Brazil? Is that far away?"

"It's in South America. Yes, it's far."

"Will we ever see them again?"

"I'm sure."

I excused myself and went to the toilet. There I sat down, did my business, and examined the tip of my penis. I guess it's because the cap is off that they tried to kill me, I thought. The shriek of the train, which sounded like an animal cry, so startled me that I quickly zipped up my pants and rushed back to my mother. When I got back she was smiling and fussing with her luggage. Then she pulled out a package.

"It's a present for you, from Wanda and Tadzo. They wanted you to have it." The package contained a book, a French translation of stories by Edgar Allan Poe. There was an inscription on the front page: "To Bobi, Love Wanda and Tadzo."

I tried to read the book on the train, but I found it hard to concentrate.

On a rainy day in the fall of 1947, soon after my arrival from Le Rosey, my father walked in with the affidavits for America. "They're here!" he announced, waving our new papers at my mother, who snatched them from his hands in her excitement.

"But there must be some mistake," she said, blanching. "These papers aren't made out to Mendelsohn, they're made out to 'Melson.'"

"That's the beauty of it," grinned my father. "'Mendelsohn' is too Jewish, too foreign. 'Melson' sounds American. That's what I called myself before the war. If we're going to start fresh in America, let's start right."

"But is it legal?"

"Legal, you ask?" my father was offended. "I don't begin my new life in America with an illegal trick. It's legal. In America they don't care about such things. From now on it's William, Nina, Robert, and Richard Melson."

It was my turn to protest. "Robert Melson, me?"

Here my father faced me with a look of triumph. "Well, you're not going to be called Bogusław in America, are you? And Bobby is the nickname for Robert. So that's it!"

It seemed impossible to argue with such logic.

Before boarding the ship we had to undergo various inspections by American immigration and consular officials. One of these was an examination for VD. We were rushed from one little room to the next until we came to a cubicle where a short, busy man was fiddling with some test tubes. "Sit down," he said in heavily American-accented French. He pulled a curtain in front of my father's chair, went behind it, and instructed him to drop his pants. After examining the tip of my father's penis out of our view, he repeated the procedure with my mother, taking a sample from her vagina. Then he sequestered himself in his makeshift lab, examining the samples under his microscope.

"Clean as a whistle," he smiled after a moment. "You can go ahead and urinate now if you wish."

The four of us stood on deck of the ship—a converted troop transport. As the shores of Antwerp and Europe receded, Richi, who had started to walk, clung to Willy's leg and Nina stroked my hair. "Bobi," she said pensively, "we're finally leaving our terrible and crazy past behind us. In America we're going to start a normal life."

I knew exactly what she meant by a "normal life." Some time before our departure, the three of us went to see a popular American movie that was playing in Brussels. It's about Margie, a teenage girl growing up in a typical midwestern American town, where people feel so safe that they never lock their doors and the one policeman is everybody's friend and neighbor. She is part of a large, warm, funny family consisting of her mom and dad, sisters and brothers, grandparents, uncles and aunts, a tabby cat, and a shaggy dog. She has lots of friends who drop by her rambling two-story colonial house, where she has a room all to herself. Her room is decorated with banners of her high school and of the colleges to which she intends to apply when she graduates. There is so much food that people pay no attention to it, but they get up in the middle of the night when they're hungry and make themselves giant sandwiches or pour themselves tall glasses of milk. Her major goals in life are to make the high school cheerleading squad and to date Chuck, a really cute guy and captain of the football team, who will invite her to the prom. Halfway through the movie, there is a crisis. She thinks that Chuck has dumped her for her best friend, but over a glass of milk late at night by the refrigerator her mom comforts her and tells her that all will be well. The movie ends with her making the cheerleading squad and Chuck throwing the long ball and winning the crucial last game of the season. Over the fadeouts we see Margie and Chuck back together again, dancing at the prom.

Once we got to America, I was going to be Chuck or "Bob." After high school I'd go to college or join the army, where I would say "it's okay" and "fuck off" like the GIs I had known in Plzeň. Then I'd come back to my hometown, where Margie, looking like Wanda when I first met her in Kraków, would be waiting for me. We'd get married and live happily ever after. That's what "normal" meant to me, and that's what I hoped for when we got to America.

When the shore finally disappeared from sight we sat on deck and examined a picture that a street photographer had taken the day of our departure. It was a photo taken in Antwerp near the docks. Nina looks tired, like she'd been packing all night, but she's hiding a grin, which could turn into a laugh. Next to her stands Ilona, a Hungarian woman who happened to be staying with us for a few weeks and had accompanied us to the ship to say good-bye. She had been a nun in Budapest who had fled the Russians and had renounced her vows. I suspected her of having a crush on my father, but I'm not sure that he reciprocated her feelings. Willy is trying to smile without much success. A few months before our journey he had lost all his money from smuggling watches, and he was facing a new life without a penny to his or our name. Richi, holding on to Willy and me, had been crying but was momentarily distracted by the camera. I'm straining to seem as big and tall as I possibly can. I was afraid of the tough American boys I'd be facing, and I was determined to look as if I could take care of myself.

We all look somewhat wan. None of us is smiling as broadly as we should. We must have forgotten for a moment that it is important to appear radiant when having your picture taken in order to make the best possible impression. You never know who might see the photograph and how that might determine your fate.

Epilogue:
A Normal Life

A few months after we came to New York, Willy went to see Schwabach, Inc., an import-export firm with offices all over the world for whom he had worked briefly before the war. We had been living at the Marseilles Hotel on 103d Street and Broadway in a room paid for by the American Jewish Joint Distribution Committee, a Jewish charity, but now our money was running out, and he had to get a job.

On the strength of his prewar connections, Willy got an interview with the head of the import division in its downtown office. Mr. Sachsel had a corner suite with a view of Wall Street. He was wearing the blue striped vest of his three-piece suit, and his broad red silk tie was loosened. He had his feet up on the desk and kept them there during the meeting. After the usual introductions, Sachsel launched himself into an analysis of the postwar situation. He told Willy, "There was hardly any flour to make bread, much less to bake cakes," but before he could tell him that there were no jobs for penniless immigrants who spoke broken English, Willy proposed a deal.

"Mr. Sachsel, I understand you perfectly, and I don't want a piece of your cake. Let us bake a cake together. I'm not looking for a job. You don't have to pay me a thing. Give me a desk in a corner and let me look through the inquiries you usually throw out. If I find a business, you'll pay me a commission. In the meantime, no salary. Okay?"

Sachsel laughed at Willy's chutzpah, but agreed to the arrangement. Willy would look through the discarded mail that was coming in from all over the world to see if he could find a deal worthy of pursuing. Should the business lead somewhere, only then would he make some money. "Very simple," Willy added as they shook hands. The next day in a dusty corner of the mail room he started poring over bins of discarded inquiries, mostly scams or crackpot schemes intended to make a buck after the war.

Then one day in the spring of 1948, Willy found a letter from Mitsubishi, a Japanese sewing machine company. It was written in the brave and improbable English of postwar Japan. After many "honorables" and "we importuning yous," the bottom line was that the company was offering a straight-stitch head for about $25. Willy had no idea what a sewing machine cost. The only sewing machine he had been familiar with before the war was made by Necchi, an Italian Jewish firm, with which his father had been in contact, but the price seemed low, and Willy smelled a business possibility.

Through the Yellow Pages he located Ike Goldstein, a sewing machine wholesaler in Brooklyn, and called him, explaining the situation but not telling him the price of the Japanese head.

"So, how much do you pay for a White or Singer straight-stitch head?" Willy got to the point.

"About $100. Retails for $130, $150."

"One hundred dollars?" Now Willy's curiosity was piqued. "If I send you a Japanese sample, will you tell me what it's worth?"

"Japanese? Are you kidding?" said the gruff voice on the other end. "They just make toys that turn into trash. Go ahead, send it. I'll tell you."

By July, Willy received a package from Japan. When he opened it he got a delicate whiff of crushed apples from the packing material, but inside he found a black straight-stitch electric sewing machine with the trademark "Mitsubishi" embossed in gold letters on its body. He called Ike Goldstein, and the next day he took the train out to Brooklyn to see the wholesaler.

New York in July can be steamier and hotter than Calcutta. Willy had taken off his jacket and tie by the time he got to Ike's warehouse. The place was dusty, suffocating in the heat, and busy, with men loading and unloading crates of merchandise. Willy was sent out back, where Ike was waiting for him in his office.

He was a big, fleshy, hirsute guy with curly steel-gray hair. He sat in his undershirt under a fan, his chair tilted backward against the wall. His arms were flung back behind him, allowing his hands to cradle his massive head. He didn't bother to get up when Willy walked in. Instead he rocked forward, stretching his hand out, and asked as they shook hands, "'Melson'? What kind of a name is that?"

"It's a Jewish name," Willy said, placing his package on Ike's desk. "It comes from 'Mendelsohn.'"

"So why don't you call yourself that? I thought you were a Swede with a funny accent when I heard you over the phone."

"I started calling myself Melson before the war in Poland. It's a long story."

"You survived Hitler?"

"Yes."

"You have a family?"

"Yes."

"You're one of the lucky ones I guess. So is this the Japanese head you were telling me about?"

"That's right." The two men stood up and unwrapped the machine from its casing. "I can see it's crap already," said Ike as he turned the black sewing machine over a few times. "But I'll have one of my girls stick a spool in it and test it. Stay here. I'll be back in a few minutes."

A half hour later, Ike walked back in. "It's shit, just as I suspected. You can use junk like this only for promotions or bait-and-switch gimmicks."

"So how much would you give me for it?" asked Willy.

"No more than $50. Tops, $55 a head."

Right then and there, Willy knew he was back in business.

When Schwabach refused to open a letter of credit for Japanese goods, Willy quit and started State Sewing Machine Corporation with Lazar Gelin, a Jew who had come to the United States from Vilna before the war. Willy had the contacts and Gelin had the money. They started modestly, importing only two hundred machines at first. They sold these to Ike Goldstein and other wholesalers in New York and around the country, and within two years of coming to America, Willy Melson was a success.

First he imported from Mitsubishi, but then he and Gelin decided that Willy would go to Japan as a buyer for State Sewing Machine Corporation to see if he could get better machines at a lower price. Wherever he went in postwar Japan he was greeted like royalty. Large and small industries were starting up everywhere, but they needed markets to sell their products, and here was Willy, an "American" businessman, actually willing to open up letters of credit to purchase their goods.

In the interim we had moved from the refugee shelter at the Marseilles Hotel to a small dingy apartment on 102d Street between Amsterdam and Columbus. While Willy was occupied with business, Nina took care of Richi and me, but she also started to make friends among the small Polish-Jewish community that had settled on the west side of Manhattan. Some people remembered her as the girl who had won beauty pageants in Warsaw and had sung at the Adria before the war. There were parties at apartments on Riverside Drive and West End Avenue. After dinner, Willy and Nina amazed their newfound friends with stories about how we managed to outwit the Gestapo and survive the war on false papers. When Nina would get too emotional and didn't want to talk about it anymore, she'd say, "Get me to a piano or get me a guitar," and she'd sing Polish, French, and Russian songs from before the war.

People would sing along, laugh, cry, and applaud. "Ninochka, sing 'Timelu Lamelu!'" She was a hit, and they loved her.

A few months after we came to New York, Willy and Nina decided that I needed a Jewish education, so they brought me down to the Jewish Center on 86th Street. Rabbi Kaminetsky had a gentle and grave manner that immediately put you at ease, and he had a neat black beard that brought to mind Abraham Lincoln. As he bent down to shake hands with me, he explained that I'd be studying Hebrew, and I'd be going to Sunday school for religious instruction. I nodded agreeably, but something else had riveted my attention: Through his study door and down the hall I could see a gym. Dressed in shorts and sneakers, some boys were laughing and shooting baskets.

"Who are those boys?" I asked the rabbi.

"Oh, they're just kids from the center," he said gently.

"Are they Jews?"

He seemed surprised by the question. "Of course they are," he replied and smiled.

I couldn't explain to him then that, in my mind, most Jews were dead, like the dead bodies in the pictures of the death camps and the dead bodies of my grandparents that I continued to see with my mind's eye. It was a revelation to me that Jews, like other people, could be young and carefree.

A month later Israel declared its independence. Every night Willy, Nina, and I, even Richi, huddled around the radio, listening for reports of the war. New pictures appeared in the papers of Jews, both men and women, rifles in hand, fighting for a homeland. It thrilled me. I wanted to join them, be like them. I begged my parents to let me go, but I was too young. "You must finish fifth grade," my father said.

Meanwhile at the Jewish Center, Rabbi Kaminetsky handed out charity boxes painted with blue and white stripes and the Jewish star. All the kids were supposed to go out and collect money for the Jewish war effort. We lived in a working-class Irish, Puerto Rican, and black neighborhood. There weren't too many Jews or rich people around, but I was out every afternoon after school collecting for Israel.

One day, I walked into an Irish tavern at the corner of 103d and Broadway. White men dressed in jeans and T-shirts were leaning against the bar. The sweet and musty smell of beer, sweat, and cigarette smoke was overpowering.

"For Israel!" I shouted as I walked in, shaking my collection box at the startled patrons. "For Israel."

"Get the fuck out of here, kid, before I cuff you one," snarled the beefy bartender as he grabbed me by the collar and threw me out. But he dropped in a quarter nevertheless.

When I wasn't collecting for Israel, I'd meet up with my fifth grade buddies from PS 179 down on a grassy knoll off Riverside Drive, where every afternoon in the summer we'd play a game of baseball. I had been introduced to the game earlier that spring when they had taken me down to the park. They had handed me a bat and told me to swing at the ball and run to something they called a "base." As the ball, tossed underhanded, slowly careened toward me, I swung at it the way I'd swing at a tennis ball back at Le Rosey. The bat made glancing contact, the ball rolled past the second baseman, my friends applauded, and I had made it to first base. From then on I was hooked on baseball. I became a passionate Dodgers fan, mostly because of Jackie Robinson, and I was well on my way to becoming "Bob—A normal American kid."

As at Le Rosey, the kids at school were curious about my past. They knew about the war and the killing of the Jews. When they asked me about it, during a game of Monopoly at Jimmy Key's house on a rainy Sunday afternoon, I tried to explain as best I could. We had fooled the Nazis by making believe we were Christians, but my grandparents had been killed.

"Why were they killed?" asked Andre Rittenhouse, a tall skinny black kid.

"Because they were Jews," I replied.

The other guys—Bobby Gutter, Peter Rosenbaum (both Jews), and Jimmy Key—nodded wisely.

The next day at school, Jimmy, a short, curly headed Irish kid, came up to me during recess and told me that he had asked his dad about it, and his dad had told him that the Jews were killed because they were all rich bankers. What did my grandfather do? I explained that my grandfather had been a tea taster and a packager of teas.

"A tea taster? What's that?"

"A guy who tastes tea," I replied, not quite knowing what a tea tast-er did. "His clothes smelled of orange pekoe," I added.

"He wasn't a banker?"

"No."

I felt I had a lot more to say, but I didn't even know where to start.

We then ran down to a corner of the yard and picked up on a softball game that was already in progress.

One day in 1949 Willy announced that it was time for us to move. He had heard that all the smart people were not staying in New York. They were going out to the suburbs in Long Island or to Westchester, where for the same money as an apartment cost in New York, you could buy a house, have a plot of land, and live near the ocean. Every weekend that spring and summer, Willy and Nina, with me looking over their shoulders, pored over real estate ads promising four-bedroom colonial, split-level, or ranch-style homes. There'd be drawings of a mom, dad, and some kids having a barbecue in their backyard, with their split-level home in back and their new Chevy parked out in front. It seemed ideal. I was all for it. In the fall of 1950, just as I was about to go into seventh grade at Booker T. Washington Junior High School, we made the move from Manhattan to New Rochelle, a suburb about a half-hour train ride away.

It wasn't a house—Willy said that he didn't want to be that tied down—but it was a spacious new two-bedroom apartment overlooking a garden, just a ten-minute walk from Hudson Park and the Long Island Sound with its beautiful beaches. Although at first I missed my friends back in Manhattan, I had few problems fitting into a new school. I was a pretty good student and athlete, and after a period of adjustment I found my bearings. Willy bought a new car—an Oldsmobile—with MELSON vanity plates, and every morning he'd drive himself to the station, where with many of the other dads of my new schoolmates he'd take the train into the city.

Meanwhile, Nina tried to adjust to her new role of suburban house-wife. She cleaned house, went shopping, and took care of Richi until he went off to kindergarten a year later. She recalled this period as being "one of the happiest of my life," but I should have been aware even then that there was something wrong. Often when I came home from school, I'd find her "resting" in bed. She had a headache or some other undiagnos-able ailment. She missed her friends in Manhattan and complained of feeling isolated. Perhaps she should go out to find a job, she said, but Willy wouldn't hear of it. His little "Ninka" was not suited for the rough-and-tumble of the business world. Anyway he was making enough money that she didn't need to work, and how would it look to his business acquaintances if she did? She took driving lessons so that she could master our new car, and she got her license, but one day when she took us out for a spin she got so flustered at an exit ramp that Willy took the wheel from her. From then on in she was so fearful about getting into an accident that she gave up driving.

Willy and Nina's more "Americanized" Jewish friends in Manhattan suggested that we join a synagogue or a temple in New Rochelle. Perhaps that way my parents could make new acquaintances. "But we're not religious," my mother said. They were told that in America Judaism had been reformed and modernized. There were Reform and Conservative congregations that they would find more congenial. So one sabbath the four of us went to services at a local Reform temple. My mother's verdict was that it left her cold.

"Did you see the men sitting there with their heads uncovered? My father would never set foot in such a place," she said with a grimace.

Willy added impatiently, "It's all *bubemeises,* nonsense," and refused to ever go back. The result was that they never made any friends in New Rochelle and continued with some difficulty to make the trip to see their Manhattan friends.

It didn't help Nina's mood when rumors reached her that my father was having an affair with Mary, one of his secretaries in the office. At first, Willy furiously denied my mother's accusations, but then one day he brought Mary over for dinner. She was a tall, full-breasted, brown-eyed brunette with a ready laugh and a sweet disposition. Willy and Mary sequestered themselves in the kitchen that night, while the rest of us went to bed, because apparently they had a lot of "work"—dictation and so forth— to complete. Then, a few weeks later, to make things easier on everyone, Willy moved Mary into an apartment of her own, two stories above us in the same building! This allowed him to get much more "work" done, he said, and he wouldn't have to stay late in the office now that his personal secretary was so close at hand. Nina and Willy had a few quarrels about Mary, but they were desultory skirmishes.

I worried that my mother hardly protested the arrangement. Where was her sparkle and grit? Why had her courage and spunk deserted her? To tell the truth, such questions only passed through my head, because I had other concerns at the time. I had discovered the world of women and girls, and nearly every waking moment of my life—that is, when I wasn't playing ball—I thought of nothing but sex. "Getting laid," we called it in eighth grade, and that's all my guy friends and I would talk about. I had a crush on one of the cutest girls in class, Connie Blum, who had auburn hair and flashing hazel eyes. When she'd pedal her bicycle in tight short shorts and bare feet and blithely wave to me in the street, my breathing would become so labored that I'd have to sit on the curb just to keep from feeling woozy with desire.

I should have resented Mary, but I didn't. At first I thought of her as another "Riya-from-Prague," but then to my chagrin and confusion, resentment yielded to unrequited yearning, and I denied to myself that my father was cheating on my mother with her.

Willy was making money, but he hated his business. He had learned from his father and his uncles in Stanisławów that only entrepreneurs and industrialists—people who founded companies and made something that others could use—were productive and worthy of emulation. According to this theory all the intermediaries—bankers, advertisers, salesmen, and buyers like him—were "useless parasites." He was disgusted with himself and his job. By 1953 he was forty-six—not old, but not young either, and he felt that it was now or never. If he was going to start his own factory, he had to make a dramatic move.

For five years he had been going out to Japan on business trips, while we waited for him, first in our flat in Manhattan and then in our apartment in New Rochelle. In the spring of 1952, after coming back from one such trip, he announced that he had bought a small plant in Osaka, where he would start assembling his own zig-zag sewing machines—no more middle men, no more State Sewing Machine Corporation. He would sell the Melson machine directly to wholesalers in New York, Europe, and Brazil. He would become a manufacturer like his father, and via Japan, he would finally make it big in America. "You don't know the Japanese," he would say to friends, only half joking. "They're the brightest, most talented, hardest working people in the world. With them I'll conquer the world!"

"Willy," his friends would reply, shaking their heads in disbelief, "now when you go to Japan, you're a big-deal American buyer. The moment you open up an assembly plant of your own, you'll wind up competing with other Japanese manufacturers. You know the market in the States, they know Japan. You'll lose. You're setting yourself up for a big fall." It took another ten years of Herculean effort and ultimate failure to prove them right.

I was fifteen years old, a sophomore in New Rochelle High School. I was doing well in English. We were reading powerful translations of the *Illiad* and the *Odyssey,* which I recalled fondly from my days at Le Rosey. I had made linebacker on the junior varsity football team and had dreams of making varsity my junior year. Although we hadn't done "it" yet, Connie and I were going steady. After college we were going to get married and live in a big house near the beach. We wouldn't do much traveling—"I've had it with moving," I told her—but we'd go often into the city to see the Dodgers play. I hated to leave New Rochelle. We had survived the war. We had just recently become naturalized Americans. We had barely started a normal life. Now Japan? *The end of the world!*

The next thing I knew, Nina, Richi, and I were passengers on the *President Cleveland,* a luxury liner in the middle of the Pacific Ocean. The first few days we were seasick, but then my sorrow about leaving New Rochelle and my anxiety about our new lives in Japan were temporarily set aside by the excitement and awe of sailing the vastness of the ocean at night. I was also busy on board ship interposing myself between Nina and various lechers. One ardent lover was a Filipino with a gold tooth, another was a tall, thin, American Air Force officer with a prominent Adam's apple who had just said good-bye to his wife and kids on the shore at San Francisco. They'd invite Nina to go dancing and then would try to get her into their cabins.

As for Nina, she'd laugh at their efforts, but she relished their attention. My father's affair with Mary was over and done with, and she was looking forward to a new adventure. She was forty-three, a beautiful woman in her prime. "*Vas banque,*" she'd say when I'd ask her about our future. "Willy is right. At times, you have to gamble it all." She'd flash me her cheerfully open and optimistic smile.

Unlike Tokyo, Yokohama, Hiroshima, Nagasaki, and other Japanese cities, Kobe, where we settled, had not been flattened into a pile of rubble by American bombers. Still, so close to the end of the war there was a lot of poverty and misery. Crippled, demobilized Japanese soldiers, still wearing parts of their imperial uniforms, could be seen begging on street corners, and mothers with children in their arms would stop me, their hands out for some change.

We moved into a freshly painted three-bedroom apartment in a brand new building situated in the hills on Yamamotodori, a section of Kobe overlooking the harbor. We had Oba San, a maid who doubled as a cook, and Willy had Hamada San, a chauffeur who picked him up every morning to drive him to the Melson assembly plant in Osaka, about forty-five minutes away. Meanwhile, Richi and I were enrolled in the Marist Brothers School in Suma, a few miles south of Kobe. It was run by an order of Catholic priests who had been expelled from Communist China. Richi went into the first grade, while I went straight into the senior year.

In the morning before going to school, I'd see the city stretched out before me and, beyond that, the port. At exactly 7:00 A.M. the train from Hiroshima would crawl north along the coast like a caterpillar circling a puddle of water. By the time it reached Sannomiya, the main railroad station, I'd be dressed and on my way. From the windows of the train you could see the ocean, and when it pulled into Suma station, we'd pass old Japanese women bowing and clapping in front of a Shinto shrine.

Brother Charles was the headmaster—a gruff, fat, but jolly old German priest from Bavaria. He wouldn't discuss the war when I brought it up in European history class. He insisted that German history had ended with Bismarck. "Hitler? Hitler wasn't even a German. He was an Austrian upstart. There's nothing more to say." I was acutely conscious that Brother Charles was a German and a priest, but for some reason he took a shine to me, and I couldn't help liking him. Marist Brothers had mandatory Bible instruction, but I insisted that as a Jew I wished to be excused, and I was. While my class pored over the Gospels and the crucifixion, I sat in Brother Charles's office and read back issues of *Time* magazine.

At first, everything seemed strange, foreign, and alien. I had fallen into my Wesely swamp, where it was difficult to breathe and my feet were sucked down by deep mud. In the evening when I'd get back from school, I'd put on the U.S. army station. When it played "The Star-Spangled Banner," I'd burst into tears.

However, we Melsons were infinitely adaptable. Within a few months we had established a pattern for ourselves among the small Jewish community in Kobe. Some were Syrian and Iraqi Jews—like the Sassoons who owned our building—whose families had had dealings with the Far East for centuries. There was also a small coterie of Russian, Polish, and Lithuanian Jews—recent arrivals who had survived the war in Japan—plus a few American Jews who were in Japan on business or on official missions. Ironically, it was in Kobe, a million miles from Warsaw, Stanisławów, and New York, that Willy, Nina, Richi, and I joined a synagogue and started going to services, especially at high holidays and for special events like bar and bat mitzvahs.

Again, as at Le Rosey and in New Rochelle, my being a fairly good

athlete helped me to get through and make some friends. I joined the
school softball team, and we played the local Canadian Academy and the
marine base. We'd beat the Canadians, but lose badly to the marines. Af-
terwards, in the evening, some of us would sneak to Shinkaichi, the red-
light district, where we'd meet for beers and ogle the local girls without
daring to make a move.

Meanwhile, Willy's factory was starting to run into trouble. He had
huge expenses and was worried about the future. He needed a big order
to establish his reputation and to make himself credible with American
buyers, most of whom he had known when he had been a buyer himself.
Then he received a call from Ike Goldstein. Ike was flying in from Brooklyn, ready "for a big deal," he had said over the long-distance connection,
so big that he wanted to check things out for himself. This was going to
be the test, because if Ike could be impressed, and if he would place a large
order, the other American buyers would too, and Willy's factory would
thrive.

The day of Ike's arrival, Willy was flushed with excitement. We were
all mobilized into the effort of charming our client from Brooklyn and
bringing him around. Nina, Richi, and I listened attentively in the backseat of the car, while Willy sat up in front next to Hamada and turned
around to lecture us on our way out to the airport to greet our American
savior. "Let him see that he's not dealing with a little Japanese, *pisschele*,
piss-pot, parts maker, but with a serious manufacturer," said Willy as he
leaned over into the backseat, adjusted my tie, and smoothed Richi's
unruly cowlick. "Goldstein is a Jew, and he's got to understand that we're
a Jewish family, survivors of Hitler, whose livelihood depends on him,"
Willy explained, allowing a note of self-righteousness to creep into his
voice.

Ike looked exhausted and disheveled after his thirty-six-hour flight
from New York, with stops in San Francisco, Hawaii, and Guam. He was
a big man with a leonine head and wore a seersucker suit with sweat
stains at the armpits. He was carrying a briefcase and a rolled-up black
umbrella. When he saw us he waved wanly. Willy crossed over to him
and pumped his hand a bit too energetically, I thought. Nina leaned over
to give him a peck on the cheek, while Richi and I hung back. "Come,
come," said Willy. "You boys remember Mr. Goldstein. Ike, come and say
hello." Only then did Richi and I shake hands with our visitor, who
seemed confused and distracted. Not a good sign, I thought. We're being
too friendly, and he's embarrassed by it all.

The next day, Willy and Ike drove to the assembly plant and let me tag along. The building, a sprawling one-story structure located on about a half acre, was in an industrial zone of Osaka. By the front entrance were Willy's offices, including a separate office for Mitzi, a delicate but perky young Japanese woman who was his head secretary and translator. She was Westernized enough not to cover her mouth when she smiled, but nevertheless she giggled almost uncontrollably when she was introduced to "this most important buyer from America." Behind Willy's offices was a large low-ceilinged hall. Under flickering neon lights sixty workers dressed in identical cotton shirts with the Melson logo inscribed on their backs sat or stood at evenly spaced workbenches. Here the Melson machines were in various stages of assembly and testing before being shipped out to customers.

After a couple of hours of talking to the workers and handling the machines, Ike seemed impressed, and Willy felt vindicated. He half expected that Ike would place an order with him right after lunch on the same day, but Ike held back. He was going to stay a week in Japan, he explained. He needed to fly up to Tokyo to check out some other outfits. "As long as I'm here I've got to look over the competition," he said, giving Willy a playful punch on the shoulder.

"Sure, Sure," replied Willy, laughing. He was disappointed, but still confident. He was certain that the Melson machine, especially the zig-zag automatic, was a good product at a fair price. He wasn't afraid of the Japanese competition.

The night before Ike's departure for Tokyo, Oba San stayed with Richi, while I came along as Willy and Nina took Ike to see the sights and nightlife of Kobe. Most of the nightclubs were raunchy affairs overrun by young American marines from the base nearby and by sailors of every nationality who were docked off shore. Their needs were simple: They wanted to get drunk and get laid. When they couldn't get either, they'd get into a fight. Although I hadn't been with a girl yet, I had been in such places on lone expeditions, fascinated by the ready sexuality but afraid of it as well. So I was relieved when Willy and Nina took Ike to the Club Rosa, a more expensive, more tastefully decorated, and slightly more sedate dive frequented by marine officers, airline pilots, and wealthy foreign businessmen.

We got a table in back, and after a few drinks, a pretty bar girl, her hair in a ponytail, came over and pulled up a chair next to Ike; then she placed a hand on his knee and started to flirt with him. At first he looked flushed and slightly dazed as the girl whispered things in his ear. After a floor show of half-clad girls mouthing lyrics and dancing to American pop songs, Willy stood up and announced that we were going home.

"You can stay," he said to Ike. "She'll come to your hotel if you want her to."

"I'll call you from Tokyo next week," said Ike, staring at his companion while waving good-bye to us.

As I glanced back before we left the club, I could see Ike and the girl in intense head-to-head conversation. They were giggling and seemed to be hatching a conspiracy.

A week later Willy came home from the office. He was unusually pale and looked shocked. He explained that he had phoned Ike at the Imperial Palace Hotel in Tokyo earlier that day and had asked him point-blank about placing an order. Ike had hesitated, but then said that he was not going to place an order with us. He had found a cheaper zig-zag automatic machine and better financing with one of Willy's Japanese competitors in Tokyo.

"But Ike, I thought we were friends," said Willy plaintively, not quite knowing what to say.

"We are," said Ike. "But friendship is one thing, and business is another. Business is business."

The year was 1954. I was sent to prep school in Boston, so as to be able to get into MIT. "You're going to become a mechanical engineer," said Willy at the Osaka airport as we were saying good-bye. "After college we'll work together at the factory. I'll take care of the business end, while you handle the technical stuff." I had no desire to become a mechanical engineer or to work with my father, but at seventeen I had no other plans. I vaguely wanted to become another Robert J. Oppenheimer and build an even more powerful H-bomb or become an actor or become a playwright or hitchhike across America or join the Air Force. So I went along with his vision, and a year later my grades were barely good enough to get me admitted to MIT. "The most prestigious engineering school in the world," Willy had said with great pride. These were nearly the identical words he had used in describing Le Rosey.

It was in 1956, the start of my sophomore year, that I received a telegram from Willy. The gist was that the factory was in deep trouble and that he couldn't afford to support me or to pay my bills at school. A letter would follow. The letter repeated the bad news, but it tried to be optimistic and upbeat as well. Richi was doing well in school. Nina had organized an evening of entertainment at the Kobe Country Club, and as expected she was a big hit. Meanwhile the sewing machine business was barely limping along, but Willy had started an exciting new venture: miniaturized portable radios. Would I help? He was going to send me a box of samples that I could show to outfits in New York.

Some weeks later I received a small crate from Japan. Inside were five portable radios, attractively housed in leather-bound cases in different shades of tan, brown, and black, with the Melson imprint embossed in gold. I plugged them in and then tested them on batteries and they sounded fine. How did he manage to start a radio assembly plant? I wondered. Whatever happened to the sewing machine business? Over the years I had learned not to question and to expect the extraordinary.

I had very little aptitude for science, and the only reason I survived at MIT was because the school had a major in literature and humanities, where those like me could find a refuge from the relentlessness of organic chemistry, vector analysis, and differential equations. I was barely hanging on to my scholarship and student loans that made attendance possible, but I tried to respond to Willy's appeal, and every week I spent a few days in New York trying to sell his radios.

After a few months of sleeping in flea-bag hotels around Times Square and schlepping my wares to various buyers in Manhattan, I ran into Harry Lefkowitz, the owner of an electronics emporium on Broadway. Harry was a tall, slim, funny guy with a rueful smile and an ironic sense of humor. I liked him immediately. He liked me too, liked the radios, and was impressed that I had come down from MIT. Somehow the connection with "The Institute" provided the Melson radios with an aura of technological validation. We met in his office with a few of his salesmen. They were intrigued with Japanese-made electronics, and when I explained that some of the financing could be arranged through Daichibussan, a Japanese multinational firm, a deal was in the making. After the meeting Harry took me aside and told me that he would be interested in starting small. "No more than twenty thousand units" the first year, he said. I didn't blink. Twenty thousand units! Was he kidding? It would make us a pile of money and save Willy's business. However, Harry explained, he had to check us out. One of his best friends happened to be in Japan on a buying trip, and Harry would wire him to take a look at the Melson radio assembly plant. Did I have any objections?

"Absolutely not," I replied. "You must." I had the vision that Willy's sewing machine factory had by some miracle been converted into a radio assembly plant and that Harry's friend would be duly impressed. We shook hands on the deal. I was to return next week to draw up the papers. I rushed back to my room at the hotel and called Willy long distance. Over a staticky connection I explained the situation. He sounded very excited and assured me that all would be well.

"You're quite the businessman," he said. These were the first words of genuine praise I had ever heard from him. When I set down the phone I was enveloped in a feeling of mission-accomplished-family-fortune-rescued-father's-regard-justly-earned. I felt ten feet tall.

The next week I showed up at Harry's store exactly as we had agreed. I had expected him to be in his office on the second floor, not in the showroom, but there he was, speaking to a customer. When he looked up he barely acknowledged me. I had a sinking feeling that something was terribly wrong, but I kept the smile pasted on my face and tried to exude the *vas banque* impression I had learned from Nina. After a few minutes Harry came over. He looked like somebody had just died and wouldn't even shake hands. He didn't waste time on preliminaries.

"There is no Melson factory in Osaka, Bob. Your father went bankrupt last year. The radio business is a fraud."

"What do you mean? What about the radios? You said you liked the way they looked and sounded." I tried to appear confident, but instead I could hear my voice crack and turn squeaky.

"He took Hitachi brand radios and placed them in Melson cases. The only thing that's his is his name. You must have known about that . . ."

"I knew no such thing. What about the financing we can provide you with?"

"That too is bullshit. Who do you think you're kidding? Never kid a kidder, kid. Leave my store and take it easy." With that he spun on his heel and went to look after another customer.

I felt as if the building had collapsed around me, and I was buried under a ton of bricks and electronic gadgets. The next day when I got back to MIT, I was called into the dean's office. I had lost my scholarship and was going to be put on probation for skipping classes and failing most of my tests. I explained that I had tried to rescue my father's business from financial ruin, that I couldn't abandon my family. But he looked at me with dull, uncomprehending eyes, as if I were a being from a foreign galaxy, which I suppose I was.

It took a while, but later that term I wrote my parents a letter saying that I was sorry, but I simply couldn't continue going to college while trying to save Willy's business. I was on the verge of flunking out, and what good would that do? My mother answered a few weeks later. She said that I should stick to my studies, but I should know that Willy had had some kind of nervous breakdown. He had momentarily lost his hearing and his power of speech and was confined to the house. It wasn't a stroke, and the doctor thought it was a condition from which he would soon recover. Meanwhile they still had a little money saved up and had many good friends who were being very helpful. Mr. Sassoon, the landlord, was kind enough to let them stay in the apartment without having to pay rent. I should not worry and should get on with my life.

I sat on my bed in my ten-dollar-a-week boarding room staring at my mother's letter. I felt as if I had abandoned my parents to their fate, but I wouldn't resume trying to sell my father's radios or quit school to help them. In 1959, the year I finally graduated from MIT, I received a telegram from Tadzo and Wanda that Pani Marylka had died of cancer. I stared dully at the words, but I couldn't even weep. A few weeks later my hair began to fall out in clumps. When I asked a dermatologist about it he said it might be a reaction to grief. I didn't know what he was talking about.

In the early spring of 1963, I received a letter from my mother saying that they were planning to return to America. They were so broke that their friends in the Kobe synagogue had passed the hat to finance their trip, she said. But all was not doom and gloom, Nina continued. Willy had fully recovered and was his old self, and Richi had been accepted at MIT! With the help of a scholarship and student loans, she hoped that he would be able to attend.

Meanwhile I had clung to MIT as if it were a raft in a stormy sea. After barely graduating, I managed to get admitted into the Ph.D. program in political science. It was the early sixties, Jack Kennedy was president, and Martin Luther King was leading the struggle for black liberation. Like so many others of my generation, I became caught up in the idealism of the moment and studied African politics out of a wish to do my small part in reaching out to the "Third World." I was also determined to graduate with a doctorate in order to prove that we Melsons had made it in America. The title and name "Doctor Melson" sounded almost as weighty as "Count Zamojski."

One of the first things I noticed about Willy when he got off the train in South Station was that he wore white socks with black shoes. I remembered him as a stylish dresser, nearly a dandy, a person who had taken great care with his appearance. When we had first come to New York, as soon as he could afford it, he had worn tailor-made or Hickey-Freeman clothes and had purchased British handcrafted shoes. While I was growing up we had not done many father-and-son things together except that he had enjoyed taking me along when he went shopping for clothes, and he had taught me the rudiments of what he considered to be good taste. One cardinal rule, almost too obvious to need explaining, he explained, was that the color of one's socks should always match or blend with the color of one's shoes. Argyle socks were a "Goyish" affectation, and white socks with black shoes were totally beyond the pale, a sure sign of a total lack of taste, he had said with contempt. And here he was energetically striding toward me after an eight-year separation, wearing white socks with cheap black shoes.

He must have let go of everything, I thought even as we embraced. My mother too seemed drastically changed. In 1963, she was only fifty-one, not old by any means, and yet she moved slowly, her face was puffy, and despite her tears of joy at seeing me, her animation seemed forced. It was as if she was in the grip of some disease that was sapping her of affect. The good news was Richi. He was totally unrecognizable. When I had last seen him he had been a nine-year-old skinny little boy. He had grown into a handsome, dark-haired, blue-eyed, strapping seventeen year old, over six feet tall, who had to bend down to kiss his older brother. Soon we bonded, exchanging our versions of Willy and Nina stories until all hours of the night.

I felt deeply moved to see them again after so many years, but I also felt apprehensive about what was expected of me. I had no money saved. I was studying for the doctoral prelims and had a small stipend that allowed me to survive as a graduate student. I was willing to share that with my family, but I was not willing to abandon my studies in order to support them. Moreover, I was determined to restart our relationships on a new footing. I would no longer be bullied by Willy, nor would I be Nina's "little confidant."

In the taxi taking us to the rooming house on Beacon Street, overlooking the Charles River, where I had rented a couple of rooms for them, my mother turned to me in the backseat and said, "Doesn't Willy look pale? I'm so worried about his health and his state of mind . . ." Before she could continue, I interrupted her and said, "*Mamusiu,* before you go on—let's not gossip about Willy anymore." I had said that with a smile, almost in jest, but she drew back as if I had slapped her and said nothing more for the remainder of the ride.

I had expected Willy and Nina to settle either in the Boston area or in New York, but they had other plans. After Richi entered MIT in the fall, they flew to Germany to hire a lawyer and to pursue their court case for reparations. Where they had found the money for the trip was a mystery. They returned two years later and moved next door to my brother in Cambridge. Soon after, my mother sank into a deep depression.

It got so bad that she stopped speaking and would hardly move. Only electroshock therapy brought her around, but the treatment had destroyed her recent memory and left her a vague, trembling, and shaky version of her former self. Years later, when I brought her grandchildren around and she could talk about the past, some of her sparkle would return, but I felt nothing but sorrow that I could never introduce my wife and children to the luminous and effervescent Nina that I remembered so clearly.

Meanwhile, Willy just barely managed to keep afloat financially. He still worked on various schemes and businesses, but the massive failure in Japan had taken its toll. Nothing ever quite panned out. For a while he sold religious bric-a-brac to Catholic churches around the Boston area, but he gave that up as too depressing for a Jew. He then tried to manage a medical clinic with my brother, but it failed because they had no experience at that kind of work. Before he died he spoke of moving to San Diego, where it was warm and sunny the year round and where he would get Hollywood money for what he called "an action center." The idea was to create a town devoted to games of chance and fantasy where whole families could come for days on end for fun and entertainment.

At about the same time that my parents returned from Japan, my life had improved dramatically. I passed my prelims in the fall of 1963 and received a grant to do research in Nigeria, but best of all I met Gail Freedman. One afternoon, I had been sitting at a desk in the far end of Widener Library at Harvard when I, and everyone else in the place, looked up to see a tall, sweet-faced, buxom young woman with a pile of frizzy hair on top of her head come striding in. In her wake came a girl who took my breath away. She was slender, of medium height, and moved with the easy grace of a dancer. Her multicolored billowing Mexican skirt only accentuated the liquid sway of her hips. Her heart-shaped face was framed by a mass of brown ringlets and curls. She was carrying a pile of books that she used unsuccessfully to hide her face and conceal an embarrassed but conspiratorial laugh.

My God, I thought, this girl is like a spring day in the fall, and I fell instantly in love with her without even knowing her name. I would see her in the library from time to time, but I didn't have the courage to approach her. What if she rejected me? The thought was too hard to bear. Finally I was introduced to her through a mutual acquaintance, and that evening I called.

"Hi. My name is Robert Melson. We met at Barclay's Burgers this afternoon."

"Yes?"

"Johnny Rubenstein introduced us."

"Oh, yes. I remember."

"Would you be interested in going out with me sometime?"

"Sure."

"How about sometime next week?"

"Okay."

"How about this week?"

"Why not?"

"How about right now?

"Okay," she laughed.

"Let's meet at the Pamplona, the cafe, in about a half hour."

"Okay."

I had called on a Thursday, late in the week, and, given the prevailing mores, I expected her to refuse a date until a week later (a girl didn't want to appear too eager for a date). Instead, she had accepted to meet me on the very day I called. This girl wasn't playing games. I was impressed by her assurance.

We met. We ordered coffee. I was in a daze—talked all sorts of nonsense about Camus and Doris Lessing, all to impress her. She didn't say much but laughed a lot. Then in the course of the conversation it turned out that she had recently returned from a year of living on a kibbutz in Israel. She spoke fluent Hebrew. Her mother was a Hebrew teacher who had come from a long line of Lithuanian rabbis. The tall, splendid girl I had first seen her with in the library was her friend, Elayne. Before attending college, she and Elayne and their friends Judy and Susie had volunteered to work for a year at Sde Boker in the Negev Desert. There she had met David Ben-Gurion and Moshe Dayan. When I asked her about Israel's prospects for survival, she said she wasn't worried. Israel was strong and dynamic, and everyone was full of hope. Not only was she beautiful and her smile melted my heart but she also carried her Jewishness with a grace and a natural ease that I envied and admired.

A few months later, before I left, I asked her if she would join me in Nigeria. She said yes, and she did. In 1964 we were married by a Yoruba judge in the Ibadan city hall, which doubled as a jail. As we entered the building a group of prisoners, one chained to the other, was being brought in. "What are you here for, man?" they asked me.

"We're getting married," I replied.

"Ah, marriage," they laughed. "You're in more trouble than we are! Good luck then!"

A few days later some Israeli acquaintances, mostly engineers who were working on the Ibadan water works, surprised us by organizing a Jewish wedding. They built us a *chuppa,* and under the immense, star-studded African night we made our vows. I crushed the traditional wine glass, which for me symbolized my former life. Life with Gail was going to be a new beginning, and it was.

For us, the interlude in Nigeria had been a happy time, but it wasn't so for the country. A year after Gail and I returned to America, the Biafran civil war broke out and more than a million people, some of whom we had known, were killed or starved to death.

More than twenty years and two children later, Gail and I were both teaching at Purdue University in Indiana, while Sara and Josh were in college out of state. By then both my parents had died, and I was worried about news from Brazil. Wanda had developed breast cancer, and Tadzo had a heart condition. They would both pass away in the next three years. I was also preoccupied with a book that compared the destruction of the European Jews to other mass destructions, such as the massacres that had occurred in Nigeria during the Biafran civil war and the Armenian Genocide. In retrospect, I see it as part of an inchoate project to find my Jewish roots and come to grips with the experience of genocide.

That spring my ruminations were interrupted by exciting news from Gail. She had been invited to attend a conference in Japan. She had heard so much about it from me, would I come along? My reaction was ambivalent. On the one hand I wanted to be with her and to see what had happened to Japan in the last thirty-four years. On the other hand, I thought of my father and the humiliating failure he had experienced there, a failure that must have contributed to my mother's later depression. And I still felt a burning anger when I thought of him.

On the long list of my grievances against Willy—at the top of which was his affair with Riya and his humiliation of my mother during the war and after—was his uprooting us from America and taking us to Japan. Why had he done it? He had survived the war and had made it to New York, to the very place he had dreamed about for years. He had started a successful business, Nina had made friends in Manhattan, and Richi and I were on our way to becoming American kids. We were on the brink of resuming a normal life—or what after the war could pass for a normal life—but then he had destroyed it all like a child wiping out a sand castle on a beach.

Why did he transplant us to an alien land where we didn't speak the language, had no friends, and had no future? What was the attraction of

Japan, especially since any child could see that competing with Japanese manufacturers on their home turf was doomed to failure? And what about Nina? In New Rochelle, she was already starting to feel the melancholy that would paralyze her years later. Willy could not be blamed for failing to recognize the onset of her serious depression, but how would moving her to Japan, after all she had been through, help her mood? I was so angry that, not for the first time, I thought of changing my name back to Mendelsohn. It would take me back to my Jewish roots and cut my ties to him. What else but memories of broken dreams would I find there? I asked myself.

"Toward the end Willy and Nina were so broke that they had to pass the hat around to return to America," I said to Gail, not making any sense.

"I know. You told me that already," she responded impatiently and urged me nevertheless to come with her.

Finally I went, but halfheartedly. I couldn't share in Gail's enthusiasm about the efficient exoticism of Tokyo. I hated its lack of open space and crowdedness. The one time we tried to get on the subway, it became so jam-packed full of people that I felt suffocated and elbowed myself out in a panic. Kyoto in July, however, was splendid, just as the tourist brochures had promised. I recalled that many years before, Willy, Nina, Richi, and I had lunch on the rooftop restaurant of the Kyoto Hotel, an elegant modern structure, with a view of the ancient city.

I was surprised that so many years later, the hotel was still there and so was the restaurant. When I explained to the headwaiter, a surprisingly tall young fellow, that years ago I had come there as a teenager, he allowed us to cross the dining room and take in the view of the old city from the picture window. In the distance against the green hills and through the delicate mist, Gail and I could make out some of the glorious ancient Zen temples we had visited earlier, but when I tried to remember what it had been like with my parents and my brother years before, I drew a blank. Did we stand by this window? Where had our table been? What did we order? What did we look like? How did we feel? I had been there in the same room years ago; presumably I had stood in the same place, but no associations came to mind. Instead of being flooded by memories I was left with a feeling of emptiness.

When we arrived in Kobe from Kyoto it was already 4:00 P.M. A light drizzle was falling on the city. My first impression after so many years was that everything, including the landscape, had changed. From the train the mountains to the west and the Inland Sea to the east seemed familiar, but the city that lay between them and before us was a mystery. I had left it as a quaint Asiatic place full of delicate wooden houses, packed close together, creating a maze of alleys. Many of the streets were covered in cobblestones, and there were open sewers on each side that ran down the mountains like muddy streams in the rainy season. I recalled that years ago I had been startled to see a middle-aged man peeing at the side of one of these sewers while his dutiful wife, dressed in a crimson kimono, had held a gigantic black umbrella over his head.

But the Kobe I remembered was gone. In its place was a prosperous, shiny, modern city. Sleepy old Sannomiya station, where Richi and I used to take the train to school in Suma years ago, was surrounded by massive glass and steel towers, shopping malls, clubs, cafes, and restaurants. A computer-guided electric train connected the station to a manufactured island called Portopia. I was told that Mt. Rokko, where we used to go on picnics in the spring, had been leveled at the cost of over a billion dollars in order to make a landfill for the island. Even as dusk was falling further up the mountains, the bright neon lights suffused the city and created a sense of synthetic daytime where evening and night should have been. After checking our bags at the hotel near the station, Gail and I set off in the direction of my old home. I was not certain that I could find my way back.

I knew that we had lived off Toa Road up the hill on Yamamotodori, but I could hardly identify the street. In the past ours had been the only European apartment building towering over the rest; now our old neighborhood had been cleared out as if by a giant crane, and in its place stood new multistoried office and apartment buildings constructed in the international, nondescript modern style. I had the sense that whole new streets had been laid over alleys where my little brother had played and that I had used as shortcuts on my way to school or to downtown Kobe.

We had been meandering through the streets for more than an hour, and we were getting tired and hungry, when I passed by a small, three-storied, decrepit old building with peeling paint and cracking walls that at first seemed abandoned. Its walls were covered with ivy and the garden in front was overgrown with weeds. As we took the path toward the entryway, I could see a shaft of light coming from the apartment on the first floor.

"This is it!" I announced to Gail as if I were presenting her with Tara.

"Are you sure?" she asked dubiously, taking my arm as we opened the door and walked into the lobby.

I was pretty sure, but not certain. As we entered the lobby, to my right I saw that the door to the first-floor apartment was open and that the space had been converted into some kind of showroom for women's handbags and accessories. A Japanese female clerk came out for a second, looked us over quizzically, and disappeared back into the showroom. I turned to Gail and motioned that we should go upstairs to the second floor, where years ago, it seemed to me, I had once lived.

I paused in front of our old apartment door and examined a copper plaque fixed to the doorpost. It was in Japanese, but I gathered that our old apartment had been converted into some kind of office or business space. Just to make sure I knocked loudly on the door, but there was no answer. Some childish part of me had half expected that Oba San, our old maid, would open the door and that I would see my father right behind her. He would be wearing a *yucata,* a light cotton Japanese robe, while sitting in his favorite easy chair. Upon seeing me he would set down his copy of *Fortune* magazine, remove his reading glasses, run his hands through his sparse black hair, dyed out of vanity. He'd rise and exclaim: "Ninka, Bobi is here!"

From the back of the apartment where the kitchen was, I'd hear my mother's voice crying out, "Bobi!" Crossing the threshold, my father would embrace me, rubbing his bristles against my face and suffusing me in a cloud of his sweat and Yardley's cologne. Then my mother would appear behind him, smiling her open-faced golden smile, her arms stretched out to me.

"No one is here." I stated the obvious, turning to Gail and avoiding her perplexed look.

We then retreated down the dusty stairs. When we reached the first-floor lobby, from out of the depths of the showroom, appeared a rumpled, middle-aged fellow with a bushy head of red hair. He was wearing a white shirt open at the neck, and his black pants sagged under his protruding belly. At first I thought he was an Arab, but then I noticed he was wearing a yarmulke.

"Who are you and what are you doing here?" he asked in English with a heavy Israeli accent, deep suspicion giving his question an edge.

"What are we doing?" I almost burst out laughing. "Who are you and what are you doing here?" I answered him in Hebrew, a language I had studied on my way to my Jewish self over the years.

When he heard the Hebrew, he relaxed somewhat. "My name is Yossi Djemal. I live in Jerusalem, but I have business in Japan," he said looking both perplexed and vaguely amused. "I own the building and this showroom, but who are you, and what do you want? Business hours start at nine tomorrow morning. We're closed."

I realized that we must have appeared as strange to him as he did to us. So I changed my tone of voice, making it more gentle and less confrontational. "My name is Robert Melson. Thirty-four years ago I lived here with my family," I said in English and pointed to the second floor. "My father, Willy, was in business in Osaka. My mother's name was Nina. I had a little brother, Richi, who was a student at the Marist Brothers school. This is my wife, Gila." I used Gail's Hebrew name to ingratiate myself further and impress him with our common Jewishness, our common fate.

Stroking his chin, Yossi looked me over quizzically, almost as if he were sizing me up for a fitting: "Melson? Melson? Your name is Melson?" he murmured. Then, without explanation, he passed Gail and me and crossed to the other side of the lobby, where we could see bulky outlines of mailboxes covered over by posters and flyers. He tore at the paper like a dog digging up dirt searching for a bone until the mailboxes were clear. Then he waved us over and proudly pointed to the second mailbox from the right. When I looked closely I could see with dazzling clarity that the name MELSON had been chiseled into the wood.

For a moment Gail and I stood still. I felt stunned as if by some apparition: decades after I had lived here, and eight years after his death, the name on the mailbox radiated my father's living presence. In my mind's eye I could see him chiseling his name into the wood of the nameplate on the mailbox. Subsequent tenants of our apartment would have had to insert their names over our own, but as long as the building stood, MELSON would remain to tell the tale that we had been the original occupants. Gail, who was thinking more clearly than I, snapped a picture of the name to verify the moment.

"Yes, that's it. That's us," I said in a tremulous voice.

"It's been here all this time," said Yossi, shaking his head. "I've often wondered, who was this 'Melson'?"

We then reminisced about friends of my parents. Yossi had heard of a few of them. Incredibly, one or two were still alive, and I made a mental note to visit them before we left Japan. As Gail and I were about to leave, Yossi pulled a dollar from his wallet: "It's for the trip," he whispered and looked down, shyness creeping into his voice for the first time. "When you get home don't forget to donate the money to charity, and it will bring you mazal tov, good luck."

I stuck the dollar in my wallet. We embraced, and then Gail and I descended the hill back to our hotel.

———————

Two days later, as we were flying home across the Pacific, with Gail dozing beside me, I thought about "my return to Japan," as we called it, and contrasted it with a trip to Warsaw we had taken years ago on our way back from Nigeria. We had stood at the edge of what once had been the ghetto, next to the gigantic heroic statue commemorating the Warsaw ghetto uprising of Passover 1943, but the moment had left me cold and bereft. I had been looking for my mother's old neighborhood, my birthplace, Nowolipki and Prosta Streets, and the dense, bustling area bursting with life. Instead I found row upon row of apartment blocks built in the dull, uniform, and oppressive style favored by the Stalinists. It was midmorning, but the neighborhood seemed deserted. In other parts of Warsaw, the Adria—the club where my mother had sung—was gone, and so was Gajewski, the coffee shop where Stefcia and Nacia had met for coffee and cake, and so were all the people who had made Warsaw alive in my thoughts. What I had experienced wasn't even a pale reflection of the past, it was its negation. I couldn't wait to get away from what seemed a gigantic desecrated graveyard.

Kobe had been different. It too had been transformed, not by mass murder, but by time, and yet through Yossi and his discovery of MELSON I had been put back in touch with my father. It was Willy's version of "Rosebud." I still didn't understand why he had dragged us to Japan, but surely part of it was that after the war Willy couldn't settle down to a "normal life." For some reason he kept on running and living on false papers after the war, as if in motion he could find safety. He must have feared that settling down and staying put was the equivalent of being identified and getting arrested, and so he had fled to Kobe.

And in some strange way, until his business failed, Kobe itself must have seemed like a sanctuary, a Japanese version of prewar Stanisławów, where the local peasants didn't hate Jews. Going to Kobe and starting a factory was Willy's way of coming home, resurrecting the Mendelsohn Brothers factory, and becoming what Julius Mendelsohn always had wanted him to be, an industrialist, a serious person. He did it to impress Julius, I thought.

Back home in Indiana, I developed our photos and was relieved to see that the picture of MELSON had come out quite clearly. The name still shouted out Willy's insistence to be noticed and to leave his mark. In the past, when I was retracing my way back to my Jewish self, I had thought of changing my name to its original, Mendelsohn, but now I decided that he had named me "Robert Melson," and "Robert Melson" I would remain. I felt relieved by the decision and hoped that wherever he was he would think well of me for it. As for Yossi, I don't know. Leib, my Hasidic grandfather, would have said that Yossi had been an angel—an intermediary between those who are still here and those who are gone.

APPENDIX: DOCUMENTS

Below are photos and translations of Jan Zamojski's and Bogusław Marian Zamojski's birth certificates. These were among the false
papers that saved our lives. I found the documents among my mother's
possessions after she died, but I failed to find her false birth certificate.
By simple inspection, one can see that Nina first impersonated Janina Zamojska and got the false papers on November 5, 1941.

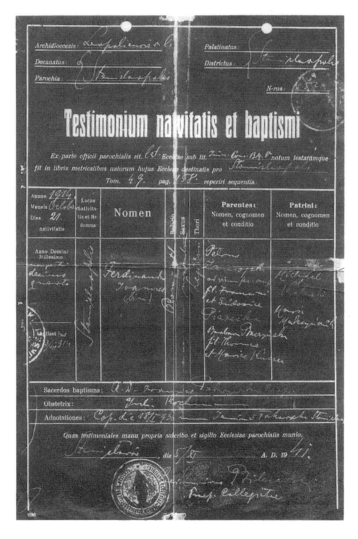

TRADUCTION DU LATIN.

Archidiocèse de Lwow. Doyennat et Paroisse de Stanisławów.
Palatinat et District de Stanisławów. Nr. 652. - - - - - -
CERTIFICAT DE NAISSANCE ET DE BAPTÊME. L'Office Paroissial du
rite latin, de l'Eglise B.V.V. certifie que, dans les registres
de naissance de cette Eglise, destinés pour Stanisławów, tome
49, page 178, est inscrit ce qui suit : - - - - - - - - - -
Année 1914, Mois Octobre, Jour de naissance 21. Année de grâces
mil neuf cent quatorze. Baptisé le 23.10.1914. Lieu de naissance
et Nr. de la maison: Stanisławów. Nom : Ferdinand-Jan /binom/
Religion : catholique romaine. Sexe : masculin. Origine : légi-
time. Nom, prénom et état des parents : Piotr ZAMOJSKI, fils de
Franciszek et de Eudozia PIASECKA - Barbara BARCZYNSKA, fille
de Tomasz et de Maria KUCZER. Nom, prénom et état des parrain et
marraine · Michał KAŁUSKI et Maria MAKSYMINCZUK. Prêtre bapti-
sant : POKRYWKA. Sage-femme : illisible. Remarques : Cet extrait
a été retiré par Janina TOKARSKA. Je signe le présent certificat
de ma propre main et je le munis du Sceau de la Paroisse. - - -
Stanisławów, le 5.XI.1941. /-/ Kazimierz BILCZEWSKI. Sceau de
la paroisse de Stanisławów. - - - - - - - - - - - - - - - - -

Nr. 238.

Le Consulat de Pologne à Bruxelles
certifie la présente traduction conforme à
l'original fait en langue latine.

Bruxelles, le 2 Octobre 1945.

LE CONSUL DE POLOGNE,

Edward PRZESMYCKI.

VISTO Nᵒ 16

TRANSLATION FROM FRENCH

Translation from Latin

Archdiocese of Lwow, Parish of Stanislawow, Palatinate and District of Stanislawow, No.652 ----------- BIRTH AND BAPTISMAL CERTIFICATE.

The Parish Bureau of the Latin rite of the B.M.V. church, certifies that in the birth registers of this church for Stanislawow, vol.49, page 158, is inscribed: Year: 1914, Month of October, day of birth: 21. Baptized on October 23, 1914. Place of birth: Stanislawow. Name: Ferdinand-Jan (compound name) Religion: Roman-catholic. Gender: masculine. Origine: legitimate. Name and christian name of parents: Piotr ZAMOJSKI, son of Franciszek and Eudozia PIASECKA - Barbara BARCZYNSKA, daughter of Tomasz and Maria KUCZER. Name and christian name of God-father and God-mother: Michal KALUSKI and Maria MAKSYMIMCZUK. Priest who baptized: POKRYWKA. Mid-wife: illegible. Remarks: This certificate has been requested by Janina TOKARSKA.

I sign the present certificate with my own hand, and seal it with the paris seal. Stanislawow, November 5, 1941 /-/ Kazimierz BILCZEWSKI

Seal of the Stanislawow Parish.

No.238

The Consulate of Poland at Brussels certifies that the present translation is in conformity with the original document in the Latin language.

Brussels, October 2, 1945.

CONSUL OF POLAND

(s) Edward PRZESMYCKI

Seal of Polish Consulate, Brussels.

Original document in Latin enclosed with the French translation.

TRADUCTION DU POLONAIS.

. . . .
Office Paroissial du Rite latin à Stanisławów. 5.XI.1941.
EXTRAIT D'ACTE DE NAISSANCE. Bogusław-Marian /binom/
ZAMOJSKI, de religion catholique romaine, fils de Ferdi-
nand et Janina, née TOKARSKA, est né le 27.12.1937, à
Lwów, bartisé à Stanisławow. signature du curé /-/ illisi-
ble. Sceau de la Paroisse de Stanisławów. - - - - - - -
. . . .

Nr.842.

        Le Consulat de Pologne à Bruxelles
certifie la présente traduction conforme à
l'original fait en langue polonaise.

Bruxelles, le 2 Octobre 1945.

              LE CONSUL DE POLOGNE,

              Edward PRZESMYCKI.

TRANSLATION FROM FRENCH

Translation from Polish Language

The Parish Bureau of the Latin rite at Stanislawow, November 5,
1941. EXTRACT OF BIRTH ACT. Boguslaw-Marian (compound name) ZAMOJSKI
of roman catholic religion, son of Ferdinand and Janina, born TOKARSKA,
was born on December 27, 1937 at Lwow, baptized at Stanislawow.

Signed by the Curate

(illegible)

Seal of the Stanislawow Parish

No. 242

The Consulate of Poland at Brussels, hereby certifies that this
translation is in conformity with the original in the Polish
language.

Brussels, October 2, 1945

CONSUL OF POLAND

(s.) Edward PRZESMYCKI

Seal of Consulate of Poland, Brussels.

Original document in Polish language enclosed with the French translation.

ROBERT MELSON is the author of *Revolution and Genocide: On the Origins of the Armenian Genocide and the Holocaust,* which won an international prize for the best book on human rights for 1993. He is a former director of the Jewish studies program at Purdue University and is currently a professor of political science there.

MICHAEL BERENBAUM is the former president of the Survivors of the Shoah Visual History Foundation and is currently the Ida E. King Distinguished Professor of Holocaust Studies at Richard Stockton College. His work as coproducer of *One Survivor Remembers: The Gerda Weissman Klein Story* was recognized with an Academy Award, an Emmy Award, and a Cable Ace Award.

University of Illinois Press
1325 South Oak Street
Champaign, IL 61820-6903
www.press.uillinois.edu